"This is the book scholars and practitioners have been waiting for. The essential theories, across risk communication, crisis communication, and other relevant areas, are infused with practical insights and actionable takeaways based on empirical evidence. This volume is a model for translational research that advances crisis research, practice, and education."

Yan Jin, *C. Richard Yarbrough Professor in Crisis Communication Leadership, Director and Co-Founder of the Crisis Communication Think Tank, University of Georgia, USA*

"For those who are curious about the theory that drives the practice, this book is a gem. It stands out as one of the most comprehensive, yet easy-to-read, books on risk and crisis communication theory. A must-have for anyone looking to deepen their understanding of the field."

Chiara Valentini, *Professor, Head of the Discipline, JSBE—Jyväskylä School of Business and Economics, Jyväskylä, Finland*

A Primer for Crisis Communication Theory

Guided by a belief that good crisis communication theory should inform and improve practice, this book makes a wide range of theories utilized in crisis communication accessible to researchers, students, and practitioners.

The book begins with an extended discussion of applied theory, including the theory building process, to help the reader appreciate how theory can connect to the practice of crisis communication. This discussion is followed by chapters each explaining a theory and using an evidence-based approach to explore how that theory illuminates and applies to crisis communication practice. The array of theories includes those that are descriptive, prescriptive, and critical and cover the areas of public crises, political crises, and corporate crises.

This book is essential reading for advanced students of public relations and strategic communication and researchers in crisis and risk communication, with practical insights suitable for interested professionals.

Finn Frandsen is Professor of Corporate Communication and Crisis Management in the Department of Management, Aarhus University, Denmark.

W. Timothy Coombs is an advisor for the Centre for Crisis and Risk Communications. His primary area of research and consulting is crisis communication.

Winni Johansen is Professor of Corporate Communication and Crisis Management in the Department of Management, Aarhus University, Denmark.

A Primer for Crisis Communication Theory

The Fusion of Theory and Practice

Finn Frandsen, W. Timothy Coombs
and Winni Johansen

Routledge
Taylor & Francis Group
NEW YORK AND LONDON

Designed cover image: Getty Images|ridvan_celik

First published 2026
by Routledge
605 Third Avenue, New York, NY 10158

and by Routledge
4 Park Square, Milton Park, Abingdon, Oxon, OX14 4RN

Routledge is an imprint of the Taylor & Francis Group, an informa business

ISBN: 978-1-032-74581-7 (hbk)
ISBN: 978-1-032-74579-4 (pbk)
ISBN: 978-1-003-46996-4 (ebk)

DOI: 10.4324/9781003469964

Typeset in Sabon
by SPi Technologies India Pvt Ltd (Straive)

Contents

Preface

A Primer for Crisis Communication Theory: The Fusion of Theory and Practice is the result of years of discussion among friends interested in advancing theory development in crisis communication. We wanted to develop a resource people could use to understand, to build, and to apply crisis communication theory. We believe that developing crisis communication theory is essential to advancing it as an academic discipline and adding value to the practice. Researchers new to crisis communication must understand the context of how theory has evolved in the field to position themselves to contribute to the field's theoretical development. Continuing to push theory development is critical in any field of study. Crisis communication is an applied field meaning the theory should have relevance and utility for those engaging in crisis communication. That is why the last part of the book's title is *The Fusion of Theory and Practice*.

Chapters 1 and 21 focus on explaining what theory is and how it is developed. We cannot expect people to build theory without giving them the ability to understand what theory is and how to construct one. The bulk of this book details theories that have relevance for crisis communication theorists and practitioners. The first part covers six risk communication theories. Risks and crises are inseparable from one another, hence the need to include risk communication theories in a book titled *A Primer for Crisis Communication Theory*. Managing risks begins with and consistently demands an understanding of risks and risk communication. The risk communication/crisis communication relationship seems to be strongest in the crisis communication subfield of public crises (public health and disasters).

The second part presents ten important crisis communication theories. These theories cover the crisis communication subfields of political and corporate crises. These crisis communication theories represent various perspectives and methods. The third part holds two general theories having applications for crisis communication. We use the label "general" because the theories do not fit neatly as risk or crisis communication but can help those interested in both. For instance, resilience has strong connections to both risk and crisis communication. Therefore, a theory about resilience is useful but more of a general theory. Crisis communication is about problem solving. Theories provide mechanisms to aid in crisis communication problem solving. We encourage readers to consider how these various theories can work together in efforts to illuminate crisis communication and to address the problems encountered by crisis communicators. Even though theories are presented in separate chapters, people must develop ways to combine them to further enhance their utility. When it comes to crisis communication theory, it is better to approach the subject as both/and rather than either/or.

Each theory chapter follows a consistent four-part structure: (1) theoretical overview, (2) theoretical conceptualization, (3) practitioner takeaways, and (4) theoretical constraints and concerns. This structure provides an understanding of the theory, its key components, how it is applied, and some of its limitations. The chapters end with the same four theoretical engagement points for those interested in the deeper structure of theory. In addition, there are five discussion questions as well to highlight important aspects of the theory. The "Requisite Readings" are works we feel are essential to understanding the theories and are marked by an asterisk (*) in the reference list. We do not claim this is an exhaustive list of all crisis communication and related theories because the book had a limit of 70,000 words. We do feel the book covers essential theories to prepare those interested in contributing to developing crisis communication theory and those interested in applying crisis communication to solving the problems that arise during the crisis management process.

Chapter 1

Introduction to and Overview of Theory

The phrase "there is nothing so practical as a good theory" is most closely associated with social psychologist Kurt Lewin (1945, p. 129). Initially, Lewin said that he heard a businessman use the phrase. Historical research has shown that the phrase was used as early as the 1870s and was part of a General Electric advertising campaign in 1920 (Bedeian, 2016). What is striking is not the origins of the phrase but that it has been used for over 100 years! People have long recognized the value of synthesizing theory and practice, because theory can be used to solve applied problems. This stands in contrast to theory being some abstraction with little practical value that is a product of ivory tower thinking. While there are many definitions of theory, a common theme is that theory serves as an explanation of phenomenon. Theory as an explanation is deceptively complex, a point we shall build upon within this book. Theory helps people organize the world by understanding and predicting outcomes (Colquitt & Zapata-Phelan, 2007).

In this first chapter, we provide an orientation to the idea of theory and its application to crisis communication. We begin by explaining how crisis communication can be considered an intervention as a foundation for theory building. From there, we explore theory by establishing why we begin our book with a discussion of theory. We review the types of theories, criteria for judging theory, and the process of theory building. This review of theory provides a foundation for exploring the various theories that have been created for and applied to crisis communication.

Crisis Communication as an Intervention

Useful theory can improve a practice by guiding effective actions such as interventions. Interventions are actions taken to improve a situation or an intentional involvement in a difficult situation. Interventions are intended to solve problems people must face (applied problems). Crises are a common problem people need to solve. Crises are disruptions to organizational

DOI: 10.4324/9781003469964-1

routines that can produce harm for those inside and outside of the organization. Crises are disruptive because they divert attention from the regular activities of the organization to the crisis situation. Managers must concentrate on the crisis and not just their normal responsibilities. Crisis management arose as a discipline to combat the negative effects of crises on stakeholders and organizations. Our position is that crisis communication is the enact of crisis management. It is through communication that the principles of crisis management are applied in practice. A crisis plan is a principle of crisis communication that is enacted through the communicative efforts of the crisis management team. A significant part of crisis communication are the words and actions taken in response to the crisis—the crisis response. It is helpful to think of the crisis response as an intervention. Crisis managers intentionally involve themselves in difficult situations and take actions (crisis communication) designed to improve the situation.

Because it is the enactment of crisis management, crisis communication encompasses a vast collection of actions. People typically take a phased view of crises, with the three phases being pre-crisis, crisis response, and post-crisis (Coombs, 2023). Crisis communication occurs during the pre-crisis, crisis response, and post-crisis phases of a crisis. Efforts to scan for crisis warnings, the creation of the crisis management plan, the training of the crisis management team, the internal decision-making of the crisis team, and the crisis response are all examples of crisis communication. In this book, we concentrate on the public aspect of crisis communication. Public communication efforts are the strategic, crisis-related communication messages sent to stakeholders. The public element of crisis communication also occurs during all three phases of a crisis.

Some will argue that the crisis messages created by an organization privilege an organization—are organization-centric. The term "organization-centric" is often abused because of its multiple meanings. One meaning is who manages the crisis. Organizations are the entities responsible for managing the crises; hence, researchers have concentrated on organizations as crisis managers. Those organizations might be corporations, government agencies, or non-profits. Researchers seek to enhance the ability of managers to manage a crisis. Stakeholders might have a voice in the crisis management efforts and even at times provide material assistance, but they are not the ones who will be critiqued for the crisis management effort.

A second meaning of organization-centric is whose interests are prioritized in crisis management. It is often assumed that by focusing on the organization as the crisis managers, the organization's concerns are the priority. This is a misrepresentation of many crisis communication theories. Most researchers and practitioners agree that the victims, those stakeholders negatively affected by a crisis, should be the priority during a crisis (Coombs, 2023). Consider how SCCT argues that the first crisis response must focus on the physical safety and psychological well-being of crisis victims. Concern for stakeholders does not preclude the organization from then pursuing some of its own interests. Mixed motives for organizational actions are common and acceptable within strategic communication. Most failed crisis communication efforts can be traced to an emphasis on organizational rather than victim concerns. The risk of failure does not prevent crisis managers from misusing crisis communication and even crisis communication theory to prioritize the pursuit of organizational objectives. Critical research has been correct in noting how organizational interests can become a priority and the harm such a prioritization creates for those affected by the crisis (Dunn & Eble, 2015).

Clearly crisis communication has a strong applied focus, because it should seek to help those negatively affected by the crisis. Hence, when we talk about crisis communication theory, we are talking about applied theory. Applied theory honors the bond between theory and practice while seeking to solve practical problems. Applied theory is similar to what Littlejohn and Foss (2010) call practical theory, theories that help to improve lives in some way by offering people various courses of action. Applied theory is comfortable with the movement from theory to practice and from practice to theory. At its core, applied theory seeks to inform how interventions affect specific outcomes. For crisis communication, theory helps to explain how and when crisis communication can create specific outcomes for those affected by the crisis. We can take the need to understand the effects of crisis interventions as the overarching goal of crisis communication theory, especially those theories related to public crisis communication.

The purpose of this book is to explicate key theories that have been applied to crisis communication. Crises manifest themselves across a variety of contexts. The four primary crisis contexts are disasters, political crises, public health crises, and organizational crises. While there are some similarities between the four contexts, there are unique dynamics within each context that prevents ideas found in some context from being applied in other contexts. For instance, not all insights from disasters are applicable in organizational crises.

Frandsen and Johansen (2020) argued that crisis communication is composed of subfields rather than being monolithic reflects the diversity of the term "crisis." The three subfields are public, political, and corporate. It is necessary to think of crisis communication as subfields, because each subfield is governed by its own specific logistics of action. The public focuses on public safety with a need to provide emergency services and to inform the citizenry. Politics is concerned about political power and the need to help in a crisis by safeguarding society. Corporate focuses on corporate reputation and stakeholder interests. Why each subfield has unique ways of operating, there can be overlap between them as well (Frandsen & Johansen, 2020). We explore an array of theories that have been applied across the three subfields and the four contexts for crises. This exploration includes theories that have been adapted for application to crisis communication (theories applied to crisis communication) and those theories developed specifically for crisis communication (theories of crisis communication).

Modern links between theory and practice are embodied in the evidence-based approach. An evidence-based approach is used in any applied field that utilizes interventions. The evidence-based approach has been used in medicine, social work, management, and crisis communication (e.g., Kovner et al., 2000; Rynes & Bartunek, 2017). Research about interventions generates evidence. That evidence indicates which interventions are effective and under what circumstances the interventions are effective. There is a contingent nature to interventions. Each intervention has specific conditions under which it is effective—improves the situation. Research addresses the question: "What works and when does it work." Ideally, the evidence is causal. That means the evidence indicates the specific outcomes connected to the use of an intervention. But at other times, the evidence can be descriptive of the situation.

Evidence is just part of the equation. The other part of the equation is the experience of the practitioner. Practitioners develop intuition through years of practice. They learn what works or what does not work in specific contexts. Practitioners interpret the evidence generated by researchers. Practitioners decide if and how to apply the new evidence to their practices (Briner, 2019).

Why Start with a General Discussion of Theory

We begin our exploration of crisis communication theory with a general discussion of theory. We cannot fully understand crisis communication theory unless we understand theory itself. As noted earlier, *theory as explanation* is a complicated process. Here, we explore the process of theory building, including the idea of theory testing. A failure to appreciate and to develop theory is a common theme in applied disciplines, including management, psychology, and public relations (e.g., Fried, 2020; Sallot et al., 2003). Researchers frequently use the term theory with little appreciation for what the term encapsulates, often confusing theories with models or simple lists or failing to appreciate there are different types of theories. The results are odd claims such as one negative finding related to a theory proves the theory wrong. Such statements ignore the larger sense of the theory and the extant body of evidence generated from theory testing. It is difficult to build and to refine theory if one does not understand what a theory is. Consider how psychologists argue how researchers conflate statistical models with theoretical models. The focus on variables being related in statistical model fitting often fails to address why those relationships should exist (Fried, 2020). This sentiment has been echoed by many communication journal editors as they lament the overdependence on statistical modeling in manuscripts seeking publication. Moreover, there are times the applied nature of crisis communication is lost. The pursuit of the relationship between specific variables often overlooks whether or not there is practical value in those relationships. By focusing on applied theories, we remind researchers of what theories are and what they can contribute to research and practice.

Types of Theories

There is not enough room in this chapter or even the book to comprehensively synthesize the various types of theories. Nor should that be focus of a book like this. Many excellent volumes have been dedicated to topic of theory. Instead, we are going to provide a few ways to think about and to categorize theory that are useful to researchers. The first way of categorizing theories we would like to offer is the basic nature of a theory.

Basic Nature of Theories

Those who study theories have argued that there are three types of theories: descriptive, relational, and explanatory. Descriptive theories seek to describe the world. These theories capture how things exist. They can include classification systems, searching for meaning creation, and be based upon grounded theory. Researchers apply descriptive theories using research methods such as rhetorical and discourse analysis. The research interprets the meaning of the descriptive concepts they are applying in the analysis. Image restoration theory (IRT) is an example of a descriptive theory. The core of IRT is its impressive list of image repair strategies. Researchers treat the image repair strategies as crisis response strategies when they analyze how an organization is responding to a crisis. The researchers then examine a variety of data sources to interpret the effectiveness or ineffectiveness of the selected responses.

Relational theories specify the relationships between concepts. Models would be an example of relational theories; however, relational theories can go beyond models. Relational theories build upon descriptive theories by adding in how concepts are related to one another. Researchers can test to see if those relationships exist. Relational theories can include reasons for why the relationships should exist, but some do not. Relational theories help to capture the dynamics of crisis communication. The integrated crisis mapping (ICM) model that mapped emotional reactions to crises is an example of a relational theory. The ICM model connected various crisis types to the emotions most likely to be associated with those crises (Jin et al., 2010).

Explanatory theories are normative and make predictions about relationships. Explanatory theories seek to identify and to validate cause and effect relationships. Explanatory theories are useful for evaluating interventions. Specific interventions should produce prescribed effects on the designated outcomes. Explanatory theories predict how the intervention will affect the outcome. Stealing thunder, for example, specifies that when the organization is the first to disclose the existence of a crisis (intervention), the organization suffers less reputational damage (designated outcome) post-crisis than if a third party discloses the crisis.

The three types of theories based on the nature of theories reflect the debate over what is a theory and what is not a theory. For example, some argue that a theory must be predictive; that would exclude descriptive theories and some relational theories from being considered theories. We are taking that wider view of theory as explanations, thereby embracing descriptive, relational, and explanatory theories.

Theories by Schools of Thought

Another way to categorize theories is to consider the schools of thought upon which the theories are based. Lynham (2002) categorized theories as empirical-analytic, interpretative, and critical. Empirical-analytic theories are driven by quantitative research (numbers) with an emphasis on explanation, prediction, and control. SCCT is an example of an empirical-analytic crisis communication theory with its reliance upon experimental methods and focus on casual relationships.

Interpretative theories seek to make sense of the world by exploring how people understand and interpret phenomena. Interpretative theories focus on language and are influenced by how meaning is socially constructed. Interpretative theories use qualitative methods but can add some quantitative methods to the mix. Qualitative methods are useful, because their utility is finding answers to questions of "why" and "how." The rhetorical arena theory (RAT) is an interpretative crisis communication theory with its need to understand how the many voices in the rhetorical arena help to create the meaning for the crisis.

Critical theories have enlightenment and emancipation as their goals and use critique to pursue those goals. Critical theories are a collection of theories that are emancipatory seeking to critique and to change society. Critical theories focus on power, power structure, oppression, and domination. Qualitative methods are the primary research device for critical theories. Dunn and Eble's (2015) use of critical discourse theory to explore how organizations use power to influence or to silence other crisis voices is an example of applying critical theory to crisis communication.

Summary

We have presented two ways to classify theories. We are not arguing that these are the best nor the most comprehensive but that are useful in guiding thinking about theories. Researchers should be cognizant that the term theory can mean many different things. This is important when critiquing a theory or comparing two theories. To be fair, a critique must consider the type of theory being examined and apply the appropriate criteria for evaluating it, a point we cover in the next section. Moreover, when two theories are compared, researchers must know if they are similar or different types of theories. Comparing apples to apples is different and more accurate than comparing apples to oranges.

Criteria for Judging Theories

Part of understanding theory is appreciating how to assess theories. Littlejohn and Foss (2010) have provided a list of six criteria for evaluating theories. As they noted, the importance and relevance of the criteria vary by the kind of theory being assessed. The criteria are not designed to rank order theories or to find the best theory; rather, the criteria help you to determine how solid a theory is.

Scope is the first criterion. Scope captures how inclusive or comprehensive a theory is. This refers to the array of phenomena to which the theory can be applied. A narrow scope means a theory might apply to single or a small number of phenomena while a broad scope can be applied to a wide range of phenomena. Is the crisis communication limited to specific crisis types or is it applicable to a broad array of crises? A narrow theory is not bad if it provides a comprehensive understanding of specific crisis types. Many of the theories in this book apply to specific forms of crises. RAT is the crisis communication theory with the broadest scope as it can be applied to disasters, political crises, public health crises, and organizational crises.

Appropriateness is the second criterion and refers to the consistency between the theory and its assumptions. There should be a logical consistency to a theory. An example of inappropriateness would be when descriptive theory is used to make causal claims. In this case, the theory does not match the outcome because description does not and is not intended to prove causation. Heuristic value is the third criterion and captures a theory's ability to generate new research. When researchers can continue to use a theory to increase our understanding of the practice, the theory has strong heuristic value. Both SCCT and IRT are crisis communication theories with proven heuristic value as indicated by the amount of research the theories have inspired since their introduction in the 1990s.

Validity is the fourth criterion and refers to the value of a theory. For applied theories, validity is evaluated by the theory's ability to illuminate the practice. A variation of validity is the ability to observe the theory's concepts in the real world. We see a connection to practice again because the concepts in the theory should be observable in the practice. Many theories, such as IRT, include lists of crisis response strategies. Those lists have validity if we can find examples of cases where crisis managers using those responses.

Parsimony is the fifth criterion and involves logical simplicity. Parsimony holds that when choosing between two explanations, the better option is the simpler one. Parsimony is the most dangerous criteria because there is the risk of oversimplification. Researchers are advised to balance parsimony against the other five criteria. Stealing thunder is very parsimonious because it focuses on who discloses the existence of a crisis. Openness is the sixth and final criterion. Think of openness as a theory's ability to play well with others. Is the theory open to additional explanations and can it accommodate new variables? RAT is an example of a very open theory. RAT can be combined with many other theories and concepts to improve the analytic contributions of the theory.

In this book, we will not attempt to rate each theory by the six criteria. Such a rating is very subjective and ultimately adds little value for the reader. The criteria are there to help you make decisions about the theories you might utilize. Keep in mind an unstated criteria when selecting a theory for research or practice is how well it fits the needs of your research endeavor or the crisis you face. Moreover, there is nothing wrong with combining theories, if those theories have a logical connection with one another. Theories are lens for viewing the world. Sometimes, multiple lens are needed to clarify your view of a crisis just as multiple lens can increase the clarity when viewing objects through a telescope.

Theory Building Process

Theory building can be defined as "the purposeful process or recurring cycle by which coherent descriptions, explanations, and representations of observed or experienced phenomena are generated, verified, and refined" (Lynham, 2000, p. 161). Applied theories can be driven by researchers who have identified a problem and a potential solution (research to practice) or be driven by ideas originating in the practice that are verified by researchers (practice to research). In many cases, applied theory building is a mix of the two because of the need to integrate theory and practice. The first published research in crisis communication were reports from practitioners about what seemed to work and what did not work in crisis communication. Many crisis communication researchers draw upon these early practitioner experiences and insights when developing a theory.

The goal of theory building is knowledge generation. Theory building creates both outcome and process knowledge. Outcome knowledge creates explanations of phenomena and the ability to make predictions about the effects of interventions. Process knowledge increases our understanding of how something works or what it means. Crisis communication theory explains the effects of crisis responses and the effects various crisis response strategies have upon the crisis situation. Moreover, crisis communication theory enhances our understanding of the dynamics involved in the crisis process, including what concepts matter and how these concepts interact with one another to shape the meaning that emerges from the crisis.

Lynham (2002) outlined a five-step, generic process for building applied theories: conceptualization, operationalization, confirmation, application, and refinement. In this chapter, the focus is on conceptualization and operationalization because the other three steps are part of theory testing. The need for theory building arises for a variety of reasons, including the need to solve practical problems and the realization that an existing theory was incomplete. The rise of social media created a practical problem for understanding how these new platforms affect crisis communication. The social mediated crisis communication (SMCC) model was developed to address this problem. When research indicated situational crisis communication theory (SCCT) recommendations were not holding for management misconduct crises, moral outrage was incorporated into the theory to address this gap (Coombs & Tachkova, 2019).

Conceptualization

Conceptualization is the first and most challenging aspect of theory building. Researchers must wrestle with the phenomenon to create a way to understand and to explain it. Conceptualization requires the identification of key concepts, explanation of the relationships between the concepts, and the identification of the boundary conditions for the relationships (when to apply and not to apply the theory). Research must identify and define the concepts, organize the concepts, explain why they are related to one another, and circumscribe the boundaries for the theory by mapping its domain of application (Chermack & Swanson, 2015).

Conceptualization fits well with what Whetten (1989) called the "what, how, and why" of a theory. What refers to identifying the concepts that are part of the explanation. There needs to be enough concepts to be comprehensive but not too many so as to violate parsimony. How specifies the relationships between the concepts. Models are used frequently to map the connections between the concepts. What and how serve to define the domain of a theory.

Why is "the most difficult avenue in theory development" (Whetten, 1989, p. 493). Why articulates the underlying dynamic that justifies why the concepts should be related to one another. It specifies why the concepts have specific relationships to one another. Whetten (1989) refers to why as the assumptions that serve as the glue to bind the theory together. Researchers often borrow perspectives from other fields to help develop the why. A theory from another discipline can be adapted to explain phenomenon in another domain. For instance, SCCT borrows from attribution theory to explain the relationship between crisis types and crisis response strategies.

Whetten (1989) includes who, where, and when as the factors that create the context for a theory. Context refers to boundary conditions, the limits for the application of a theory. Whetten (1989) notes the need to "set the boundaries of generalizability, and as such constitute the range of the theory" (p. 492). No theory is applicable everywhere all the time. It is important to know the limits of a theory. For applied theory, it is essential to know when to apply the theory and when not to apply the theory. However, boundary conditions may not be known from the start of a theory and emerge only through subsequent testing of a theory. For example, it was from addition testing that moral outrage emerges as a boundary condition for SCCT. That is why Chermack and Swanson (2015) argue "theory is always in progress" (p. 39). It is useful to think of theories as being in a dynamic rather than a static state. This does not mean the central elements of the theory keep changing; rather, it means theories can evolve as new evidence emerges, and new concepts are added.

Operationalization

Operationalization serves to link theory to practice. It is also the way to create and to measure the key concepts in the theory. For instance, how does one measure post-crisis reputation for an organization? Operationalization specifies the real-world context for the theory. Researchers need to specify the nature of the intervention for the practice. Operationalization explains how a theory is applied and empirically confirmed by practitioners. SCCT, for instance, identifies the cues that can be used by practitioner to identify the type of crisis they are managing. IRT defines the various crisis response strategies practitioners might employee when responding to a crisis. If a theory is too esoteric for practitioners, that would be a failure of operationalization. For researchers, operationalization provides a means of measuring each variable. Consider how crisis researchers have created measures to assess the various emotions associated with crises (Jin et al., 2014; Schoofs et al., 2019).

Operationalization reflects the duality of theory. Theory must be useful to both researchers and to practitioners. Researchers must understand the concepts, relationships, and measures if they are to apply the theory to their own research. A common problem within academic research is the misrepresentation and misapplication of theories. Misinterpretation involves a lack of understanding of the concepts and/or their relationships in a theory; while misapplication occurs, the theory is applied to an inappropriate domain. Practitioners need to understand when and how to apply the theory to their problems. That is why so many research articles seek to clarify the implications of the research for the practice. Such articles include potential guidance or lessons for practitioners.

Summary of Theory Construction

We have begun our exploration of crisis communication by clarifying what we mean by crisis communication and theory, the two essential terms in the book's title. While we define crisis communication as the enactment of crisis management, we limit its scope to a focus on public communication efforts. We created this limitation, because the crisis communication can include so many forms of communication. Theory needs to be discussed, because too often the term is present as a given—that people know what it means. Experts in theory cannot agree on its meaning, so it would be foolish to discuss various crisis communication theories without providing a context for what theory can be. We then began to explore theory building through its first two steps, conceptualization and operation. The next section continues the discussion of theory by moving to the theory testing process.

Theory building does not end with the construction of the theory. The last three steps in theory building involve testing the new theory: confirmation, application, and refinement. This chapter begins by detailing the last three steps in theory building designed to determine the strength of the theory development (conceptualization and operationalization).

Confirmation

Confirmation involves designing studies that will confirm or disconfirm a theoretical framework. Theory confirmation is about accuracy, how well the theory can capture and explain a phenomenon. Accuracy relates to the predictive aspect of theory. Relational theories make predictions about how concepts are related to one another while explanatory theories explain how independent variables, such as crisis intervention, affect dependent variables, such as crisis outcomes. Researchers can test if the relationships between concepts exist as prescribed in the theory and if predicted outcomes occur or not. Quantitative research is the common way to assess this aspect of accuracy. The numerical data can determine relationships, such as correlations between concepts, and the effects of a crisis intervention on specific outcome variables. Quantitative testing is based upon significance, the likelihood the effects are not a result of chance. Typically, the acceptance level for significance is .05, meaning the odds of the finding being a result of chance are only 5% (Vermeulen et al., 2015).

Significance is not the ultimate test, however. Researchers should also ask if the result is important. One measure of importance is effect size. Effect size indicates how much variance is being explained. Crisis interventions are a helpful example to illustrate this point. A crisis intervention can be significant, but if the effect size is small, the crisis intervention is adding little to our understanding of crisis communication. We know the crisis intervention has an effect but that effect will be hard to notice and may not warrant the use of the crisis intervention. For practitioners, accuracy is the confidence they can place in the proposed relationships, including the effects of crisis intervention on the specified crisis outcomes. Statistics require interpretation and do not speak for themselves. For instance, the findings from stealing thunder are significant and typically have large effect sizes. That means stealing thunder is worth the effort, and practitioners can rely upon that effect occurring if they are the first to disclose a crisis exists. Confirmation can indicate the degree to which practitioners can trust the theory to help provide guidance for the practice.

Descriptive theories are still concerned about accuracy but would assess it differently. For descriptive theories, accuracy reflects the degree to which the theory reflects the actual phenomenon. For example, did the list of crisis responses derived from IRT capture the array of crisis response appearing in the study?

Application

Application examines what happens when a theory is applied to phenomenon such as a crisis. Case studies are used to examine real-world application of the theories. The case studies can shed light on whether or not the application of the theory improved a crisis communication effort. Research related to application collects naturally occurring data generated during a crisis to determine the effects of a theory. For instance, one consulting firm used their longitudinal reputation data to support the recommendation from SCCT that accommodative strategies produce the strongest, positive effect on post-crisis organizational reputations (Gregory & Moran, 2014).

We can think of application as an extension of confirmation. An extension that moves the theory beyond academic study to the real world.

Refinement

Refinement is a continual process for any theory, because "a theory is never 'complete'" (Chermack & Swanson, 2015, p. 41). Refinement is the process of improving a theory and its applications. Additional research finds ways to adapt the theory and improve its rigor and relevance. As Whetten (1989) noted, the only way to map the boundaries of a theory is through additional testing. Research indicates when a theory is no longer applicable, a boundary condition has been identified.

It is important to remember that theories should not be static, especially in social science where the object of study is complex human behavior. As a theory is tested, results often indicate a need to refine the theory by adjusting it to account for the new findings if a rethink of the theory is not required (Gioia & Pitre, 1990). One contrary finding involving a non-core aspect of a theory does not disprove an entire theory but may lead to a revision of the theory. One variation of building theory involves introducing a new construct or significantly reconceptualizing an existing construct (Colquitt & Zapata-Phelan, 2007).

Problematizing is what drives theory building when using the reconceptualizing concepts approach. Researchers problematize a concept by exploring a weakness in the theory. To build theory, the reconceptualization must be both original and useful. Original means we learn something we did not know, and that finding can even be a surprise. Useful means that the reevaluated concept adds specificity and rigor to the theory and its application to problem solving (the practice). To problematize a concept, researchers must understand the research domain and be open minded to possible changes. Once a problem is identified, the researchers must articulate the problem so as to feature its potential contribution to theory and practice (Shepherd & Suddaby, 2017).

Summary

Lynham's (2002) growth cycle for applied theory building is captured in Figure 1.1. Note the theory building process reflects the connection between theory and practice. Theory building involves creating and testing theory. The first step is to create a theory. Theory creation can be done inductively or deductively. Inductive theory construction begins with a collection of specific observations. Theory is then developed by identifying the patterns that emerge in these observations. The theory is created based upon specific observations. This is a common route from practice to

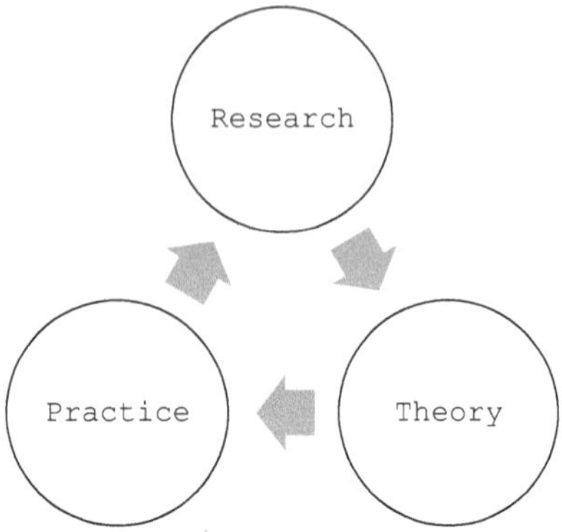

Figure 1.1 Lynham's Theory Building Growth Cycle.

theory. Deductive theory construction begins with articulating a theory and then collecting data to test the theory. The theory begins with a problem, and the theory is developed to solve the problem. This is a common route from theory to practice. We argue that applied theory is usually a mix of the two. Even deductive theory requires some understanding of the practice to begin articulating a theory, and an inductive theory requires some insights into other theories to inform the identification of patterns. Regardless of the route taken, once created, a theory must be tested.

Conclusion

Corley and Gioia (2011) have written about theoretical contributions in academic research. Their ideas are relevant to our discussion of applied theory. Corley and Gioia (2011) created a two-by-two matrix for evaluating theoretical contributions. The first dimension is originality. Originality can be revelatory or incremental. Revelatory refers to unique and often unexpected insights from the theory. The theory offers something new and different in what it reveals about or how it conceptualized a phenomenon. Incremental extends our current insights by building upon the existing theory. An example would be adding a new variable to a theory. The advancement of science is often described as incremental additional of knowledge. Utility, a point we will return to shortly, can be scientific or practical. Scientific utility means that the theory is helpful to future researchers examining the phenomenon. Practical utility means the theory can offer possible guidance to those tasked with managing a phenomenon.

They concluded that in management, major journals were forcing researchers toward theory that was revelatory and scientific. This was considered a problematic outcome mainly because it separated management research from its roots in the practice. (Corley & Gioia, 2011). They argue that management research should be problem driven and address problems in the practice directly or indirectly. Their position is that management research should be pragmatic and should include a focus on practical matters as well as scientific ones—theory should address research and practice. Good theory does not merely find gaps in the literature but seeks to solve real-world problems (Corley & Gioia, 2011). The critique of the management literature is a cautionary tale for crisis communication research. Researchers should not lose sight of the applied nature of crisis communication and the need for theory and research to be relevant to the practice and not just academic pursuits.

Earlier in the chapter, we provided a list of various criteria that can be used to evaluate a theory. The criteria vary in relevance depending upon the nature of a theory. This is to say that no criterion has strong relevance to every theory. Hence, comparing different types of theories is neither productive nor very insightful, because different types of theories provide different ways of creating insights.

As Lynham (2002) echoed Corley and Gioia (2011) by noting, utility is a critical criterion to apply to any theory. Utility captures how well a theory can explain a phenomenon, for our purposes that would be crisis communication. A useful theory illuminates a phenomenon. For researchers, utility involves the ability to create new insights into crisis communication with the theory. What do we learn about crisis communication that we did not know before the research? For practitioners, utility involves the ability to apply the findings to the practice of crisis communication. Are the insights useful in the practice? Utility is a concern for descriptive, relational, and explanatory theories as well as empirical-analytic, interpretative, and critical theories.

The key to utility is its application to your problem—theory and research should seek to solve problems. For researchers, how can a particular theory or combination of theories help you to understand the problem at the center of your research effort. Are you interested in capturing how people make sense of a crisis, the way powerful actors on a crisis, or the effects of a crisis intervention on specific crisis outcomes? You need to pick the theory or theories that are right for your problem and the research questions you have derived from that problem. Similarly, practitioners need to pick a theory that can provide some insight into the practical problems emerging from their crisis. Do they need to help stakeholders understand how to protect themselves physically from a crisis, find ways to assess the other crisis voices impacting the crisis communication effort, or understand the structural features in society that allow a crisis to repeat itself? Different crisis communication theories provide insights into different aspects of crisis communication. For both researchers and practitioners, utility is the relevance of the theory to the questions they need to answer. As we move to the exploration of theories of crisis communication and theories applied to crisis communication, we will feature both the nature and utility of the various theories.

Discussion Questions

1. How can the concept of crisis communication as an intervention inform the development of more effective crisis management strategies, and what are some potential challenges in applying this perspective in real-world situations?
2. The chapter distinguishes between different types of theories (descriptive, relational, and explanatory) and schools of thought (empirical-analytic, interpretative, and critical). How might understanding these different approaches help researchers and practitioners to select the most appropriate theoretical framework for a specific crisis situation or research question? Consider how the nature of a theory impacts its utility.
3. The chapter outlines a five-step theory building process. Considering the steps of conceptualization and operationalization, how do they contribute to the development of useful and applicable crisis communication theories? How does the duality of theory for researchers and practitioners affect this process?
4. The chapter emphasizes the importance of both evidence and practitioner experience in the application of theory. How can these two elements be effectively integrated to ensure that crisis communication strategies are both theoretically sound and practically effective?
5. The chapter mentions that theories are not static and can be refined through testing. How does the process of confirmation, application, and refinement contribute to the continuous improvement of crisis communication theory and practice, and what are the implications of viewing theories as dynamic rather than static?

References

Bedeian, A. G. (2016). A note on the aphorism "there is nothing as practical as a good theory". *Journal of Management History*, *22*(2), 236–242.

Briner, R. (2019). The basics of evidence-based practice. Retrieved from https://cebma.org/assets/Uploads/Briner-The-Basics-of-Evidence-Based-Practice-v2.pdf

Chermack, T. J., & Swanson, R. A. (2015). When methodologies become theologies, applied disciplines falter. *Human Resource Development Review*, *14*(4), 509–513.

Colquitt, J. A., & Zapata-Phelan, C. P. (2007). Trends in theory building and theory testing: A five-decade study of the Academy of Management Journal. *Academy of Management Journal*, *50*(6), 1281–1303.

Coombs, W. T. (2023). *Ongoing crisis communication: Planning, managing, and responding* (6th ed.). Sage.
Coombs, W. T., & Tachkova, E. R. (2019). Scansis as a unique crisis type: Theoretical and practical implications. *Journal of Communication Management*, *23*(1), 72–88.
Corley, K. G., & Gioia, D. A. (2011). Building theory about theory building: What constitutes a theoretical contribution?. *Academy of Management Review*, *36*(1), 12–32.
Dunn, C., & Eble, M. (2015). Giving voice to the silenced: Using critical discourse analysis to inform crisis communication theory. *Journal of Business Ethics*, *132*, 717–735.
Frandsen, F. & Johansen, W. (2020). Reframing the field: Public crisis management, political crisis management, and corporate crisis management. In *Crisis communication*, edited by F. Frandsen and W. Johansen (pp. 59–102). Boston: De Gruyter.
Fried, E. I. (2020). Lack of theory building and testing impedes progress in the factor and network literature. *Psychological Inquiry*, *31*(4), 271–288.
Gioia, D. A., & Pitre, E. (1990). Multiparadigm perspectives on theory building. *Academy of Management Review*, *15*(4), 584–602.
Gregory, J.R. & Moran, R. (2014). Post crisis: Engage or fly low? *Brunswick Review*, *8*, 32–34.
Jin, Y., Liu, B. F., Anagondahalli, D., & Austin, L. (2014). Scale development for measuring publics' emotions in organizational crises. *Public Relations Review*, *40*(3), 509–518.
Jin, Y., Pang, A., & Cameron, G. T. (2010). The role of emotions in crisis responses: Inaugural test of the integrated crisis mapping (ICM) model. *Corporate Communications: An International Journal*, *15*(4), 428–452.
Kovner, A. R., Elton, J. J., & Billings, J. (2000). Evidence-based management. *Frontiers of Health Services Management*, *16*(4), 3–24.
Lewin, K. (1945). The research center for group dynamics at Massachusetts Institute of Technology. *Sociometry*, *8*(2), 126–136.
Littlejohn, S. W., & Foss, K. A. (2010). *Theories of human communication*. Waveland Press.
Lynham, S. A. (2000). Theory building in the human resource development profession. *Human Resource Development Quarterly*, *11*(2), 159–178.
Lynham, S. A. (2002). The general method of theory-building research in applied disciplines. *Advances in Developing Human Resources*, *4*(3), 221–241.
Rynes, S. L., & Bartunek, J. M. (2017). Evidence-based management: Foundations, development, controversies and future. *Annual Review of Organizational Psychology and Organizational Behavior*, *4*, 235–261.
Sallot, L. M., Lyon, L. J., Acosta-Alzuru, C., & Ogata Jones, K. (2003). From aardvark to zebra: A new millennium analysis of theory development in public relations academic journals. *Journal of Public Relations Research*, *15*(1), 27–90.
Schoofs, L., Claeys, A. S., De Waele, A., & Cauberghe, V. (2019). The role of empathy in crisis communication: Providing a deeper understanding of how organizational crises and crisis communication affect reputation. *Public Relations Review*, *45*(5), 101851.

Shepherd, D. A., & Suddaby, R. (2017). Theory building: A review and integration. *Journal of Management*, *43*(1), 59–86.

Vermeulen, I., Beukeboom, C. J., Batenburg, A., Avramiea, A., Stoyanov, D., van de Velde, B., & Oegema, D. (2015). Blinded by the light: How a focus on statistical "significance" may cause p-value misreporting and an excess of p-values just below. 05 in communication science. *Communication Methods and Measures*, *9*(4), 253–279.

Whetten, D. A. (1989). What constitutes a theoretical contribution?. *Academy of Management Review*, *14*(4), 490–495.

Part I

Risk Communication Section

Chapter 2

Protective Action Decision Model

Before and during crises, crisis managers will want constituents to engage in behaviors that will be beneficial to them. An example would be the need to shelter-in-place during hazardous chemical release or to take steps to reduce the risk of wildfires. Yet people often fail to engage in these desired behaviors, what are termed protective actions. The protective action decision model (PADM) was developed to help understand why people choose to engage in protective actions as a means of helping them to improve compliance with protective behavior requests before and during crises.

Theoretical Overview

Risk communication intertwines with crisis communication in many ways. One such connection involves efforts to encourage people to reduce risks. This includes actions people can take both before and during a crisis. For instance, people can prepare for crises by creating home emergency kits and personal emergency plans. During crises, people can follow official recommendations to evacuate or to shelter-in-place. The actions people take to reduce risks from hazards fall under the concept of protective actions. Lindell and Perry (2012) noted, "Researchers have long been interested in explaining the process by which people respond to environmental cues or socially transmitted warnings about environmental hazards and disasters" (p. 616). The PADM was developed to explain how and why people adopt protective actions. PADM is applicable to the development of risk communication messages, evacuation modeling, and long-term hazard adjustment.

PADM builds upon earlier research, including the health belief model (HBM) (Rosenstock, 1974) and protective motivation theory (PMT) (Floyd et al., 2000). Both HBM and PMT help to explain if people engage in protective actions. Central to these approaches are response efficacy (the belief actions will reduce the threat), self-efficacy (people belief in their ability to execute the behavior), and response cost (perceived cost of the

DOI: 10.4324/9781003469964-3

action). PADM provides "a more detailed set of variables to define efficacy beliefs and response costs" (Terpstra & Lindell, 2012). Strahan and Watson (2019) observed that PADM is used widely, especially in North America as a way to understand how people make decisions and enact behaviors when facing hazards.

Theoretical Conceptualization

PADM is a detailed conceptualization of how people make decisions about protective actions. PADM begins with environmental cues, social cues, and warnings (the environmental and social context). Environment cues refer to what your senses tell you about a threat. You can feel the wind or see the funnel cloud of a tornado. Social cues are observations of the actions of others. You can see other people seeking shelter from the tornado. Warnings are messages transmitted by various channels about the threat (Lindell & Perry, 2012). You might receive a text message about a tornado warning or hear a warning siren. These three factors can trigger the predecisional process for protective action, the first step in the psychological process that produces protective action decisions.

The predecisional process involves three factors necessary for protective action. First, a person must be exposed to environmental or social cues. Second, people must attend to these environmental and social cues. Third, a person must comprehend and accurately interpret the environmental cues (Lindell & Perry, 2012). Those familiar with information and persuasion will recognize these key factors. People will not consider taking protective action if they do not know there is a threat. To know there is a threat, people must be exposed to cues about the threat, attend to those cues, and interpret those cues properly. People will not take protective actions if they do not encounter the proper cues, ignore those cues, or misinterpret the cues.

If people do properly process the environmental and social cues, the three types of core perceptions in PADM can be activated. Those three types of core perceptions are threats, protective actions, and stakeholders. Once people perceive a threat, they will evaluate the threat. Common evaluations of threats are based on the probability of the threat manifesting and the consequences the threat will have on the individual if the hazard is realized. These are the well-known evaluative factors of likelihood and impact. Hazard intrusiveness can be a factor here. Hazard intrusiveness is the frequency of thinking about or talking about a threat as well as seeking information about the threat. Is the treat a part of your daily life? Do you think and talk about tornados with others or do you not think about them? Hazard intrusiveness should make a person more sensitive to a threat (Lindell & Perry, 2012).

Next are perceptions of hazard adjustments—efforts to mitigate a threat. If people feel a threat is serious, they will assess hazard-related efficacy and hazard-related resources. Efficacy is the ability of an action to mitigate the potential negative effects of the hazard. Hazard-related resources are the costs of the protective actions as well as the knowledge and skills needed to engage in the protective actions (Lindell & Perry, 2012). People will not choose a protective action if it is perceived as ineffective. Nor will they use an effective protective action if they feel it is too costly or they lack the knowledge and/or skill to enact it. Consider the action of evacuating a coastal area due to an approaching hurricane. People will not evacuate if they feel staying at home is a safe option. Or people will not evacuate if they feel evacuation is too costly. During a recent hurricane, a young couple did not evacuate because they could not find a hotel they could afford in the evacuation areas.

The final core element is the perception of social stakeholders. Social stakeholders include authorities such as government officials, experts on the hazard (valuators), watchdog groups like the news media and citizen groups, and households. Any of these social stakeholders might affect how people perceive the protective actions. Messages from these social stakeholders might reinforce engaging in the protective action or discourage use of the protective action. The influence of these social stakeholders is primarily a function of trust. People typically are more influenced by trustworthy sources (Lindell & Perry, 2012). If government authorities tell you to evacuate but your friends and family all say to stay, you are unlikely to evacuate the area.

Following these various perceptions, people will begin the protective action decision-making process which is a series of decision stages. People might not follow all of these actions nor follow the actions in any particular order (Lindell & Perry, 2012). The first action is risk identification; the threat perceptions prompt people to attend to the risk. The second action is risk assessment, "determining the expected personal impacts that the disaster could cause" (Lindell & Perry, 2012, p. 621). People consider the personal relevance of the risk and make assessments about probability, severity, and immediacy (how soon they could feel the effects).

The third action is the protective action search. If the threat is real and a personal risk, people must find what that can do to protect themselves. People can learn about protective actions through experience, social cues (what others are doing), and from warning messages. The fourth action is protective action assessment. People will evaluate the alternatives and decide which one will work best for them. Protective actions are adaptive plans and can vary from vague to detailed. Lindell and Perry (2012) note that people always have two choices. They can either take protective actions or follow their normal actions.

The fifth action is protective action implementation. People use their resources to engage in the protective actions. Timing does matter because protective actions can be taken too late. For example, hesitating to evacuate during a wildfire can be a serious mistake. Fires spread rapidly and can cutoff potential evacuation routes. The sixth action is information needs assessment. People will seek additional information if they perceive the existing information to be insufficient. The need for information can slow reactions by delaying decision-making at any of the stages of the decision-making process (Lindell & Perry, 2012).

The seventh action is communication action assessment. People must decide where and how to get their information. This includes what channels to use in formation collection and what sources to use for their information. Sources can include the news media, authorities, or peers. The eighth action is communication action implementation. This reflects the urgency of information need. Is it something people need immediately or can it wait (Lindell & Perry, 2012)? Information is more urgent during a crisis than during preparation for a crisis.

Summary

PADM provides a detailed consideration about how people choose to engage or to not engage in protective actions before and during crises. PADM can improve risk communication by identifying factors that can facilitate or inhibit the adoption of protective actions. Furthermore, we learn improved risk communication can enhance crisis management and communication efforts.

Applications to Subfields

PADM has been used most often within the public subfield. Because of the focus on hazards, PADM has been applied widely to the study of disasters, including flooding (Lindell & Perry, 2012; Terpstra & Lindell, 2012), hurricanes (Lindell, 2020; Lindell et al., 2007), wildfires (Strahan & Watson, 2019), earthquakes (Lindell & Prater, 2000), shelter-in-place behaviors (Sorensen et al., 2004), and heatwaves (Beckmann et al., 2021). The research helps to improve preparation for disasters and crisis communication during disasters. Terpstra and Lindell's (2012) examination of flood preparedness among people in the Netherlands illustrates PADM's application to preparation. Lindell's (2020) research into improving the utility of hazard maps in risk communication is an example of efforts to improve risk communication during crises. PADM has been applied to public health crises as well. Wang et al. (2018) examined H7N9 public health crisis through the PADM lens, while Gonzalez et al. (2021) and

Silver et al. (2024) applied it to protective decision-making during the COVID-19 pandemic.

The hazard element makes PADM applicable to the corporate crisis subfield as well. Researchers have utilized PADM when studying issues surrounding nuclear facilities (Lindell, 2000) and hazardous chemicals (Lindell & Hwang, 2008). For instance, Heath et al. (2018) applied PADM to understanding shelter-in-place decisions for chemical releases. PADM does not appear to be applicable to all types of corporate crises but does apply to those involving hazards. PADM seems to have little utility for application to political crises.

Practitioner Takeaways

PADM provides practitioners with a great understanding of the process involved when people decide to accept or reject protective actions. Yes, protective actions do help people so that people should embrace them. However, people fail to engage in protective actions for a myriad of reasons. PADM helps to explain why people are making these "problematic choices" and suggests ways to improve risk messages to increase the likelihood of protective action adoption both before and during crises. Risk communication must address the perceived threat. If people do not sense that a hazard is a personal threat, they will ignore protective behaviors. People may need to be convinced that a hazard is a personal threat. Social influence matters as well. If trusted others disregard the protective actions, individuals are likely to do the same. Risk communication might need to address why a community is reluctant to embrace certain protective actions.

Response efficacy and resources matter as well. People must believe that the protective actions will make them safer. The benefits of protective actions are not always obvious and may need to be sold to people. Remember protective actions take resources and have costs (expenditure of effort or resources). People cannot evacuate an area if they lack transportation, a point authorities often fail to appreciate during hurricanes. Marginalized groups often lack the resources necessary to engage in protective actions (e.g., Choi et al., 2022). Those managing a crisis must consider how to provide people with the necessary resources as part of the crisis preparation phase and to be sure the resources are delivered during the crisis phase. The PADM research also has found a gender difference in assessments of hazards. Females tend to have higher risk perceptions and hazard-related attributes (Liddell et al., 2020; Terpstra & Lindell, 2012). Crisis managers need to consider how gender differences might affect the efforts to promote the use of protective actions.

Theoretical Constrains and Concerns

Some concerns have been raised about PADM. A primary concern is with the theory's application across a range of contexts. This includes PADM's fit across cultures. Also, PADM is focused on the individual-level and may not provide much insight into community-level decision-making (Tierney, 2007). Another concern is the strong rational focus of PADM and limited consideration for the affective element of crises (Silver et al., 2013). Finally, some consider PADM to be static and incapable of capturing the dynamic aspects of crises (Lindell & Perry, 2012).

Theoretical Engagement Points

1 What type of research methods are most closely associated with PADM?
2 Is PADM primarily a descriptive, relational, or explanatory theory?
3 Is PADM primarily an empirical-analytic, interpretative, or critical theory?
4 How would you evaluate PADM in terms of scope, appropriateness, heuristic value, validity, parsimony, and openness?

Discussion Questions

1 How does the PADM model contribute to our understanding of why individuals might choose not to engage in protective actions during crises?
2 What are the key differences between the Health Belief Model (HBM), Protective Motivation Theory (PMT), and the PADM? How does PADM build upon these earlier models?
3 Discuss the role of social stakeholders and trust in influencing individuals' decisions to adopt protective actions. Provide examples.
4 How can crisis managers utilize PADM to develop effective risk communication strategies that encourage individuals to take appropriate protective actions?
5 What are some of the limitations of PADM? How might these limitations affect its applicability in different cultural contexts or community-level decision-making?

References

Beckmann, S. K., Hiete, M., Schneider, M., & Beck, C. (2021). Heat adaptation measures in private households: an application and adaptation of the protective action decision model. *Humanities and Social Sciences Communications*, *8*(1), 1–12.

Choi, S., Powell, T. M., Muller, J. M., & Lux, E. A. (2022). Exploring the disproportionate impact of disasters: Social service providers' perceptions of factors increasing vulnerability Among hurricane survivors. *Families in Society*, *103*(3), 314–327.

Floyd, D. L., Prentice-Dunn, S., & Rogers, R. W. (2000). A meta-analysis of research on protection motivation theory. *Journal of Applied Social Psychology*, *30*(2), 407–429.

Gonzalez, K. F., Bull, M. T., Muñoz-Herrera, S., & Robledo, L. F. (2021). Determinant factors in personal decision-making to adopt COVID-19 prevention measures in Chile. *International Journal of Environmental Research and Public Health*, *18*(15), 8131.

Heath, R. L., Lee, J., Palenchar, M. J., & Lemon, L. L. (2018). Risk communication emergency response preparedness: Contextual assessment of the protective action decision model. *Risk Analysis*, *38*(2), 333–344.

Liddell, J. L., Saltzman, L. Y., Ferreira, R. J., & Lesen, A. E. (2020). Cumulative disaster exposure, gender and the protective action decision model. *Progress in Disaster Science*, *5*, 100042.

Lindell, M. K. (2000). An overview of protective action decision-making for a nuclear power plant emergency. *Journal of Hazardous Materials*, *75*(2–3), 113–129*.

Lindell, M. K. (2020). Improving hazard map comprehension for protective action decision making. *Frontiers in Computer Science*, *2*, 27.

Lindell, M. K., & Hwang, S. N. (2008). Households' perceived personal risk and responses in a multihazard environment. *Risk Analysis: An International Journal*, *28*(2), 539–556.

Lindell, M. K., & Perry, R. W. (2012). The protective action decision model: Theoretical modifications and additional evidence. *Risk Analysis: An International Journal*, *32*(4), 616–632*.

Lindell, M. K., & Prater, C. S. (2000). Household adoption of seismic hazard adjustments: A comparison of residents in two states. *International Journal of Mass Emergencies & Disasters*, *18*(2), 317–338.

Lindell, M. K., Prater, C. S., & Peacock, W. G. (2007). Organizational communication and decision making for hurricane emergencies. *Natural Hazards Review*, *8*(3), 50–60.

Rosenstock, I. M. (1974). The health belief model and preventive health behavior. *Health Education Monographs*, *2*(4), 354–386.

Silver, A., Koratty, N., Penta, S., & Clay, L. (2024). The influence of environmental cues on behavioral response: An assessment of the protective action decision model in the context of COVID-19. *Risk, Hazards & Crisis in Public Policy.*

Silver, R. C., Holman, E. A., Andersen, J. P., Poulin, M., McIntosh, D. N., & Gil-Rivas, V. (2013). Mental- and physical-health effects of acute exposure to community violence in the context of a disaster. *Journal of the American Medical Association*, *290*(5), 603–610. DOI: 10.1001/jama.290.5.603

Sorensen, J. H., Shumpert, B. L., & Vogt, B. M. (2004). Planning for protective action decision making: Evacuate or shelter-in-place. *Journal of Hazardous Materials*, *109*(1–3), 1–11.

Strahan, K., & Watson, S. J. (2019). The protective action decision model: When householders choose their protective response to wildfire. *Journal of Risk Research*, 22(12), 1602–1623*.

Terpstra, T., & Lindell, M.K. (2012). Citizens' perceptions of flood hazard adjustment: An Application of the protective action decision model. *Environment and Behavior*, *45*(2), 993–1018.

Tierney, K. J. (2007). From the margins to the mainstream? Disaster research at the crossroads. *Annual Review of Sociology*, *33*, 503–525. DOI: 10.1146/annurev.soc.33.040406.131743

Wang, F., Wei, J., & Shi, X. (2018). Compliance with recommended protective actions during an H7N9 emergency: A risk perception perspective. *Disasters*, *42*(2), 207–232.

*Requisite Readings

Chapter 3

Social Amplification of Risk

Early on, risk communication treated risk as objective. Risks were facts, and people were supposed to accept them once communicated to them (Palenchar, 2020). The more enlightened view treats risk as subjective. The social amplification of risk framework (SARF) unpacks the subjective nature of risk by explaining how people's perceptions of risk are influenced by social and cultural factors. Risk communication messages can alter perceptions of risk and the consequences of risks (Kasperson et al., 1988). Given the importance of risk communication to crisis communication, SARF is a valuable framework for crisis managers to appreciate.

Theoretical Overview

People are faced with various risks daily such as taking a shower or commuting to work. Experts know risks matter in people's lives and communicate to people about these risks. Examples of risk communication include encouraging people to wear seatbelts and to avoid texting and driving. Initially, risk communication focused on technical evaluations of risk, meaning the probability and magnitude of a risk. The belief was that if people understood the technical meaning or a risk, they understood the risk. However, how people experienced risk frequently did not match the technical evaluation of a risk. People would either undervalue or overvalue a risk. In the 1970s and 1980s, risk researchers began to explore this difference between technical and perceived risk. Roger Kasperson, Ortwin Reen, and Paul Slovic were among those exploring how people actually perceived risk and effects of those perceptions upon risk communication. Eventually, their work would coalesce to form what became known as SARF (Kasperson et al., 1988).

Simply defining risk based upon technical information about a hazard is not good enough—it is inaccurate. Public reaction to a risk frequently does not reflect the technical evaluation of the hazard with people overestimating minor risks and underestimating serious risks. SARF seeks to explain

DOI: 10.4324/9781003469964-4

how the public (people) react to risks. SARF holds people perceive risk through the interaction of technical and social experiences with risk. Those social experiences involve psychological, social, institutional, and cultural processes. In SARF, risk perceptions are both objective and a social construction. Initial risk perceptions can change as risk messages become transmitted to and circulate among people. The risk might become intensified or attenuated as it passes through various sources (amplification stations). For instance, in 1989, the chemicals in the pesticide Alar were a relatively low risk, but extensive media news coverage of the dangers it posed to children eating apples and apple products portrayed Alar as a significant cancer risk. The coverage was orchestrated through a public relations campaign built around the National Resource Defense Council's (NRDC's) study tilted "Intolerable Risk." Alar was quickly banned even though the government acknowledged the risk was on the low side (Herrmann et al., 1997).

The seminal article for SARF was written by Kasperson et al. (1988), titled "The Social Amplification of Risk: A Conceptual Framework" and appearing in *Risk Analysis*. This was followed by Renn & Levine's (1991) influential work. These pioneers continued to develop SARF, and a wide array of researchers have joined them in its exploration and application. More recently, interest in SARF has been heightened through explorations of how the digital environment is, especially social media platforms (Vijaykumar et al., 2015).

Theoretical Conceptualization

SARF is about how the public—people—experience/perceive risk. Risk communication initially relied upon technical definitions of risk comprised of assessments of probability and magnitude. The technical analysis of risk indicated how likely a risk was to occur and how bad the risk would be (Kasperson et al., 1988). However, early research by Slovic and others found technical risk to be inaccurate, because it did not reflect how the public perceived the risk. Risk spreads through the public via social amplification stations. Social amplification stations are actors who both collect and respond to risk information. A social amplification station can be an individual or a collective (a social station of amplification). Actors become amplification stations through their behavioral and communicative responses to the risk. Moreover, their reactions are shaped by personal values or the nature of the collective. The news media are an example of a social amplification station, and their interpretations are shaped by news routines and values. The social amplification stations generate and transmit risk information through various channels (Renn et al., 1992).

Amplification can result in intensifying perceptions of a risk or attenuating perceptions of a risk. Amplification is a result of the information used in a risk message and how people filter that information (respond to the risk information). Social amplification of risk results in one of two behavioral patterns, overreactions or downplaying of risks. These behavioral patterns have consequences, because they influence how people respond to the risk (Kasperson et al., 2022; Renn et al., 1992). "The roots of social amplification lie in the social experience of risk, both in direct experience, through information received about risk, risk events, and management systems" (Kasperson et al., 1988, p. 184)

SARF has been presented as a six-step process. Step one is a risk event involving a physical event or recognition of an adverse effect. Step two involves people interpreting the risk event based upon how they perceive the cues related to the risk event. Step three occurs when people translate their interpretations of a risk event into messages and communicate them to others. Step four involves people collecting and responding to risk information. These people then become social amplification stations through their actions and communications about the risk event. Step five represents the spread of the impact of the risk information. There is a ripple effect as the risk information moves through society. Each social amplification station serves to expand the ripple. Step six represents the societal impacts from the risk perceptions. During this step, additional social amplification stations can emerge allowing the ripple effect to expand further (Renn et al., 1992).

Message characteristics do influence social amplification. Social amplification can be enhanced by the volume of messages, the extent of dramatization in the message, and the symbolic connotations of the information. However, we should not assume all social amplifications stations agree in how they interpret the risk event. Uncertainty, this can increase the degree of dispute between social amplification stations. Message disputes result in a weakened effect because there are competing views of the risk resulting in varying interpretations of the risk event within society (Renn et al., 1992). Consider how many countries had contradictory interpretations about social distancing messages during the COVID-19 pandemic (Thu et al., 2020).

Key concepts in SARF include the physical consequences of a hazard, media coverage, risk perception, public response, and political and social impacts. The physical consequences of a hazard reflect a technical assessment of a risk event that includes the number of people exposed (exposure), the amount of area exposed (area), the number of people injured or killed (casualties), and financial damage (property damage). Media coverage is composed of the number of stories about the risk, the duration of the time between the first and last story about the risk, and the half-life which is the number of days until half the news stories are generated. Risk perceptions include how others could be harmed in the future (future risk), how strongly a hazard is tied to negative consequences (dread), the degree to which people blame an entity for the risk (blame), and how people believe similar events might be mismanaged (managerial incompetence). Public response includes if people want further media investigations (follow-up), people desire political action to reduce the risk (political involvement), people being willing to take actions to reduce the risk (action), and how experts rate the likelihood of people mobilizing for action (potential for social mobilization). Political and societal impacts include litigation, indirect costs, protests, and political changes (Renn et al., 1992). The political and societal impacts are outcome variables, while the other factors are predictor variables.

Renn et al. (1992) tested the relationship between the five groups of variables. They found the following relationships: the physical consequence of casualties was related to media coverage's number of news stories and to societal impacts. The number of news stores was related to societal impacts and to the risk perception of dread. The risk perception of dread was related to the public response of action, and action was related to societal impacts. They concluded:

> [T]he social and economic impacts of an adverse event are determined not only by the direct physical consequences of the event, but by the interaction of psychological, cultural, social, and institutional processes that amplify or attenuate public experience of risk and result in secondary impacts.
>
> (Renn et al., 1992, p. 154)

Their data demonstrated public risk perceptions, and the consequences of those perceptions were a function of both objective risk assessments and the social construction of risk perceptions.

Social Media Addition

Social media platforms, as part of the digital communication environment, have added to thinking about SARF. Social media platforms increase the speed and reach of risk information dissemination and provide a greater diversity of social amplification stations. Potentially, social media can increase engagement and interactivity with messages but that potential is often unrealized (Pizzi et al., 2021). Finally, social media allows for the real-time monitoring and response to risk messages. Monitoring and response can be used to counter misinformation that enters into the risk communication discussion (Lee, 2022; Lee et al., 2023).

Vijaykumar et al. (2015) integrated social media with SARF to create the risk amplification through media spread (RAMS) model for application to public health authorities communication about public health risks. RAMS offers an alternative to the traditional top-down model of public health by embracing the wide array of communication channels now available to public health officials. They argue the virality of a message is the key. Virality can shape perceptions of risk directly and indirectly. Direct is from the message itself, while indirect is from social conversations related to the message. RAMS provides a basis to begin integrating social media into SARF, thereby expanding our understanding of how publics perceive risk (Vijaykumar et al., 2015).

Summary

SARF provides a useful framework for understanding social perceptions of risk, how risk perceptions influence behaviors, and how risk communication can affect those perceptions. Social amplification stations (individuals or collectives) can play an important role in shaping risk perceptions. Social amplifications can attenuate or intensify perceptions of risk. Social media platforms have increased the potential number of social amplification stations and the relevance of SARF to understanding risk communication.

Applications to Subfields

SARF has been applied primarily to public crises. SARF is commonly used to analyze public health crises, including A/H1N1 in Europe (Rossmann et al., 2018) and COVID-19. For COVID-19, SARF has been applied to Twitter and risk information (E. Lee et al., 2024) and warning messages (Guo et al., 2022). Applications to disasters include the focus on maritime stakeholders for Fukushima (Wang et al., 2013) and facilitating planning for earthquakes (Stanciugelu et al., 2013). Corporate crises have been explored with SARF as well. Song et al. (2019) explored a ferry sinking in South Korea utilizing SARF. Shahrabani et al. (2020) examined the effects of political crises on tourism. Though political crises were mentioned, the focus was on corporate crises given the concern with tourism. Liu et al. (2017) explored product recalls using SARF.

Practical Takeaways

Practitioners can utilize the insights into risk perceptions from SARF to improve risk and crisis communication with constituents. SARF helps crisis managers to understand how constituents are perceiving risks including how those perceptions may be changing before, during, and after a crisis. Crisis managers can develop messages built upon an understanding of how constituents are perceiving a risk, including social and psychological factors influencing risk perceptions, and crafting messages that addresses the risk perceptions and provides constituents with options to help cope with the risks as they perceive them. Crisis managers can think of themselves as amplification stations and work to build trust with constituents prior to a crisis so that constituents turn to their messaging during the crisis. For instance, public health offices should establish their expertise and concern for citizens so that during a public health crisis, the citizens turn to them for information.

SARF provides opportunities to identify and to address misinformation related to a risk. Crisis managers can identify potential amplification points (social amplification stations) to monitor and intervene if misinformation is appearing. Furthermore, crisis managers can monitor and respond on social media to misinformation becoming part of the conversation about risk perceptions. Crisis managers can also use monitoring to simply find points at which they can add useful information to the risk perception conversation independent of misinformation concerns. In general, SARF helps crisis managers to understand risk perceptions during a crisis and to develop more nuanced messages designed to facilitate constituents coping with the various risks.

Theoretical Constraints and Concerns

SARF views itself more as a framework than a traditional theory (Renn et al., 1992). Hence, it is not surprising that the SARF has limited predictive power. Some believe SARF may be too linear and simplistic for capturing the nature of risk perceptions. Moreover, SARF may place too much importance on risk amplification over personal experience and the role of emotion in risk perceptions. Finally, more work is needed to integrate digital channels and social media into SARF (Sutton & Veil, 2017).

Theoretical Engagement Points

1 What type of research methods are most closely associated with SARF?
2 Is SARF primarily a descriptive, relational, or explanatory theory?
3 Is SARF primarily an empirical-analytic, interpretative, or critical theory?
4 How would you evaluate SARF in terms of scope, appropriateness, heuristic value, validity, parsimony, and openness?

Discussion Questions

1 How does the SARF framework challenge the traditional view of risk as objective?
2 Explain how social amplification stations can either intensify or attenuate risk perception. Provide examples to illustrate your point.
3 What are the key message characteristics that influence social amplification? How can uncertainty and message disputes impact the effectiveness of risk communication?
4 Discuss the impact of social media on SARF. How has social media affected the speed, reach, and diversity of risk information dissemination?
5 What are some of the theoretical constraints and concerns associated with SARF? How might these limitations be addressed in future research?

References

Guo, Y., An, S., & Comes, T. (2022). From warning messages to preparedness behavior: The role of risk perception and information interaction in the Covid-19 pandemic. *International Journal of Disaster Risk Reduction*, *73*, 102871.

Herrmann, R. O., Warland, R. H., & Sterngold, A. (1997). Who reacts to food safety scares?: Examining the Alar crisis. *Agribusiness: An International Journal*, *13*(5), 511–520.

Kasperson, R. E., Renn, O., Slovic, P., Brown, H. S., Emel, J., Goble, R., Kasperson, J.X., & Ratick, S. (1988). The social amplification of risk: A conceptual framework. *Risk Analysis*, *8*(2), 177–187*.

Kasperson, R. E., Webler, T., Ram, B., & Sutton, J. (2022). The social amplification of risk framework: New perspectives. *Risk Analysis*, *42*(7), 1367–1380*.

Lee, E. W., Zheng, H., Goh, D. H. L., Lee, C. S., & Theng, Y. L. (2024). Examining COVID-19 tweet diffusion using an integrated social amplification of risk and issue-attention cycle framework. *Health Communication*, *39*(3), 493–506.

Lee, J. (2022). When web add-on correction comes with fear-arousing misinformation in public health crisis: focusing on the role of risk perception in belief in misinformation. *Journal of Applied Communication Research*, *50*(1), 70–90.

Lee, J., Choi, J., & Britt, R. K. (2023). Social media as risk-attenuation and misinformation-amplification station: How social media interaction affects misperceptions about COVID-19. *Health Communication*, *38*(6), 1232–1242.

Liu, Y., Busby, J. S., & Onggo, B. S. (2017, April). Modeling social risk amplification during recall crises. In *SpringSim (ADS)* (pp. 4–12). The Society for Computer Simulation International.

Palenchar, M. J. (2020). Historical trends of risk and crisis communication. In R.L. Heath & H.D. O'Hair (Eds), *Handbook of risk and crisis communication* (pp. 31–52). New York: Routledge.

Pizzi, S., Moggi, S., Caputo, F., & Rosato, P. (2021). Social media as stakeholder engagement tool: CSR communication failure in the oil and gas sector. *Corporate Social Responsibility and Environmental Management*, *28*(2), 849–859.

Renn, O., Burns, W. J., Kasperson, J. X., Kasperson, R. E., & Slovic, P. (1992). The social amplification of risk: Theoretical foundations and empirical applications. *Journal of Social Issues*, *48*(4), 137–160*.

Renn, O., & Levine, D. (1991). *Credibility and trust in risk communication* (pp. 175–217). Springer Netherlands.

Rossmann, C., Meyer, L., & Schulz, P. J. (2018). The mediated amplification of a crisis: Communicating the A/H1N1 pandemic in press releases and press coverage in Europe. *Risk Analysis*, *38*(2), 357–375.

Shahrabani, S., Teitler-Regev, S., Desivilya Syna, H., Tsoukatos, E., Ambrosio, V., Correia Loureiro, S. M., & Voulgaris, F. (2020). The effects of socio-political context on tourism. *EuroMed Journal of Business*, *15*(1), 22–38.

Song, M., Jung, K., Kim, J. Y., & Park, H. W. (2019). Risk communication on social media during the Sewol Ferry disaster. *Journal of Contemporary Eastern Asia*, *18*(1), 189–216.

Stanciugelu, I., Frunzaru, V., Armas, I., Duntzer, A., & Stan, S. (2013). Social amplification of risk and crisis communication planning-a case study. *Scientific Bulletin-Nicolae Balcescu Land Forces Academy*, *18*(2), 197–205.

Sutton, J., & Veil, S. R. (2017). Risk communication and social media. In *Risk conundrums* (pp. 96–111). Routledge.

Thu, T. P. B., Ngoc, P. N. H., & Hai, N. M. (2020). Effect of the social distancing measures on the spread of COVID-19 in 10 highly infected countries. *Science of the Total Environment*, *742*, 140430.

Vijaykumar, S., Jin, Y., & Nowak, G. (2015). Social media and the virality of risk: The risk amplification through media spread (RAMS) model. *Journal of Homeland Security and Emergency Management*, *12*(3), 653–677*.

Wang, X., Kato, H., & Shibasaki, R. (2013). Risk perception and communication in international maritime shipping in Japan after the Fukushima Daiichi nuclear power plant disaster. *Transportation Research Record*, *2330*(1), 87–94.

*Requisite Readings

Chapter 4

Covello's Risk Communication Theories

Vincent Covello has been a driving force in the creation and advancement of risks communication. This includes being the president of the Society for Risk Analysis. In Covello & Allen (1988), he co-authored with F.W. Allen the important pamphlet, "Seven Cardinal Rules of Risk Communication" for the Environmental Protection Agency (EPA) that is still accessible today (Covello & Allen, 1988). The pamphlet was part of the growing recognition of the psychological factors that shaped risk perception and provided a foundation for engaging in effective risk communication. Covello established the Center for Risk Communication in 1992. Covello has gone on to write numerous articles and books on risk communication and advise a wide array of governmental agencies around the world on risk communication matters as well as provide training for improving risk communication. His articles include "Best Practices in Public Health Risk and Crisis Communication" appearing in the *Journal of Health Communication* (Covello, 2003). His most recent book is *Communicating in Risk, Crisis, and High Stress Situations: Evidence-Based Strategies and Best Practices* (Covello, 2022).

Theoretical Overview

Covello posits that risk communication is built around four theories: trust determination theory, negative dominance theory, mental noise theory, and risk perceptions theory (Covello, 2022). Combined, these four theories provide insights into how people process risk information, how people perceive risks, and how people make risk decisions (Covello et al., 2001). Covello's work embraces the connections between risk and crisis communication. He envisions the two being connected through the situational factors of high concern and high stress. High-concern situations create unique challenges for communication. These challenges are a result of situations evoking strong emotions, including frustration, anger, fear, anxiety, and helplessness (Covello et al., 2001). High-concern situations

DOI: 10.4324/9781003469964-5

promote the use of Kahneman's (2011) fast thinking (System 1). Fast thinking tends to be automatic, intuitive, and emotional. High concern leads to high stress. Stress reduces a person's ability to process information and comprehend messages. Risk communication occurring in high-concern and stress conditions means that the attempt to transfer and exchange information must occur because the situation is emotionally charged (Covello, 2022).

Theoretical Conceptualization

Trust determination theory holds that trust is the most important factor when people make risk-related decisions. People are more willing to engage in recommended actions when the information comes from a trusted source. Trust is built overtime through interactions and communication. Covello lists the following factors as predicting high levels of trust: acknowledging uncertainty, being transparent about negative information, quickly disseminating risk information, providing technical information that is easy to understand, soliciting input from stakeholders through engagement, providing consistent messaging by coordinating communication activities among risk managers, avoiding sending out conflicting information, and using multiple communication channels for delivering risk information (Covello, 2022; Peters et al., 1997). Risk communication ideally serves to build trust but can erode trust when ineffective.

Third-part endorsements are useful for establishing trust. When a trusted source endorses a risk message, trust transference occurs. The high trust of the source causes people to view the message as trusted. For instance, a trusted local physician can be used to enhance the trust in messages from the local public health agency by publicly endorsing the risk messages.

Negative dominance theory is predicated on the idea that people feel loss more than they feel gains. This means that people in high-stress and concern situations place greater emphasis on negative messages than on positive messages—there is an asymmetry between positive and negative information. Covello (2022) argues that it takes three to five pieces of positive information to offset one negative piece of information. Negative dominance theory helps to shape the crisis messages in two ways. First, whenever negative information enters the discussion, a larger amount of positive information (those that are solution-oriented) needs to be provided by risk communicators. Second, try to avoid using negative terms such as never or nothing in the risk messaging. People will pay more attention to these negative terms, and that can result in people ignoring the positive risk messaging. Risk communications should focus on the positive of what is being done and solutions, not on the problems and what has not been done (Covello et al., 2001).

Mental noise theory involves information processing during high stress and concern situations. Under stress, a person's information processing ability can be reduced by as much as 80% (Covello, 2022). Psychology has documented how stress serves as a distraction, resulting in the reduced ability to process information. This is due in part to the heightened emotional state experienced during high stress and concern situations. The implications are that people will have a reduced ability to understand and to remember risk messages (Covello et al., 2001).

Covello's message mapping approach to risk communication is designed to combat the problems identified in the mental noise theory. Message maps are a systematic approach to identifying the concerns of stakeholders and developing messages to address those concerns. The risk communicator begins by identifying the relevant stakeholders and creating a list of the concerns and questions they will have about the risk situation. Key messages are then developed to address the concerns and questions. The key messages must be mindful of the reduced information processing of the stakeholders and therefore be simple. Covello argues for the rule of three. There should be just three key messages for each concern/question or one key message that has three parts (Covello, 2006). There is a need for risk communication to be concise and brief. The key messages should be brief lasting about 3 seconds and less than 9 words. That means the three messages combined should be about 9 seconds and 27 words. The messages should be at a readability level of between 6th and 8th grades. Using graphics can improve the reception and understanding of the key messages (Covello, 2022).

Risk perception theory reflects the subjective nature of risk evaluations. Risk perceptions are not shared objective assessments of risk but are subjective interpretations of risk shaped by personal experience, social, economic, political, and cultural factors (Covello, 2022). A number of factors that can shape and alter risk perceptions have been identified. Moreover, these factors affect the decisions people make about risks. The list of the 20 most salient risk perception factors identified by Covello (2022) is presented in Table 4.1. The more of the characteristics from Table 4.1 a risk possesses, the "more worrisome, more fearful, and less acceptable" the risk becomes (Covello, 2022, p. 54). Risk perceptions can be significantly influenced by the risk perception factors and shape how people respond to the risk. Risk perception involves the acceptability of a risk. Covello (2022) emphasizes that risk acceptance is not a function of technical data but a subjective assessment related to social and cultural factors.

Table 4.1 Covello's Risk Perception Factors

1	Trust in authorities: people perceive risk as more serious risk when they lack trust in the risk manager than when they trust the risk managers.
2	Voluntariness: people perceive risk as more serious when the risk is involuntary or imposed on them in some way rather than voluntary risks.
3	Scope/catastrophic potential: The amount or harm a risk can generate will increase concern about that risk. Risk events that are cataclysmic or produce groupings of casualties are viewed as more serious than those that are random or casualties are spread out over time.
4	Familiarity/exotic: people perceive risk as more serious when the risks is unfamiliar, especially those that seem exotic than risks that are more familiar and routine.
5	Understanding/visibility: people perceive risk as more serious when the risks are hard to see or difficult to understand than those that are visible and understandable.
6	Uncertainty: people perceive risk as more serious when the risks are ambiguous, including unknown causes, than risks have known causes and detailed data about the risk.
7	Controllability: people perceive risk as more serious when the risks are out of their control than risks they believe they can control.
8	Effects on children: people perceive risk as more serious when the risks can affect children than those that pose a risk to an adult population.
9	Effects manifestation: people perceive risk as more serious when the risks produce delayed effects than risks product an immediate effect.
10	Effect on future generations: people perceive risk as more serious when the risk poses a threat to future generations than when the risk seems to pose no real threat to future generations.
11	Victim identity: people perceive risks as more serious when there are identifiable victims than when the risk relates to statistics that are nameless.
12	Pleasurable/dread: people perceive risk as more serious when it is unpleasant and can produce dread than when the risk is perceived as pleasurable and not associated with dread.
13	Awareness/media attention: people perceive risk as more serious when there is a larger amount of media coverage and high public awareness than risks that create little media coverage or public attention.
14	Fairness: people perceive risk as more serious when there is an unfair distribution of risk indicating inequities (certain groups suffer the risk more than others) than when the risks are consider equitably distributed among the population.
15	Benefits: people perceive risk as more serious when there are no clear or questionable benefits related to the risk than when the risk can create specific benefits.
16	Reversibility: people perceive risk as more serious when the negative effects are permanent than when the negative effects can be reversed.
17	Person stake: people perceive risk as more serious when they feel it can affect them or those close to them than risks that do not seem to affect them or those close to them.
18	Nature of evidence: people perceive risk as more serious when the data is based on human studies than data based on lab studies of animals.
19	Morality: people perceive risk as more serious when they violate moral principles than risks perceived to be consistent with moral principles.
20	Human vs natural origin: people perceive risk as more serious when they are created by human actions than risks occur naturally.

Applications to Subfields

Covello's risk communication theories have been applied most often to public crises. There is a strong historical link between Covello's risk communication work and public health (1992). We can see this connection to the public subfield most clearly in his 2003 article detailing best practices in public health risk and crisis communication. Jang and Baek (2019) examined the MERS outbreak in South Korea, while Tagliacozzo et al. (2021) analyzed the COVID-19 pandemic in Italy, Sweden, and US, drawing upon Covello's work. Covello's risk communication theories have been applied to disasters (Coombs & Tachkova, 2022; Covello, 2006; Marlowe et al., 2018; Morgan, 2023). More recently, researchers have linked Covello's risk communication theories to corporate crises (e.g., Coombs, 2023). There has been no clear application of Covello's risk communication theories to political crises save for some application to terrorism (Covello et al., 2010). However, the application to terrorism seems better suited to public than to the political crisis subfield.

Practitioner Takeaways

Covello's (2022) theories of risk communication are designed to be applied; hence, there are many takeaways for crisis communicators. First, crisis managers must seek to understand how their stakeholders are perceiving risk because crisis managers cannot assume that stakeholders share their risk perceptions. Risk perceptions are subjective not objective so be sure to understand stakeholder perceptions of risks. Crisis managers must establish trust with stakeholders and that can be facilitated by listening to their concerns and demonstrating empathy for the stakeholders. Crisis managers must speak with compassion as well as being honest and transparent when discussion risks. People must know you care about them before they will listen to you. Second, risk communication requires careful preparation. Message maps provide organizing guidance by identifying the relevant stakeholders, their needs, and how communication can be used to meet those needs. Third, people work to enhance the effectiveness of risk messages through simplicity (remember the rule of three) and third-party endorsements. Keep the risk messages clear and short because stakeholders have reduced information processing during crises. Moreover, credible third parties will boost the credibility of crisis messages. Finally, avoid using negative language in crisis messages and know that when negative messages enter the crisis discussion, they will draw the most attention and require significant effort to counteract. High concern and stress situation create unique demands that crisis managers must understand if they are to create effective risk messages as part of their crisis communication efforts.

Theoretical Constraints and Concerns

Researchers have been concerned about a lack of nuance to Covello's risk theorizing. While there is value in simplified risk messages, oversimplification of complex risk information could result in a loss of important nuances in the risk information (Rowan, 1994). Covello pays little attention to socio-political dimensions that can shape risk perceptions such as power dynamics, inequalities, and cultural differences (Leiss, 1996). This can include issues with translation of risk materials into multiple languages (Coombs & Tachkova, 2022). His focus on individual risk perceptions does not give enough consideration to systemic and structural factors that influence risk communication (Kasperson et al., 1988). Finally, some have argued trust determination theory oversimplifies the complexities required in building and maintaining trust (Renn, 2008). While others recognize the value of Covello's contributions to risk communication theory, there is a push from others to provide great nuance to the theories.

Theoretical Engagement Points

1 What type of research methods are most closely associated with Covello's theories of risk communication?
2 Are Covello's theories of risk communication primarily a descriptive, relational, or explanatory theory? Consider each of the four separately.
3 Are Covello's theories of risk communication primarily an empirical-analytic, interpretative, or critical theory? Consider each of the four separately.
4 How would you evaluate Covello's theories of risk communication in terms of scope, appropriateness, heuristic value, validity, parsimony, and openness? Consider each of the four separately.

Discussion Questions

1 How can trust be built and maintained in risk communication, especially during high-stress situations? Provide examples.
2 How can negative dominance theory be used to shape effective risk messages? What strategies can be employed to counteract the effects of negative information?
3 Explain Covello's message mapping approach and discuss its effectiveness in addressing the challenges of mental noise theory. How can the "rule of three" be used to enhance message clarity and retention?
4 Select three risk perception factors from Table 4.1 and discuss how they can influence public responses to a specific risk event, such as a natural disaster or a health epidemic.

5 What are the ethical considerations that crisis communicators should be aware of when applying Covello's risk communication theories? How can these theories be used responsibly to promote public safety and well-being?

References

Coombs, T. W., & Tachkova, E. R. (2022). Extending the value of crisis translation in crisis communication. In S. O'Brien & F.M. Federici (Eds.), *Translating crises* (pp. 37–48). London: Bloomsbury Publishing.
Coombs, W. T. (2023). *Ongoing crisis communication: Planning, managing, and responding* (6th ed.). SAGE Publications.
Covello, F., Battazza, F., Coletta, A., Lopinto, E., Fiorentino, C., Pietranera, L., Valentini, G., & Zoffoli, S. (2010). COSMO-SkyMed an existing opportunity for observing the Earth. *Journal of Geodynamics*, *49*(3–4), 171–180.
Covello, V. T. (1992). Risk communication: An emerging area of health communication research. *Annals of the International Communication Association*, *15*(1), 359–373*.
Covello, V. T. (2003). Best practices in public health risk and crisis communication. *Journal of Health Communication*, *8*(S1), 5–8*.
Covello, V. T. (2006). Risk communication and message mapping: A new tool for communicating effectively in public health emergencies and disasters. *Journal of Emergency Management*, *4*(3), 25–40*.
Covello, V.T. (2022). *Communicating in risk, crisis, and high stress situations: Evidence-based strategies and practice*. Hoboken, NJ: Wiley*.
Covello, V. T., & Allen, F. H. (1988). Seven cardinal rules of risk communication. Retrieved from https://archive.epa.gov/publicinvolvement/web/pdf/risk.pdf
Covello, V. T., Peters, R. G., Wojtecki, J. G., & Hyde, R. C. (2001). Risk communication, the West Nile virus epidemic, and bioterrorism: Responding to the communication challenges posed by the intentional or unintentional release of a pathogen in an urban setting. *Journal of Urban Health*, *78*, 382–391.
Jang, K., & Baek, Y. M. (2019). When information from public health officials is untrustworthy: The use of online news, interpersonal networks, and social media during the MERS outbreak in South Korea. *Health Communication*, *34*(9), 991–998.
Kahneman, D. (2011). *Thinking, fast and slow*. New York: Macmillian.
Kasperson, R. E., et al. (1988). The social amplification of risk: A conceptual framework. *Risk Analysis*, *8*(2), 177–187.
Leiss, W. (1996). Three phases in the evolution of risk communication practice. *Annals of the American Academy of Political and Social Science*, *545*, 85–94.
Marlowe, J., Neef, A., Tevaga, C. R., & Tevaga, C. (2018). A new guiding framework for engaging diverse populations in disaster risk reduction: Reach, relevance, receptiveness, and relationships. *International Journal of Disaster Risk Science*, *9*, 507–518.
Morgan, B. (2023). Building a career from crisis responder to crisis communicator: A journey of learning and growth through Canda's costliest natural disasters and

largest peacetime evacuations. In W.T. Coombs & S.J. Holladay (Eds.), *The handbook of crisis communication* (pp. 545–552). West Sussex: Wiley Blackwell.

Peters, R. G., Covello, V. T., & McCallum, D. B. (1997). The determinants of trust and credibility in environmental risk communication: An empirical study. *Risk Analysis*, *17*(1), 43–54.

Renn, O. (2008). *Risk governance: Coping with uncertainty in a complex world.* Earthscan.

Rowan, K. E. (1994). The technical and democratic approaches to risk situations: Their appeal, limitations, and rhetorical alternative. *Argumentation and Advocacy*, *31*(1), 40–56.

Tagliacozzo, S., Albrecht, F., & Ganapati, N. E. (2021). International perspectives on COVID-19 communication ecologies: Public health agencies' online communication in Italy, Sweden, and the United States. *American Behavioral Scientist*, *65*(7), 934–955.

*Requisite Readings

Chapter 5

The Anger Activism Model

An important focal point in risk communication is convincing people to engage in a desired, prosocial behavior. Health communication, for instance, depends upon risk communication for communicative efforts desired to decrease behavior harmful to a person's health and increasing behaviors beneficial to a person's health. We find a similar need to encourage and discourage certain behaviors during crises. People should benefit from the behavior such as evacuating a coastal area at risk of flooding and wind damage during a hurricane or sheltering-in-place during a hazardous chemical release. The anger activism model (AAM) explores the role of anger in behavior change.

Theoretical Overview: Anger Activism Model

Researchers have studied the effects of positive and negative emotions on persuasion for a very long time. One of the more recent foci has been on the negative emotion of anger. Anger is created when people feel a sense that their goals are being blocked and an emphasis on injustice (Lerner & Tiedens, 2006). Turner's (2007) AAM seeks to explicate the relationship between anger and persuasion. AAM focuses on the link between attitude and behavioral intentions and is influenced by Lazarus's (1991) cognitive appraisal approach. Anger can be a motivator for action, and those actions can be utilitarian (adaptive). Anger can be created by a threatening situation and create a need to regain control. AAM combines anger with efficacy. The idea is that anger is adaptive when people believe that they can do something about the situation that has caused the anger. Why take action if you feel you cannot change the situation? Anger motivates through the systematic processing of information. The effect of anger is mediated by information processing (Turner, 2007).

Persuasion is relevant to crisis communication. There are times when crisis managers try to persuade the attitudes and/or behaviors of stakeholders. Reputation management involves efforts to shape attitudes about the

DOI: 10.4324/9781003469964-6

organization. Safety warnings, such as evacuation orders, seek to persuade people to engage in behaviors designed to increase safety. Furthermore, people can be persuaded to engage in behaviors that can create a crisis. People can be convinced to oppose possible governmental actions, such as proposed changes to laws or regulations, that could precipitate a crisis. Or people might protest or boycott a corporation to pressure the corporation to change its practices. The boycotts and protests can be paracrises or escalate into actual crises (Coombs & Holladay, 2012).

Theoretical Conceptualization

Anger, efficacy, and information processing are the primary concepts in AAM. Both anger and efficacy can be considered as high or low in a situation. The two factors can be combined to create a two-by-two matrix representing four different types of audiences: (1) high anger and high efficacy (activists); (2) high anger and low efficacy (angry), (3) low anger and high efficacy (empowered), and (4) low anger and low efficacy (disinterested). Activists audiences will engage in the highest levels of information process and should be the most willing to engage in behaviors. They should be motivated to regain control and feel that they have the abilities to do so. Angry audiences feel powerless and are likely to engage in non-utilitarian behaviors. Empowered audiences believe they could do something about the situation but that the situation is not important enough to warrant their efforts. Disinterested audiences lack any motivation to take action. AAM holds that people need a suitable outlet for their anger and confidence in their ability to affect change if anger is to result in utilitarian behaviors (Turner, 2007).

The interaction between anger and efficacy is the starting point for AAM. Information processing mediates the relationship between anger and efficacy on behavioral intentions. People with high anger and high efficacy are more likely to engage in systematic information processing and that "translates into greater intentions to engage in activism" (Turner et al., 2020). In short, anger and efficacy can increase information processing which can then lead to intentions to act (Turner, 2007). [add about not interactive]

Applications to Subfields

AAM has applications for the public, political, and corporate subfields. The earliest application of AAM was to the public crisis subfield with the study of public health. The threat to public health can be a result of the actions of others. An example of that is how tobacco companies benefitted from the unhealthy behaviors of their customers. Ilakkuvan et al. (2017) studied the effects of anger toward tobacco companies to change health-related attitudes and behaviors. The rationale was how anger can trigger coping behaviors designed to remove obstacles and to regain control of a situation. The study found that high anger and high efficacy can move people to action. Those with high anger and high efficacy showed greater receptivity to the messages (had more message-related cognitions), found the message more persuasive, and were more likely to speak to others about the message. Low-anger and low-efficacy respondents showed the weakest effect on the same variables (Ilakkuvan et al., 2017). Jang et al. (2021) applied AAM to vaccinations, another aspect of public health.

In the political crisis subfield, Bessarabova et al. (2023) examined student activist related to campus policies (a form of political behavior). Information processing was assessed through message-relevant cognitions (thought-listing). The message cognitions were coded with a focus on positive-related and negative-related message cognitions. Anger and efficacy did increase attention, information processing, and behavioral intentions. Message-relevant cognitions were found to be mediators on intentions to act. However, anger and efficacy had independent rather than an interaction effect on intentions to act (Bessarabova et al., 2023).

Skurka (2019) examined how anger and efficacy can influence activism intensions and policy support for resolving an issue. Because issues can become crises and crisis can generate issues, the study has relevance to crisis communication (Coombs, 2023). The issue under examination was childhood obesity and how sugary drink marketing by the soda industry was contributing to the issue. Anger was evoked by noting how the soda industry was predatory because children have limited ability to identify the persuasive intent of their marketing efforts as well as using more intense language in the anger-inducing messaging. Both anger and perceived efficacy were found to increase support for obesity-prevention policies and intention to engage in five activism activities. Moreover, the results found anger and efficacy worked separately and lacked an interaction effect (Skurka, 2019).

Cho and Cho (2012) provided the most direct application of AAM to the corporate crisis subfield. The research explored how anger can be a motivator for online consumer activism. The study drew upon part of AAM and cognitive appraisal theory. The results found a positive relationship between anger and communication activities. Efficacy was not part of the study (Cho & Cho, 2012). Zhou and Zhang's (2023) use of AAM to examine CSR crises has implications for the corporate crisis subfield too.

Many corporate crisis communication researchers have drawn directly upon the AAM model or fear as a motivator. However, the corporate crisis communication researchers tend to look at anger generated by a crisis rather than messages designed to create anger. Jin et al. (2012) used the AAM in their discussion of anger as part of their integrated crisis model (ICM). AAM is part of the discussion of SMCC as well (Jin et al., 2014).

Coombs and Holladay (2007) identified anger as a motivator for generating stakeholder negative word-of-mouth following a crisis, what they called the negative communication dynamic. The crisis is a message that can evoke anger which can affect how stakeholders then react toward the organization. Hence, one objective of crisis communication is to reduce anger, thereby reducing the negative effects crisis-generated anger can have on stakeholder attitudes and behavioral intentions (Coombs, 2023). Anger and AAM have been a part of the broader theoretical discussion in crisis communication.

AAM has potential application to the study of corporate paracrises. Paracrises are driven primarily by stakeholder concerns about corporations acting irresponsibly (Chen & Holladay, 2023; Coombs & Holladay, 2012). Essentially paracrises can be viewed as a form of activism. AAM can be used to better understand how paracrises might develop by exploring the roles of anger and efficacy in paracrises. How do anger and efficacy contribute to the development and impact of paracrises? Furthermore, anger-related insights could help to develop more appropriate and effective responses to paracrises.

Researchers have also delineated how AAM can be used to understand misperceptions and misinformation. The results of the study found that high-anger partisans were the most likely to support claims by their party regardless of the veracity of the information. Moreover, anger was shown to increase avoidance of counterattitudinal sources and stronger use of pro-attitudinal sources (Carnahan et al., 2023). This data suggests that anger could be a factor in misinformation/disinformation, a problem that plagues all three subfields of crisis communication.

Practitioner Takeaways

Practitioners can benefit from a greater understanding of how anger matters in crisis communication. First, anger can be used to persuade stakeholders to support a certain position and/or to engage in a desired behavior. Anger can be used to win support for specific policies and to enact specific health behaviors. Second, practitioners must be aware of the level of anger a crisis is likely to evoke from stakeholders because the crisis can serve as an anger-inducing message. A premium can be placed on crisis response strategies that serve to reduce anger such as accommodative response strategies, adjusting information, and instructing information (Coombs, 2023).

Theoretical Constraints and Concerns

While anger is recognized as a motivator, there are some concerns about the AAM and anger as an explanatory variable. One concern is how anger becomes an isolated emotion and does not explain how anger can interact with other emotions. There is also a concern with anger having the potential to lead to anti-social behavior (Turner, 2020). A constraint includes how AAM is affected by cultural difference (Williams, 2017).

Theoretical Engagement Points

1 What type of research methods are most closely associated with AAM?
2 Is AAM primarily a descriptive, relational, or explanatory theory?
3 Is AAM primarily an empirical-analytic, interpretative, or critical theory?
4 How would you evaluate AAM in terms of scope, appropriateness, heuristic value, validity, parsimony, and openness?

Discussion Questions

1 How does the AAM differ from traditional models of persuasion that focus on positive emotions or fear appeals?
2 What are some examples of "utilitarian" behaviors that might result from anger, as described in AAM? How do these differ from "non-utilitarian" behaviors?
3 The chapter discusses the application of AAM to various subfields of crisis communication. Which subfield do you find most compelling for using AAM? Why?
4 How might cultural differences influence the effectiveness of anger appeals based on AAM? Can you provide specific examples?
5 What ethical considerations should practitioners be aware of when leveraging anger in crisis communication strategies?

References

Bessarabova, E., Turner, M. M., & Richards, A. S. (2023). Anger, efficacy, and message processing: A test of the anger activism model. *Southern Communication Journal*, *89*(1), 1–14*.

Carnahan, D., Ahn, S., & Turner, M. M. (2023). The madness of misperceptions: Evaluating the ways anger contributes to misinformed beliefs. *Journal of Communication*, *73*(1), 60–72*.

Chen, F., & Holladay, S. J. (2023). Identifying and responding to social media risks: Towards an organizational paracrisis communication framework. *Corporate Communications: An International Journal*, *28*(1), 103–117.

Cho, S. H., & Cho, S. H. (2012). The effect of situational perceptions and anger on a consumer's communication activeness. *Journal of Digital Convergence*, *10*(9), 111–122.

Coombs, W. T. (2023). *Ongoing crisis communication: Planning, managing, and responding* (6th ed.). SAGE Publications.

Coombs, W. T., & Holladay, J. S. (2012). The paracrisis: The challenges created by publicly managing crisis prevention. *Public Relations Review*, *38*(3), 408–415.

Coombs, W. T., & Holladay, S. J. (2007). The negative communication dynamic: Exploring the impact of stakeholder affect on behavioral intention. *Journal of Communication Management*, *11*(4), 300–312.

Ilakkuvan, V., Turner, M. M., Cantrell, J., Hair, E., & Vallone, D. (2017). The relationship between advertising-induced anger and self-efficacy on persuasive outcomes. *Family & Community Health*, *40*(1), 72–80.

Jang, Y., Turner, M. M., Heo, R. J., & Barry, R. (2021). A new approach to audience segmentation for vaccination messaging: Applying the anger activism model. *Journal of Social Marketing*, *11*(4), 424–452.

Jin, Y., Liu, B. F., & Austin, L. L. (2014). Examining the role of social media in effective crisis management: The effects of crisis origin, information form, and source on publics' crisis responses. *Communication Research*, *41*(1), 74–94.

Jin, Y., Pang, A., & Cameron, G. T. (2012). Toward a publics-driven, emotion-based conceptualization in crisis communication: Unearthing dominant emotions in multi-staged testing of the integrated crisis mapping (ICM) model. *Journal of Public Relations Research*, *24*(3), 266–298.

Lazarus, R. S. (1991). Cognition and motivation in emotion. *American Psychologist*, *46*(4), 352–367. https://doi.org/10.1037//0003-066x.46.4.352

Lerner, J. S., & Tiedens, L. Z. (2006). Portrait of the angry decision maker: How appraisal tendencies shape anger's influence on cognition. *Journal of Behavioral Decision Making*, *19*(2), 115–137.

Skurka, C. (2019). You mad? Using anger appeals to promote activism intentions and policy support in the context of sugary drink marketing to kids. *Health Communication*, *34*(14), 1775–1787*.

Turner, M. M. (2007). Using emotion in risk communication: The anger activism model. *Public Relations Review*, *33*(2), 114–119*.

Turner, M.M. (2020). Harnessing anger for social change. Retrieved from https://researchoutreach.org/articles/harnessing-anger-social-change/

Turner, M. M., Richards, A. S., Bessarabova, E., & Magid, Y. (2020). The effects of anger appeals on systematic processing and intentions: The moderating role of efficacy. *Communication Reports*, *33*(1), 14–26*.

Williams, R. (2017). Anger as a basic emotion and its role in personality building and pathological growth: The neuroscientific, developmental and clinical perspectives. *Frontiers in Psychology*, *8*, https://doi.org/10.3389/fpsyg.2017.01950

Zhou, Z., & Zhang, X. (2023). Applying the Anger Activism Model (AAM) to CSR crises: From the perspective of the 2022 Russian invasion of Ukraine. *Journal of International Crisis and Risk Communication Research*, *6*(2), 53–86*.

*Requisite Readings

Chapter 6

The Extended Parallel Process Model

Crisis managers are often tasked with convincing people to engage in behaviors designed to protect themselves. Examples include evacuating an area, not consuming a food product that may be contaminated with a foodborne illness, or sheltering in place. It seems odd, but crisis managers do need to persuade people to help themselves. Fear appeals have a very long history in persuasive efforts designed to help people dating back to the 1950s. Fear is a negatively valenced emotion created by a relevant and significant threat (Witte, 1992). Fear appeals work by noting something bad will happen to people if they do not follow the recommended actions. You could be injured if you do not evacuate an area or get sick if you eat a contaminated food product. Essentially, you try to scare people into changing behaviors.

Theoretical Overview

In 1992, Kim Witte published an article in *Communication Monographs* titled "Putting the Fear Back into Fear Appeals: The Extended Parallel Process Model." The model became known as EPPM for short. Witte and others began applying the model in the health communication campaign context. Later, researchers extended EPPM to other risk communication contexts, including crisis communication (Roberto et al., 2020).

EPPM was developed by Kim Witte as a way to harness fear more effectively in efforts to persuade people to engage in behaviors that will help them. EPPM's original focus was on health behaviors such as getting vaccinations or medical check-ups. Witte (1992) synthesized the fear-as-acquired drive model, parallel process model, and protection motivation theory to create EPPM. Fear-as-acquired drive model is a learning model that argues people will change behaviors once they learn to fear a threat. For instance, you wear a seatbelt when you learn not wearing one can result in injury. However, people can react to fear in an adaptive way by following the recommended action or in a maladaptive way through

DOI: 10.4324/9781003469964-7

defensive avoidance (Hovland et al., 1953). The parallel process model posits that people have cognitive and emotional reactions to fear. A cognitive response is when people think about and try to avoid the threat (Leventhal, 1971). You decide not to hike in the area where a grizzly bear has been spotted. An emotional response involves fear control efforts, including avoidance or denial. You decide to hike in the area because you deny the grizzly will attack you.

Protection motivation theory refined thinking about threat messages. The effect of a threat is a function of the likelihood of a threat occurring, the magnitude of the threat, how effective the recommended action is, and a person's ability to execute the recommended action (self-efficacy) (Rogers, 1975; Popova, 2012). By building upon previous research, Witte (1992) hoped to increase the understanding of why fear appeals fail, re-focus persuasive research on fear as a central variable, and clarify the relationship between threat and efficacy.

Theoretical Conceptualization

EPPM centers on fear, "a negative reaction to perceived threat" (Popova, 2012, p. 457). Threat and efficacy are the key concepts necessary to understand how fear affects behaviors. A threat is an external stimulus that people need to perceive as dangerous to themselves. A threat cannot create fear if you do not know it exists. A threat involves a message component and perceived threat. The message component are elements of a message that create the impression that a threat is severe, and a person is susceptible to the threat (Popova, 2012). Messages can be used to increase perceptions of a threat. Perceived threat is comprised of perceived severity and perceived susceptibility. Perceived severity is how serious the threat appears to be. Is the threat something can have a serious negative effect or just a minor inconvenience? Perceived susceptibility is whether or not people believe the threat will affect them (Witte, 1992). Can this threat affect me?

Efficacy involves message characteristics and perceived efficacy. Message characteristics emphasize the effectiveness of a response (recommended action) and a person's ability to engage in that response (self-efficacy). Efficacy messages should enhance perceived efficacy. Perceived efficacy is a function of perceived response efficacy and perceived self-efficacy (Popova, 2012). Perceived response efficacy is how people perceived the effectiveness of the recommended response. Perceived response efficacy is high when people believe that the recommended response will allow them to avoid threat—it will work. For example, people need to believe a vaccine will help to prevent the disease. Perceived self-efficacy is the degree to which people believe they can actually do the recommended response (Witte, 1992). Can the person perform the desired behavior or not?

There are three possible responses to a fear appeal in EPPM: danger control, fear control, and no response. Danger control is a form of protective motivation where people engage in the recommended response. For instance, people decide to get their annual flu shot. Fear control is a form of defensive motivation where people believe that they can do nothing about the threat, so they engage in denial, avoidance, or reactance (Popova, 2012; Witte, 1992). No response is when people simply ignore the messages and view them as irrelevant. Using the threat and efficacy factors, EPPM can be used to diagnosis why people selected one of the three outcomes. The diagnostic value of EPPM resides in the relationship between threat, efficacy, and response.

Perceived threat is the first assessment people make about a message. Again, a threat must matter for people to take some action. If people either perceive the threat is not severe or the threat is not relevant to them, they will do nothing. Why pay any attention to something you do not see as a threat or do not see as a threat that can affect you? Research finds that over 50% of people will consume a food produce event when they know the product has been recalled due to a risk of it containing a foodborne illness. People might not see a foodborne illness as a serious threat or that it will not affect them. If people do perceive the threat to be serious and relevant to themselves, they then assess efficacy.

People select the danger control response when they believe the recommended action will work and they can perform the action. For instance, people will get. A flu shot if they believe the shot can prevent the flu and they have easy access to the vaccine. People are responding to the danger and not to the fear. People select fear control if they think the recommended action will not work and/or they cannot perform the recommended action. The threat has created fear, and the recommended response cannot alleviate the fear, so people need to cope psychologically with the fear through avoidance, denial, or reactance. In such cases, people are responding to the fear and not the danger (Witte, 1992).

The critical feature in EPPM is the threat-to-efficacy ratio. If threat is greater than efficacy, people opt for fear control. If threat is less than efficacy, people opt for danger control. Researchers have examined the ratios and found that high threat and high efficacy do produce the optimal effect on changing behavioral intentions. Threat and efficacy did not influence behavioral intentions, while threat with no efficacy had a limited effect on intentions (Carcioppolo et al., 2013). A survey instrument has been developed that allows researchers to assess perceived threat severity, perceived threat susceptibility, perceived response efficacy, and perceived self-efficacy. The data helps to explain why people engaged or did not engage in the recommended response. The failure of the messaging might be in perceptions of the threat and/or perceptions of efficacy. Knowing where the message failed allows crisis managers to revise the messages and potentially increase the likelihood of people engaging in the recommended action.

EPPM provides a framework to diagnose the threat and efficacy factors that are critical to convincing people to follow a recommended action. Threat can be assessed using perceptions of severity and susceptibility of a threat. For a threat to motivate people, they must perceive the threat as severe and that it can affect them (susceptibility). To engage in the recommended action, people must perceive that the plan will alleviate the threat (plan efficacy) and that they themselves can perform the recommended action (self-efficacy). EPPM provides a means of evaluating each of these four factors which provides greater insight into why people did or did not follow the recommended actions during a crisis.

Application to Subfields

EPPM has been applied to public and corporation crises. Political is the only crisis subfield where it does not seem to fit well. EPPM was developed with a focus on health communication; hence, there was a natural application to public health crises, part of the public crisis subfield. Public health crises create a need for people to follow recommended actions. EPPM was widely utilized in research related to the COVID-19 pandemic. For instance, Tsoy et al. (2022) examined intentions to stay home during the COVID-19 pandemic using EPPM. Their US data found that threat and efficacy did were positively related to the recommended action of staying. The findings were consistent with the tenets of EPPM.

Disasters require people to follow recommended actions too and represent another facet of the public crisis subfield. People need to evacuate for hurricanes and to go to designated shelters, and other behaviors intended to help them through the situation. EPPM has been used to examine disaster communication intended to shape behaviors. Ashida et al. (2016) utilized EPPM to understand the lack of compliance for disaster preparation among older adults in rural areas. The researchers explore how fear control and danger control responses emerged among the target population. Their findings supported EPPM's argument for the importance of threat and efficacy perceptions. Efficacy emerged as a focal point in the data analysis and informed the recommendations for future preparedness efforts (Ashida et al., 2016).

Corporate crises are just beginning to explore the application of EPPM. Risk communication is a natural part of crisis communication and becomes relevant during many facets of the crisis communication process. Liu et al. (2016) used EPPM to explore crisis communication within the cruise tourism industry. The focal crisis was contracting Norovirus while on a cruise. The data indicated that the perceived threat of Norovirus did affect the perceived danger of cruising and cruise travel intention. Instructing information was included in the study because it tells people how to protect themselves physically from a crisis (Holladay, 2009; Sturges, 1994). Instructing information was found to build self-efficacy and serve to lessen the effects of threat on the perceived danger of a cruise and cruise travel intentions. The study reinforced the value on instructing information in crisis communication because of its potential to increase perceived self-efficacy for recommended actions (Liu et al., 2016).

Practitioner Takeaways

EPPM has message construction guidance and diagnostic value for practitioners. EPPM holds that perceptions of threats and efficacy can be cultivated through risk messages. As guide, EPPM indicates the key factors that must be included in crisis communication designed to garner adherence to recommended actions. These persuasive messages must create the perceptions that a threat is serious and that the target audience is susceptible to the threat. If there is no threat, there is no need to comply with recommended actions. However, threat is just the start. The message also must enhance perceptions of both plan and self-efficacy. The target audience must believe that the recommended action will alleviate the threat and that they can engage in desired behaviors.

EPPM's diagnostic value can be used to evaluate the effectiveness of risk messages intended to gain compliance with recommended actions. Such evaluations can be useful in the pre-crisis, crisis response, and post-crisis phases of crisis management. During the pre-crisis phase, training can be used to increase perceptions of threat and efficacy. One aspect of preparation is training people how to respond to a crisis situation. For instance, people living near a facility that utilizes hazardous materials may need to learn to how to shelter-in-place. EPPM can help to identify any barriers to community members sheltering-in-place as well potential recommendations for overcoming these barriers. Part of training can include explaining why the threat is serious and how people are vulnerable to it. Virtual reality has been used to help people realize the threat posed by flooding and their susceptibility to the threat (Purnomo et al., 2022). Moreover, training is a chance to demonstrate the efficacy of a plan and for people to realize that they can execute the desired action. An example would be employees learning the proper way to evacuate a building (Zlateva et al., 2020).

Pre-drafting messages is another facet of preparation. Crisis managers can pre-test compliance messages to see if they have the desired effect to increase threat and efficacy perceptions. Message testing would increase confidence of the effectiveness of compliance messages during a crisis.

A crisis response should contain instructing information (Coombs, 2023), advice on what people should do to protect themselves physically during a crisis. As noted earlier, product harm crises require product recalls and for consumers to comply with the request to not use or to not consume a product. Hence, there is a need to persuade people to follow recommended actions.

EPPM can be used as part of the post-crisis evaluation. Crisis managers can review reactions to their compliance messages. This review can include actual compliance rates with the recommended actions and reactions from those in the target audience to the compliance messages. The reactions can be any combination of social media posts, focus groups, or survey responses designed to assess perceptions of threat and efficacy.

Constraints and Concerns about EPPM

Concerns about EPPM center around its rationality. EPPM reflects a rational decision-making model. Emotions, social influences, past experiences, and other psychological factors influence human decision-making as well. EPPM can overlook the emotional reactions people can have to fear appeals, another aspect of the rationality concern. The fear appeals can have unintended consequences when people "overdose" on fear and engage in negative behaviors (Lu & Jin, 2023). There is also a risk of fatigue if the fear appeal is used repeatedly in the crisis messaging. One constraint is EPPM's limited predictive power. While EPPM has proven its utility, the model has limited predictive power for accurately and consistently predicting when fear-based messages will promote behavior change. A second constraint is that EPPM may not capture the full complexity of human decision-making (Popova, 2012).

Conclusion

EPPM is a theory of risk communication that is most closely associated with health communication and disaster communication. The focus is understanding why people often fail to follow recommended actions intended to help them such as getting an annual flu vaccine. EPPM has application in crisis communication because of the strong ties between risk and crisis communication. Public health crises and disaster communication require risk communication as part of crisis communication. For instance, any public health or disaster warning message is a form of risk communication. The warning messages seek to inform and to persuade people to take the desired actions necessary to avoid the negative consequences of a disease or disaster—a mix of risk and crisis communication. Crisis messaging is frequently infused with elements of risk communication (Coombs, 2023).

EPPM has been widely applied to public crises, including public health crises and disasters. The potential for EPPM's application in corporate crises has just begun to be tapped (e.g., Coombs & Tachkova, 2022; Liu et al., 2016). EPPM is a risk communication theory that should also be considered a crisis communication theory.

Theoretical Engagement Points

1 What type of research methods are most closely associated with EPPM?
2 Is EPPM primarily a descriptive, relational, or explanatory theory?
3 Is EPPM primarily an empirical-analytic, interpretative, or critical theory?
4 How would you evaluate EPPM in terms of scope, appropriateness, heuristic value, validity, parsimony, and openness?

Discussion Questions

1 How can crisis managers effectively use EPPM to design persuasive messages during a public health crisis?
2 Discuss the ethical considerations of using fear appeals in crisis communication. What are the potential risks and benefits?
3 How can EPPM be applied to address vaccine hesitancy in a community? Provide specific examples of messages that could be used.
4 Compare and contrast the effectiveness of danger control and fear control responses in different crisis situations. Provide examples.
5 Critique EPPM's assumption of rationality in human decision-making. How do emotions and other psychological factors influence responses to fear appeals?

References

Ashida, S., Robinson, E. L., Gay, J., & Ramirez, M. (2016). Motivating rural older residents to prepare for disasters: Moving beyond personal benefits. *Ageing & Society*, *36*(10), 2117–2140.

Carcioppolo, N., Jensen, J. D., Wilson, S. R., Collins, W. B., Carrion, M., & Linnemeier, G. (2013). Examining HPV threat-to-efficacy ratios in the extended parallel process model. *Health Communication*, *28*(1), 20–28.

Coombs, W. T. (2023). *Ongoing crisis communication: Planning, managing, and responding* (6th ed.). SAGE Publications.

Coombs, W. T., & Tachkova, E. R. (2022). Elaborating the concept of threat in contingency theory: An integration with moral outrage and situational crisis communication theory. *Public Relations Review*, *48*(4), 102234.

Holladay, S. J. (2009). Crisis communication strategies in the media coverage of chemical accidents. *Journal of Public Relations Research*, *21*(2), 208–217.

Hovland, C., Janis, I., & Kelly, H. (1953). *Communication and persuasion*. New Haven, CT: Yale University Press.
Leventhal, H. (1971). Fear appeals and persuasion: The differentiation of a motivational construct. *American Journal of Public Health*, *61*(6), 1208–1224.
Liu, B., Pennington-Gray, L., & Krieger, J. (2016). Tourism crisis management: Can the Extended Parallel Process Model be used to understand crisis responses in the cruise industry?. *Tourism Management*, *55*, 310–321.
Lu, X., & Jin, Y. (2023). Integrating strategy and dosage: A new conceptual formula for overcoming unintended effects of public health crisis communication (PHCC). In W.T. Coombs & S.J. Holladay (Eds.), *The handbook of crisis communication* (2nd ed., pp. 263–284), West Sussex: John Wiley and Sons.
Popova, L. (2012). The extended parallel process model: Illuminating the gaps in research. *Health Education & Behavior*, *39*(4), 455–473.
Purnomo, F. A., Yoeseph, N. M., Koesuma, S., Hartono, R., Ristania, S., & Riasti, B. K. (2022, August). Virtual reality flood disaster with variations of water levels in the early warning system. In *2022 1st International conference on smart technology, applied informatics, and engineering (APICS)* (pp. 180–185). IEEE.
Roberto, A. J., Goodall, C. E., & Witte, K. (2020). Raising the alarm and calming fears: Perceived threat and efficacy during risk and crisis. In Robert L. Heath & H. Dan O'Hair (Eds.), *Handbook of risk and crisis communication* (pp. 285–301). Routledge.
Rogers, R. (1975). A protection motivation theory of fear appeals and attitude change. *Journal of Psychology*, *91*, 93–114.
Sturges, D. L. (1994). Communicating through crisis: A strategy for organizational survival. *Management Communication Quarterly*, 7(3), 297–316.
Tsoy, D., Godinic, D., Tong, Q., Obrenovic, B., Khudaykulov, A., & Kurpayanidi, K. (2022). Impact of social media, Extended Parallel Process Model (EPPM) on the intention to stay at home during the COVID-19 pandemic. *Sustainability*, *14*(12), 7192.
Witte, K. (1992). Putting the fear back into fear appeals: The extended parallel process model. *Communications Monographs*, *59*(4), 329–349*.
Zlateva, P., Velev, D., & Galabov, M. (2020). Research on the applicability of virtual reality for emergency evacuation training in business buildings. *International Multidisciplinary Scientific GeoConference: SGEM*, *20*(5.2), 417–423.

*Requisite Readings

Chapter 7

Warning Response Model

In 2022, the United Nations launched the "Early Warning for All" project. The goal is to provide early warnings for hazardous weather, water, or climate events to everyone in the world by 2027. Early warning systems save lives and are cost-effective. The world needs more early warning systems because intense weather events will only increase as a result of climate change. About one in three people in less developed areas is not covered by early warning systems (UN, 2022). However, having a warning system is most effective when people receive complete warning messages that facilitate people taking the necessary protective actions. Research derived from Mileti and Sorensen' (1990) work on the warning response model (WRM) seeks to provide guidance on creating complete and effective warning messages. Understanding the work inspired by the WRM is valuable to crisis managers.

Theoretical Overview

Researchers have been exploring the warning notification used in the US. This research centers on the utilization of wireless emergency alerts (WEAs). According to FEMA (2023), "Wireless Emergency Alerts (WEAs) are short emergency messages from authorized federal, state, local, tribal and territorial public alerting authorities that can be broadcast from cell towers to any WEA-enabled mobile device in a locally targeted area" (para 1). WEAs are used in the area distributed through the Integrated Public Alert & Warning System (IPAWS). IPAWS is a communication tool that allows public safety agencies to notify people about disasters and to provide emergency and public safety information (FEMA, 2024).

The WRM is at the heart of research into enhancing warning messages. The WRM has five core components: (1) source, (2) hazard, (3) location, (4) guidance, and (5) time. Source identifies the organization or person issuing the warning message. The more credible people receiving the message perceived the source to be, the more likely they are to take the

DOI: 10.4324/9781003469964-8

recommended protective actions (Sutton & Kuligowski, 2019). Hazard identifies the specific threat such as tornado or wildfire. The hazard message should include a description of how the hazard will affect people. The location specifies where the hazard is occurring and who might be affected by it. Location should provide specific information for people about the location such as streets or landmarks. Guidance instructs people what precisely they should do to protect themselves from the hazard. The guidance must be easy to understand and for people to execute. Time involves the timing of the hazard including when it might affect people, when people should engage in the protective actions, and when the warning message might expire (Kuligowski et al., 2023).

In addition to the core components, the WRM includes style because style does affect the effectiveness of the warning messages. The style of the warning message involves its presentation and how the message is composed. The style of the warning message includes specificity (exact information about location, hazard, and timing), consistency (use consistent language in the messaging), accuracy (information is up-to-date and accurate), and clarity and simplicity (avoid jargon, technical terms while writing is style that is easy to understand) (Sutton et al., 2024, 2023). Some researchers refer to the WRM as the message optimization paradigm (Bean et al., 2024). Working from this basic model, researchers have developed ways to operationalize the elements of the WRM, analyzed existing warning messages, and provided insights into how to improve warning messages.

Theoretical Conceptualization

The WRM has guided research seeking to improve warning messages. The idea is for the messages to warn people about hazards and not just alert them to the existence of hazards (Sutton et al., 2023). As noted in the previous section, the warning message research has explored the utility of the WRM model by establishing the value of complete hazard messages (Sutton et al., 2024). Important outcome variables related to the WRM include message understanding, message belief, agreeing or disagreeing with the message, the ability to make quick and effective decisions about protective actions, self-efficacy, and response efficacy (Sutton et al., 2024).

The research also has studied the degree to which actual WEAs are complete and utilizing ideas from WRM to create a warning lexicon designed to enhance the ability of public safety officials to develop more effective warning messages. WEAs are used in a wide range of emergency settings, including earthquakes, tsunamis, explosions, active shooters, radiological releases, and even for improvised nuclear device detonation (Sutton et al., 2023).

Because there is value in complete warning messages, researchers have examined WEAs to determine the degree to which these messages are complete. One of those studies examine a set of WEAs from 2012 to 2022 containing 6,080 messages. The analysis found only 8.5% of the WEAs were complete. Source and timing information elements of the WRM appear the least often. The results found that the 90-character WEAs were less complete than the 360-character WEAs (Sutton et al., 2023).

One effect of incomplete messages is milling. Milling is when people get the warning message but then seek additional information rather than acting on the warning—they delay their response to the warning (Wood et al., 2018). People might search the Internet for additional information, ask family and friends about the warning, or look for environmental and social ques relevant to the hazard (Bean et al., 2024; DeYoung et al., 2019).

WRM research has found that there is limited training about message developed for those responsible for creating and distributing WEAs (Bean et al., 2024). The lack of training is problematic because those using WEAs do not have the resources to quickly create warning messages. WRM was used as a guide to develop message warning templates (predesigned messages) for those officials who need to create WEAs. The research resulted in the creation of a Warning Lexicon (Sutton et al., 2024).

The Warning Lexicon has three primary components: hazards, protective action statements, and hazard impact statements. The first component is a list of possible hazards. Using FEMA guidelines, the researchers defined hazards as being urgent (action needed within an hour), severe (significant threat to life or property), and certain (likelihood of happening 50% or higher). The analysis resulted in the identification of 48 hazards. The 48 hazards were organized into seven hazard categories: atmospheric, geophysical, law enforcement, public health, public safety, technological, and wildfire (Sutton et al., 2024).

Protective action statements inform people about how the actions they should take to protect themselves from the hazard. The researchers analyzed 372 protective actions that were grouped into broader categories. The analysis identified 112 protective actions. There were ten action categories: shelter, evacuate, protect, decontaminate, refrain, avoid, obtain, listen, rearrange, and contact. Of those protective actions, 68 could be used for multiple hazards, while 44 were for specific hazards (Sutton et al., 2024).

Hazard impact statements were the final element. Hazard impact statements are the "effects, outcomes, or consequences of hazardous events" (Harrison et al., 2021, p. 2). Hazard impact statements can be pre-event or during/post-event. Pre-event hazard impacts are uncertain while those during/post-event are more certain. The researchers created 93 impact statements to cover all the identified hazards. A series of prompts were developed to help people use the warning lexicon more effectively (Sutton et al., 2024).

Researchers have attempted to connect warning messages to crisis communication in general because of the strong connection between risk and crisis communication (Cain et al., 2024). The researchers noted the overlap between warning messages, exemplified by WEAs, and crisis communication recommendations from situational crisis communication theory (SCCT) calling for the first crisis response to be a combination of instructing information and adjusting information (Coombs, 2007). Instructing information has a natural connection to WEAs because it seeks to tell people how to protect themselves physically from the negative effects of a crisis. Adjusting information helps people to cope psychologically with the crisis (Holladay, 2009; Sturges, 1994). WEAs were analyzed to determine if they used instructing and adjusting information, the types of adjusting information, difference in uses between 90-character and 360-character WEAs, and if instructing and adjusting information varied by hazard. Instructing information appeared in 72.2% of WEAs, while adjusting information appeared in 13.7%. The most common type of adjusting information were official orders (95) and official actions (4.6%). Both instructing information (62%–88%) and adjusting information (7.1% and 24%) appeared more frequently in 360-character WEAs than 90-character WEAs. Instructing information was found more often in public safety and public health hazards, while adjusting information was more common in law enforcement hazards (Cain et al., 2024).

The results reinforced the overlap between the WRM and SCCT through instructing information. Instructing information does improve understanding and self-efficacy, establishing its value in a communicative effort. However, the researchers did not see a compelling reason to include adjusting information in WEAs. This was due to the limited space in WEAs and the lack of research establishing the benefits of adjusting information (Cain et al., 2024).

Bean et al. (2024) developed and refined the concept of public warning failures because the concept was ill defined. A public warning failure as was defined to occur "When a message is issued by a public safety official for a threat that does not exist, is not issued for a threat that does exist, or does not adequately follow evolving best practices for public warning" (Bean et al., 2024, p. 3). The first two failures are obvious. Unwarranted message failure occurs when a warning is sent but there is no hazard. Unsent messages involve a hazard existing but no message being sent. The failure to follow best practices is more complicated and divided into three types. Message content failure is the first type. The warning message can be incomplete (not meet the requirements of WRM), conflicting, or inconsistent. Idle alerts are included as well—alerts that simply ask people to be more alert. Message dissemination is the second type. Insufficient message dissemination can occur if distribution is inconsistent or not widely sent. Untimely message dissemination constituents failure as well. Message context failure is the third type. Message context failure can be a function of inadequate public education about warnings (people are not prepared to understand the warnings) or inadequate local adaptation such as not understanding the language needs of the target audience (Bean et al., 2024).

Application to Subfields

The WRM is limited to crises that involve hazards, which is an important domain because of the risk to human life. The public communication subfield has been the primary application of WRM. WRM has been applied to a wide range of public crises, including hurricanes, floods, tsunamis. Earthquakes, tornadoes, blizzards, severe thunderstorms, wildfires, disease outbreaks, and terrorism (Sutton et al., 2023). Examples of applications include Kuligowski et al.'s (2023)) analysis of wildfires, Sutton et al.'s (2018) development of tsunami warning messages, and Riel and Miczo's (2024) exploration of response to tornado messages. The subfield of corporate crises can produce crises warranting public warnings. Corporate crises that evoke hazards include industrial accidents such as the release of hazardous materials and transportation accidents such as aviation crashes. For instance, Lindell's (1983) work on nuclear hazards fits within the corporate crisis subfield. Crises in the political subfield might involve hazards as well. An example would be terrorist attacks. WRM can be applied across the three crisis subfields whenever a crisis produces a hazard requiring a public warning.

Practitioner Takeaways

The WRM research demonstrates the value of complete warning messages in crisis communication about hazards. Complete warning messages contain the five core components: (1) source, (2) hazard, (3) location, (4) guidance, and (5) time. Complete warning messages provide the critical information people need to make decisions about protective actions. The WRM research has produced a rich set of resources to help crisis managers needing to develop complete warning messages. The warning lexicon is a comprehensive set of templates to guide message development. Moreover, crisis managers can access The Warn Room, an online resource to help with warning messaging construction (https://www.thewarnroom.com/free-tools). The web site is free and helps guide crisis managers through the warning message development process. Practitioners also be alert to the problem of milling.

Theoretical Constraints and Concerns

While templates have value crisis managers needing to deliver alerts, some are cautious about templates. The concern is the potential to oversimplify messages and the potential to miss nuances related to complex hazards and diverse audiences (Mowbray et al., 2024). The point is there is a need to balance context-specific communication with the basic information in the templates (Kim et al., 2019). Others have argued that the WRM does not give enough attention to individual differences such as culture or trust in government and overlooks the problems of the digital divide (Bean et al., 2024; Kuligowski et al., 2024). Relevant individual differences include perception of the threats (DeYoung et al., 2019), people's emotional reactions to the situation (Gutteling et al., 2018; Liu et al., 2017), prior exposure to warning messages (Smith et al., 2022), and language spoken at home (Kim et al., 2019). The concerns do not question the value of the WRM, rather they explore ways to enhance it (Mowbray et al., 2024). There is also a debate over what constitutes the desired outcome for warning messages/measure of success. Some argue that the effectiveness of warning message is measured as compliance with protective behaviors (Bean et al., 2024). This can include the intention to comply. Others posit that a warning message is successful if it provides the information people need to make decisions (Sutton et al., 2025).

Theoretical Engagement Points

1 What type of research methods are most closely associated with WRM?
2 Is WRM primarily a descriptive, relational, or explanatory theory?
3 Is WRM primarily an empirical-analytic, interpretative, or critical theory?
4 How would you evaluate WRM in terms of scope, appropriateness, heuristic value, validity, parsimony, and openness?

Discussion Questions

1 What are the five core components of a complete warning message, according to the WRM?
2 What is milling, and why is it a problem in crisis communication?
3 What are some of the limitations of using templates for warning messages?
4 What are some of the individual differences that the WRM does not adequately consider?
5 What are some of the different ways to measure the effectiveness of a warning message?

References

Bean, H., Hasinoff, A., & Fields, S. (2024). Defining public warning failure. *Journal of Contingencies and Crisis Management*, *32*(3), e12602*.

Cain, L. B., Sutton, J., & Olson, M. K. (2024). Wireless emergency alerts and organisational response: Instructing and adjusting information in alerts. *Journal of Contingencies and Crisis Management*, *32*(1), e12516.

Coombs, W. T. (2007). Protecting organization reputations during a crisis: The development and application of situational crisis communication theory. *Corporate Reputation Review*, *10*, 163–176.

DeYoung, S. E., Sutton, J. N., Farmer, A. K., Neal, D., & Nichols, K. A. (2019). "Death was not in the agenda for the day": Emotions, behavioral reactions, and perceptions in response to the 2018 Hawaii Wireless Emergency Alert. *International Journal of Disaster Risk Reduction*, *36*, 101078.

FEMA (2023). Wireless emergency alerts. Retrieved from https://www.fema.gov/emergency-managers/practitioners/integrated-public-alert-warning-system/public/wireless-emergency-alerts

FEMA (2024). Integrated emergency alert & warning system. Retrieved from https://www.fema.gov/emergency-managers/practitioners/integrated-public-alert-warning-system

Gutteling, J. M., Terpstra, T., & Kerstholt, J. H. (2018). Citizens' adaptive or avoiding behavioral response to an emergency message on their mobile phone. *Journal of Risk Research*, *21*(12), 1579–1591. https://doi.org/10.1080/13669877.2017.1351477

Harrison, S. E., S. H. Potter, R. Prasanna, E. E. H. Doyle, and D. Johnston. 2021. "'Where oh where is the data?': Identifying data sources for hydrometeorological impact forecasts and warnings in Aotearoa New Zealand." *International Journal of Disaster Risk Reduction*, *66* (Dec), 102619. https://doi.org/10.1016/j.ijdrr.2021.102619

Holladay, S. J. (2009). Crisis communication strategies in the media coverage of chemical accidents. *Journal of Public Relations Research*, *21*(2), 208–217.

Kim, G., Martel, A., Eisenman, D., Prelip, M., Arevian, A., Johnson, K. L., & Glik, D. (2019). Wireless Emergency Alert messages: Influences on protective action behaviour. *Journal of Contingencies and Crisis Management*, *27*(4), 374–386.

Kuligowski, E. D., Sutton, J., Olson, M. K., & Cain, L. B. (2024). Alerts and warnings in emergency communication. In Brooke F. Liu & Amisha M. Mehta (Eds.), *Routledge handbook of risk, crisis, and disaster communication* (pp. 130–145). Routledge*.

Kuligowski, E. D., Waugh, N. A., Sutton, J., & Cova, T. J. (2023). Ember alerts: Assessing wireless emergency alert messages in wildfires using the warning response model. *Natural Hazards Review*, *24*(2), 04023009.

Lindell, M. K. (1983, October). Analysis of emergency staffing for nuclear power plants. In *Proceedings of the human factors society annual meeting* (Vol. 27, No. 2, pp. 184–186). Los Angeles, CA: SAGE Publications.

Liu, B. F., Wood, M. M., Egnoto, M., Bean, H., Sutton, J., Mileti, D., & Madden, S. (2017). Is a picture worth a thousand words? The effects of maps and warning messages on how publics respond to disaster information. *Public Relations Review*, *43*(3), 493–506.

Mileti, D. S., & Sorensen, J. H. (1990). Communication of emergency public warnings. *Landslides*, *1*(6), 52–70*.

Mowbray, F., Mills, F., Symons, C., Amlot, R., & James Rubin, G. (2024). A systematic review of the use of mobile alerting to inform the public about emergencies and the factors that influence the public response. *Journal of Contingencies and Crisis Management*, *32*(1), e12499*.

Riel, Z., & Miczo, N. (2024). Responses to a WEA Tornado warning text message: A health belief model approach. *Western Journal of Communication*, *89*, 1–26.
Smith, K. R., Grant, S., & Thomas, R. E. (2022). Testing the public's response to receiving severe flood warnings using simulated cell broadcast. *Natural Hazards*, *112*(2), 1611–1631.
Sturges, D. L. (1994). Communicating through crisis: A strategy for organizational survival. *Management Communication Quarterly*, 7(3), 297–316.
Sutton, J., Kuligowski, E., Olson, M., Walpole, H., & Wood, M. M. (2025). Measuring the effectiveness of disaster warning messages: A forum. *Natural Hazards Review*, *26*(1), 02524001*.
Sutton, J., & Kuligowski, E. D. (2019). Alerts and warnings on short messaging channels: Guidance from an expert panel process. *Natural Hazards Review*, *20*(2), 04019002.
Sutton, J., Olson, M. K., & Waugh, N. A. (2024). The warning Lexicon: A multi-phased study to identify, design, and develop content for warning messages. *Natural Hazards Review*, *25*(1), 04023055*.
Sutton, J., Vos, S. C., Wood, M. M., & Turner, M. (2018). Designing effective tsunami messages: Examining the role of short messages and fear in warning response. *Weather, Climate, and Society*, *10*(1), 75–87.
Sutton, J., Wood, M. M., Huntsman, D. O., Waugh, N., & Crouch, S. (2023). Communicating hazard location through text-and-map in earthquake early warnings: A mixed methods study. *Natural Hazards Review*, *24*(4), 04023035.
UN. (2022). Early warning for all. Retrieved from https://www.undrr.org/implementing-sendai-framework/sendai-framework-action/early-warnings-for-all
Wood, M. M., Mileti, D. S., Bean, H., Liu, B. F., Sutton, J., & Madden, S. (2018). Milling and public warnings. *Environment and Behavior*, *50*(5), 535–566*.

*Requisite Readings

Part II

Crisis Communication Section

Chapter 8

Corporate Apologia/ Terminological Control Theory

Apologia is an established rhetorical genre that examines self-defense. Dionisopoulos and Vibbert (1988) were the first to argue apologia could be applied to corporate discourse thereby create the theory of corporate apologia. Hearit's (1994) application of corporate apologia to crisis communication resulted in people considering corporate apologia as crisis communication theory. Hearit (2006) later expanded beyond the basics of corporate apologia to focus more specifically on apology with an infusion of Burke's (1966) notion of terminological control. This terminological control theory explores how individuals and organizations use apologia to restore legitimacy in society following accusations of wrongdoing in public relations crises, as well as on how to perform an ethically correct apology and control terminology

Theoretical Overview

This theory takes a social constructivist approach to crisis and emphasizes the key role of terminological control or definitional hegemony (Frandsen & Johansen, 2017). The terminological control theory includes a process model that explains the whole process of apologia from wrongdoing, *kategoria* (accusations), to response strategies, *apologia*, and the ending of a crisis. Furthermore, based on casuistry, viewing ethics as a kind of practical wisdom, the theory also includes a more practical-oriented apologetic ethics model that describes the manner and content of an ethically correct apology.

The theory belongs to what has been named a rhetorical and text-oriented research tradition, as it is also the case of William Benoit's theory on image repair (1995, 2020), as opposed to the strategic and context-oriented research tradition within crisis communication research (Frandsen & Johansen, 2017). Hearit perceives organizational rhetoric

DOI: 10.4324/9781003469964-10

and crisis communication to be a matter of defending and repairing the social legitimacy of an organization during public relations crises.

Accordingly, Hearit is inspired by Suchman (1995) and his theory of social legitimacy, that is based on the idea that companies are dependent on their environment and can only survive and attract needed resources for their business activities if they live up to the norms and values of society. Hearit applies Suchman's distinction between pragmatic legitimacy and ethical (moral) legitimacy to describe how an organization may end up in a legitimacy crisis, when it is accused of wrongdoing. Lack of *pragmatical legitimacy* is when an organization is considered incompetent or unprofessional, and lack of *ethical legitimacy* is when an organization violates laws, rules, norms and values of society (Suchman, 1995; Frandsen & Johansen, 2020).

Terminological control theory has a focus on corporate apologia. In crisis communication, attempts can be made to strategically control terminology and frame the way people understand a crisis. According to Hearit (2006), to strategically name an act of wrongdoing means that the apologist engage in a persuasive act acknowledging with Burke:

> Even if a given terminology is a reflection of reality, by its very nature as a terminology it must be a selection of reality, and to this extent it must function also as a deflection of reality.
>
> (Burke, 1966: 45)

In his early work, Hearit and his co-authors mostly studied corporate crises (e.g., Hearit, 1996, 1999; Hearit & Courtright, 2003, 2004). The most comprehensive presentation of Hearit's theory and studies of apologies can be found in his book *Crisis Management by Apology: Corporate Response to Allegations of Wrongdoing* (2006). It is here Hearit sharpens his focus on the apology and presents his ideas on how to make an apology that lives up to the apologetic ethics in a paradigm case. Furthermore, he expands his studies on corporate cases and includes case studies on not-for-profit organizations, politicians, sports figures, media celebrities, and religious and governmental institutions. The book also presents a case study that shows how difficult it can be to live up to expectations and cultural differences in offering a right apology in different parts of the world (Hearit, 2006).

Theoretical Conceptualization

Terminological control theory consists of at least two components: a process model of terminological control and a rhetorical model of apologetic ethics that consists of a set of normative guidelines on how to perform a correct apology.

The Process Model

The process model of terminological control contains five phases: An action is committed that is considered wrongful by parts of society, followed by accusations of wrongdoing against an organization. This is also named *kategoria*. Consequently, the organization ends up in a legitimacy crisis. Next, the organization starts defending itself, using corporate apologia strategies (see Table 8.1), and this may lead to the ending of the crisis for the organization, if a performed apologia allows to restore legitimacy and to continue its business.

Based on his first corporate case studies, Hearit identified three main strategies for corporate apologia: persuasive accounts, expressing sorrow, and dissociation that include three substrategies (Hearit, 1994, 1995a, 1995b).

Persuasive accounts consist in an organization's attempts to offer convincing accounts of a crisis situation, for instance to counter news medias' framing of the crisis. This is a way to regain terminological control over competing "proto-definitions" (Hearit & Courtright, 2003, p. 88) and to exercise definitional hegemony over competing interpretations (Frandsen & Johansen, 2017). To *express sorrow* for what has happened is a way to show empathy and is often used to try to minimize or reduce responsibility.

The third strategy is *dissociation* and is a strategy used by an individual or organization in an attempt to distance itself from the wrongdoing. Inspired by Perelman and his idea about separating or distancing appearance (what looks like reality) from reality (what actually is reality), Hearit distinguishes between three basic types of dissociation referring to denial, differentiation, and explanation. The first type uses an *opinion/knowledge dissociation*. In this case, an organization describes the accusations of wrongdoing as merely opinion, that people do not have real or actual knowledge on what has created the crisis. It can be considered a denial.

The second type is an *individual/group dissociation*. This constitutes an attempt to use differentiation as a strategy, e.g., by claiming that only a few employees were responsible for the wrongdoing, not the organization as such. Finally, *act/essence dissociation* is used by an individual or organization in an attempt to explain itself. The organization admits that it has done something wrong but explains that this is not the true nature or essence of the organization, e.g., by stating: "If you think this happened because we left our employees to themselves, you could not be more wrong. We have always tried to be there and to assist our employees during challenging times".

Hearit (2023) has recently begun applying Seeger and Sellnow's (2016)) concept of blame narratives within apologia strategies, as it aligns well with the assignment of guilt or blame ascribed to an organization when it is accused of wrongdoing by various actors. An organization may offer counter-narratives (i.e., attempts of terminological control) to justify actions, meet audience expectations, and restore legitimacy in society, and three forms of blame narratives can be used for such a purpose: denial, differentiation, and apology stances (Hearit, 2023, p. 88) that corresponds to the above-mentioned dissociation strategies.

Apologetic Ethics

An apology is a speech act, applied within the process model of terminological control, and it is part of the strategy used to potentially end a crisis. Hearit developed the apologetic ethics model to offer normative guidelines on how to produce the best and ethically correct apology (Hearit, 2006).

The model is based on casuistry and the use of paradigm case. Casuistry is viewed as a kind of practical wisdom, as ethical rules do not cover all cases without exceptions. Specific circumstances must be taken into consideration and may differ from case to case, as reflected in the term: casuistry. The use of casuistry allows for taking complicating considerations into account, and they may allow for communication that is not living fully up to the ethical ideal (Hearit, 2006, p. 215). A paradigm case is a case where ethical considerations are so clear-cut that everybody can agree on whether an act or situation is ethically acceptable or not. Hearit is based on the idea of a paradigm case serving as a standard against which complicated ethical situations can be measured. According to him, a paradigm case includes two dimensions that must be accomplished: manner of communication and content of communication, although complicating circumstances may justify deviations from the standard. The model is presented in Table 8.1.

As it appears from Table 8.1, the model includes three main dimensions: manner of communication, content of communication, and complicating circumstances. As for *manner of communication*, an ethical apology must be truthful, sincere (not faking an apology), timely (offered at the right point in time: not too quick, not too late), voluntary, address all stakeholders (not just the "ones that feel offended"), and performed in an appropriate context (e.g., in news media prime time or another appropriate place for people to learn about the apology)

As for *content of communication*, an ethical apology must observe the ten elements presented in Table 8.1, including: accept full responsibility; address injured stakeholders showing empathy and regret; explain why it happened to the public not withholding any details, and explain what will be done to correct the action, compensate, etc.

Finally, Hearit also points to a list of *complicating circumstances* that may justify deviations from the paradigm case or standard. Catastrophic financial

Table 8.1 Normative Guidelines for Apologetic Ethics

Manner of the Communication	*Content of the Communication*
• Truthful • Sincere • Timely • Voluntary • Addresses all stakeholders • Is performed in an appropriate context	• Explicitly acknowledges wrongdoing • Fully accepts responsibility • Expresses regret • Identifies with injured stakeholders • Asks for forgiveness • Seeks reconciliation with injures stakeholders • Fully discloses information related to the offense • Provides an explanation that addresses legitimate expectations of the stakeholders • Offers to perform an appropriate corrective action • Offers appropriate compensation
Complicating Circumstances • Catastrophic financial losses • Grave liability concerns • A moral learning curve • The problem of full disclosure • Discretion	

Source: Frandsen and Johansen (in press), 2026, Table 5.5.

losses, serious concerns about liability, problem of full disclosure (e.g., to what extent does an organization or top management fully know the extent of wrongdoing), and discretion (e.g., confidentiality issues, such as respect for victims, can make it impossible to go public with a full disclosure or apology). A fifth complicated circumstance is related to what is named a "moral learning curve," and it has to do with the nature of the relationship to the injured parties. Sometimes, it is only later in time that an organization becomes fully aware of its harmful wrongdoing, feels guilt, and/or accepts full responsibility, acknowledging the moral need for an apology, recognizing that "a late apology is better than no apology at all" (Hearit, 2006, p. 75).

Applications to Subfields

Terminological control theory and the rhetorical model of apologetic ethics have been applied by Hearit not only to the study of corporate crises and corporate rhetorics but also to other subfields of public and political crises. His work and theories have been applied in various ways by other scholars within the field of rhetorics and crisis communication (cf. Coombs et al., 2010). Ihlen (2002) used his theory for the study of the crisis response of Daimler-Benz defending their Mercedes A-Class in 1997; Towner (2009) gave an overview of rhetorical apologia theories, including a detailed presentation of Hearit's theoretical framework; and Frandsen and Johansen (2020) were inspired by Hearit's perspectives on the relationship between apologia and social legitimacy in a study on the restoration of organizational legitimacy of a large bank.

Frandsen and Johansen did two studies on apologetic ethics in an attempt to test and expand terminological control theory. Frandsen and Johansen (2007) applied the rhetorical model of apologetic ethics in the case of a renowned handball coach who during a handball match told her players to leave the ground because she disagreed with a verdict of the sports referees. And they studied a misunderstanding of a quote from a lecture of Pope Benedict in Regensburg in 2006 that made Muslims claim an apology and the pope to offer a 'meta-apology', not apologizing for his words in the lecture but only for the negative effects the misunderstanding had possibly caused (Frandsen & Johansen, 2010).

Scholars studying terminological control and apologies primarily use case studies and conduct rhetorical, text analysis, framing or narratives to identify format, content and frames applied to the study of verbal defense and apologizing for wrongdoing and transgressions of a socio-cultural order.

Practitioner Takeaways

The primary takeaway from the terminological control theory and apologetic ethics is that it is crucial to be able to defend yourself in an appropriate way, using disassociation strategies in a correct way for people to accept and understand the crisis response, such as a denial or excuse. This includes competences in dealing with competing frames and interpretations among actors occurring in a crisis, through terminological control. It also includes the ability to perform an ethically correct apology for people to forgive an organization for wrongdoing and restore social order.

Furthermore, crisis managers need to be aware of the role of terminological control and ethical expectations in maintaining social legitimacy in society. Only if the activities and behavior of an organization are considered legitimate, that is, an organization has a "license to operate," it will get the needed resources from the environment. If an organization lacks pragmatical legitimacy, it will be considered incompetent, not able to perform its activities, and score low on corporate ability. If an organization lacks ethical legitimacy, it will be considered irresponsible, as someone who is violating norms and values, and score low on corporate social responsibility.

Theoretical Constraints and Concerns

Terminological control theory primarily concentrates on one crisis response strategy: the apology. Although, the theory recognizes difficulties in apologizing when an organization is hit by a crisis involving actors from different cultures having different expectations as to the performance of an ethically correct apology, the theory does only, to a less extent, deal with dilemmas and situations of conflicting expectations, e.g., if an organization is perceived of wrongdoing in one culture but has not done something wrong according to its own cultural order (Frandsen & Johansen, 2010). In this case, no matter how the organization responds, it will face criticism. More research is needed within this field. Moreover, there is a lack of concern with power issues in the theory.

Theoretical Engagement Points

1 What type of research methods are most closely associated with terminological control theory?
2 Is terminological control theory primarily a descriptive, relational, or explanatory theory?
3 Is terminological control theory primarily an empirical-analytic, interpretative, or critical theory?
4 How would you evaluate terminological control theory in terms of scope, appropriateness, heuristic value, validity, parsimony, and openness?

Discussion Questions

1 How can organizations effectively balance the need for terminological control with the ethical considerations of a sincere and truthful apology?
2 In what ways might cultural differences impact the success of an apology, and how can organizations navigate these challenges?
3 How do the three strategies for corporate apologia—persuasive accounts, expressing sorrow, and dissociation—differ in their effectiveness and ethical implications?
4 What role does social legitimacy play in an organization's crisis communication strategy, and how can organizations rebuild legitimacy after accusations of wrongdoing?
5 What are the potential limitations of terminological control theory, particularly regarding power dynamics and conflicting expectations, and how might these be addressed in future research?

References

Benoit, W. L. (1995). *Accounts, excuses and apologies: A theory of image restoration strategy* (2nd ed.). Albany, NY: State University of New York.

Benoit, W. L. (2020). Image repair theory. In F. Frandsen & W. Johansen (Eds.), *Crisis communication, Vol. 23. Handbooks of communication science* (pp. 105–119). Berlin: De Gruyter Mouton.

Burke, K. (1966). *Language as symbolic action: Essays on life, literature, method.* Berkeley, CA: University of California Press.

Coombs, W. T., Frandsen, F., Holladay, S. J., & Johansen, W. (2010). Why a concern about corporate apologia? *Corporate Communication: An International Journal, 15*(4), 337–349.

Dionisopoulos, G. N., & Vibbert, S. L. (1988). CBS vs. mobil oil: Charges of creative bookkeeping in 1979. In H. R. Ryan (Ed.), *Oratorical encounters* (pp. 241–251). New York: Greenwood.

Frandsen, F. & Johansen, W. (2007). The apology of a sports icon: Crisis communication and apologetic ethics. *Hermes: Journal of Language and Communication Studies, 38*, 85–104.

Frandsen, F., & Johansen, W. (2010). Apologizing in a globalizing world: Crisis communication and apologetic ethics. *Corporate Communication: An International Journal, 15*(4), 350–364*.

Frandsen, F., & Johansen, W. (2017). *Organizational crisis communication. A multivocal appraoch.* London: Sage.

Frandsen, F., & Johansen, W. (2020). Crisis communication and organizational legitimacy. In J. D. Rendtorff (Ed.), *The handbook of business legitimacy: Responsibility, ethics, and society* (pp. 707–725). Springer. doi:10.1007/978-3-030-14622-1_27

Frandsen, F., & Johansen, W. (in press, 2026) *Organizational crisis communication. A multivocal approach* (2nd ed.). London: Sage.

Hearit, K. M. (1994). Apologies and public relations crises at Chrysler, Toshiba, and Volvo. *Public Relations Review, 20*, 113–125. https://doi.org/10.1016/0363-8111(94)90053-1

Hearit, K. M. (1995a). "Mistakes were made:" Organizations, apologia, and crises of social legitimacy. *Communication Studies, 46*, 1–17. https://doi.org/10.1080/10510979509368435

Hearit, K. M. (1995b). From "we didn't do it" to "it's not our fault": The use of apologia in public relations crises. In W. N. Elwood (Ed.), *Public relations inquiry as rhetorical criticism*, (pp. 117–131). New York: Greenwood.

Hearit, K. M. (1996). The use of counter-attack in public relations crises: The case of General Motors vs. NBC. *Public Relations Review, 22*, 233–248. https://doi.org/10.1016/S0363-8111(96)90047-8

Hearit, K. M. (1999). Newsgroups, activist publics, and corporate apologia: The case of Intel and its Pentium chip, *Public Relations Review, 25*, 291–308.

Hearit, K. M. (2006). *Crisis management by apology: Corporate responses to allegations of wrongdoing.* Mahwah, NJ: Lawrence Erlbaum*.

Hearit, K. M. (2023). Corporate apologia as crisis communication. In W. T. Coombs & S. J. Holladay (Eds.), *The handbook of crisis communication* (pp. 81–97). Chichester: John Wiley & Sons*.

Hearit, K. M., & Courtright, J. L. (2003). A social constructionist approach to crisis management: allegations of sudden acceleration in the Audi 5000. *Communication Studies*, *54*(1), 79–95*.

Hearit, K. M., & Courtright, J. L. (2004). A symbolic approach to crisis management: Sears defense of its auto repair politics. In D. P. Millar & R. L. Heath (Eds.), *Responding to crisis: A rhetorical approach to crisis communication*, (pp. 201–213). Mahwah, NJ: Lawrence Erlbaum Associates.

Ihlen, O. (2002). Defending the Mercedes a-class: combining and changing crisis response strategies. *Journal of Public Relations Research*, *14*, 185–206.

Seeger, M. W., & Sellnow, T. L. (2016). *Narratives of crisis: Telling stories of ruin and renewal*. Stanford: Stanford University Press.

Suchman, M. C. (1995). Managing legitimacy: Strategic and institutional approaches. *Academy of Management Review*, *20*(3), 571–610.

Towner, E. B. (2009). Apologia, image repair, and reconciliation. The application, limitations, and future directions of apologetic rhetoric. *Annals of the International Communication Association*, *33*(1), 431–468, doi:10.1080/23808985.2009.11679093

*Requisite Readings

Chapter 9

Image Repair Theory

When accused of wrongdoing, rightly or wrongly, most people or organizations try to defend themselves by using various verbal and/or non-verbal rhetorical strategies to repair an image that may have been damaged by such accusations. Choosing the right self-defense strategies, named crisis response strategies within the field crisis communication, are central to image repair. Thus, the image repair theory was developed to understand such persuasive defense. The theory is mainly inspired by the disciplines of rhetoric and the sociology of accounts, but social psychology and the theory of reasoned action also serve as inspiration.

Theoretical Overview

Image repair theory (Benoit, 2015, 2024), originally named image restoration theory (Benoit, 1995), by William L. Benoit belongs to what has been named a rhetorical and text-oriented research tradition, as opposed to the strategic and context-oriented research tradition within crisis communication research (Frandsen & Johansen, 2017). The theory is interested in understanding what people say and how they say it; that is, the rhetoric or rhetorical strategies that people use when they try to defend themselves against accusations of wrongdoing or suspected wrongdoing.

William L. Benoit, alone or together with colleagues, have conducted numerous qualitative case studies, since Benoit, 1982 on how politicians (e.g., Reagan, Clinton, Bush, Obama, Biden, and Trump), corporations (e.g., CocaCola, the tobacco industry, USair, British Petroleum, Apple, Walmart), actors (e.g., Hugh Grant), sports people (e.g., Tonya Harding, Tiger Woods, Lance Armstrong), religious institutions (e.g., the Vatican), royals (Queen Elizabeth), and countries (the US and Japan; China and SARS) defend themselves more or less successfully using rhetorics, when they are accused or suspected of having done something wrong. Benoit published one of his first image repair studies, using the case of Richard M. Nixon's rhetorical strategies in his public statements on Watergate, in 1983.

DOI: 10.4324/9781003469964-11

Based on all these case studies, Benoit developed his theory and has since confirmed its value again and again.

The most comprehensive presentation of Benoit's theory can be found in his book *Accounts, Excuses, and Apologies* (Benoit, 1995) that was revised in 2015 (2nd ed.) and again in 2024 (3rd ed.). In these books, Benoit presents the theory of image repair and shows how the theory may be applied in all sorts of areas, including politics, corporate, sports, religion, health and education, where people or organizations attempt to defend themselves against accusations of wrongdoing. As a rhetorician, Benoit concentrates on the wordings and the self-defense: what do people say when they get attacked and criticized of wrongdoing? However, William Benoit has also, together with Dorries (Benoit & Dorries, 1996), studied the persuasive attacks, that is, the type of accusations or attacks on their behavior or character that individuals and organizations are dealing with when accused of wrongdoing (see Table 9.2). However, it is the verbal crisis response strategies that constitute the cornerstone of image repair theory.

Image repair theory is inspired by three rather different theoretical traditions which have been interested in studying verbal self-defense or image repair through communication: rhetoric (in particular, neo-rhetorical theory), sociology of accounts, and social psychology.

Within rhetoric, Benoit is first and foremost inspired by Ware and Linkugel (1973) and their theory of *apologia* that originated in the generic criticism tradition (Black, 1965) and Bitzer's article on the rhetorical situation (Bitzer, 1968). The apologia theory studies the specific forms or genres of verbal self-defense and has been applied in a series of analyses of political speeches, sports rhetoric and organizational communication. Ware and Linkugel distinguish between four rhetorical basic strategies: deny, support, differentiate, and transcend that can be combined into four potential apologetic stances: absolutive (deny and differentiate), vindicative (deny and transcend), explanative (support and differentiate), and justificative (support and transcend). However, Benoit is also inspired by Kenneth Burke and his neo-rhetorical *theory of purification* (Burke, 1970), in particular, his idea of the importance of guilt that occurs when an undesirable state of affairs or feelings of guilt appear when expectations are violated. An attack on the image or reputation of an individual or an organization may provoke this feeling of guilt. Burke indicates two types of purification strategies: *victimage strategy* where the blame is transferred to somebody or something else turning that person or instance into victim or *mortification strategy* where the accused accept responsibility and ask for forgiveness.

Within sociology, Benoit has been inspired by Scott and Lyman (1968) and their theory of accounts. They define an account as "a statement made by a social actor to explain unanticipated or untoward behavior" (p. 46), distinguishing between two types of accounts: excuses and justifications. When you excuse, you admit that the action was bad, wrong, or inappropriate but deny having full responsibility. When you justify, you accept responsibility but deny that it is a bad, wrong, or inappropriate act. Both strategies contain a number of sub-strategies.

Within social psychology, Benoit (2015) is inspired by Fishbein and Ajzen (2010) and their social psychological *theory of reasoned action.* According to this theory, persuasive communication will always try to influence, create, and change attitudes, such as beliefs (descriptions or knowledge of the world) and values (positive or negative evaluations). This means that image repair strategies can be perceived as attempts to change or create new beliefs or values about an offensive act and the accusation of wrongdoing.

Theoretical Conceptualization

Image repair theory is based on two assumptions (1) that communication is a goal-oriented activity and (2) that a key goal of communication is to maintain a favorable image/reputation. As Benoit puts it: "People try to reach the goals that seem to be the most important at the time they act, or to be the best possible mix of goals" (Benoit, 1995: 65). When people communicate, they always have a goal of some kind, whether it is to make students listen and give feedback in a teaching situation or to keep a dialogue (phatic communication) between people ongoing on a mobile phone or to attempt to persuade others about a specific stance, etc. Maintaining a positive image seems to be one of the goals, because a favorable image strengthens positive self-esteem and is important to the position and influence of an individual or organization. Thus, if your image is threatened, you will spontaneously try to protect the image, and one way of doing this is to avert an attack or repair a damaged image.

The image repair theory is a crisis communication theory (Benoit, 2004) that can be presented as a process moving from an attack leading to a crisis and from a crisis to image repair of the damage done to an image, see Table 9.1 for an overview of the process.

Through the analyses of a high number of case studies conducted by Benoit and fellow scholars since Benoit, 1982, Benoit has identified 5 main strategies and 14 strategies in total (5 main strategies and 11 sub-strategies). However, in his recent third version of his book *Accounts, Excuses and Apologies*, (Benoit, 2024), he states that he has discovered another two frequently used denial sub-categories: *deflecting the blame* and *straw blaming*. Studies of accusations of wrongdoing, for example, of American presidents, have shown that when they try to deny wrongdoing, they sometimes attempt to deflect attention away from what they did by referring to

Table 9.1 Image Repair Process Model

From attack to crisis

- An undesired event or wrongdoing takes place
- Somebody/the public thinks that X (company/organization/actor) is responsible for this event
- The image of X is threatened

From crisis to image repair

- X reacts using verbal response (response strategies—from denial to mortification)
- Someone/the public thinks that X is not responsible for the event or wrongdoing or has justified its part in the case
- The image of X is repaired

others. Benoit is also naming this strategy for "Whataboutism," that is, a strategy where the accused points to others: what about the others, what are they doing? When Trump was accused of dealing wrongly with documents when in office, he asked: What about Hillary's emails? (Benoit, 2024: 18). Straw blaming is denying an accusation by claiming that an attack is misleading, exaggerated, or more extreme than it really is to create the false impression that X denied an accusation. To illustrate: during Covid-19, Trump was asked why he did not support a mask mandate? And he answered: I sometimes wear a mask (Benoit, 2024: 18). A full overview of the list of image repair strategies is seen in Table 9.2.

As it appears from Table 9.2, the model includes five main strategies: the first is the *denial strategy* which has four sub-categories, all intended to convince accuser/public that the accused has not performed the act/wrongdoing or that the act is not harmful in any way. The second main strategy, *evade responsibility*, and its four sub-categories are used to reduce the responsibility for the act by explaining that the act occurred due to: provocation, lack of information, accidentally or for the sake of somebody/something else, that is, good intentions. Third main strategy, *reducing offensiveness of the event*, has six sub-categories. They are all meant to mitigate the negative effect of the event or action, by either stressing the good character of the accused, criticizing the credibility of the accuser, offering compensation to the offended, reducing the seriousness of the event by minimizing, differentiation or transcendence, that is, changing the context (doing it for a bigger cause, such as society). The last two main strategies have no sub-categories. *Corrective action* is used to convince accuser/public that this action is not going to happen again by communicating about the plans or about what has been done to avoid this from happening again in the future. No matter whether an individual or organization is responsible or not, people want to make sure that it is not going to happen again. Hence, this is an important strategy to use together with

Table 9.2 Image Repair Strategies

Main Strategies	*Sub-categories*	*Definition/Explanation:*
Denial	Simple denial	X denies having performed an undesirable event and/or being responsible for it
	Shifting the blame	X blames another actor for being guilty of the undesirable event
	Deflecting the blame	X stresses unrelated criticism, deflect attention away from damaging accusations
	Straw blame	X characterizes an attack as exaggerated, misquoted or more extreme than it really is, to make it easier to refute
Evading of responsibility	Provocation	X claims that X was provoked to act/ was a scapegoat/others share the blame
	Defeasibility	X claims due to lack of information or ability
	Accident	X claims the event occurred accidentally
	Good intentions	X claims it was meant well
Reducing offensiveness	Bolstering	X tries to reduce offensiveness by reminding about good character, and past actions
	Minimization	X tries to minimize negative effect, by stressing the act was not serious
	Differentiation	X tries to distinguish the event from other similar but less desirable events or actions
	Transcendence	X tries to place the act in a new positive context
	Attack accuser	X criticizes the accuser/questions the credibility of the accuser
	Compensation	X remunerates the offended part
Corrective action		X plans or attempts to correct the problem
Mortification		X accepts responsibility, apologizes, express remorse, and ask for forgiveness

Source: Benoit (2015, 2024); Frandsen and Johansen (2017).

one of more of the other strategies. Finally, the fifth main strategy is *mortification* where the accused accepts responsibility, apologizes, and shows remorse.

The multiple analyses of case studies conducted by Benoit and colleagues show that most individuals or organizations are using several strategies to restore a damaged image. To deny does not necessarily repair an image, and it may be important to add bolstering, attacking the accuser or other kinds of reducing offensiveness. According to Benoit, it is a matter of not putting all the eggs in just one basket (Benoit, 1995, p. 157). It may also be a matter of point in time. Some defensive strategies may be useful at the onset of a crisis but may be changed for more accommodative strategies over time. However, Benoit also states that in some cases, the response strategies cannot repair a damaged image. In such a case, there is nothing else to do but to wait until people hopefully forget about the event. Furthermore, different people may have different sets of beliefs and values and a defense that may repair a damaged image to one group may fail or backfire with another group of people (Benoit, 2024). However, as reality is socially constructed, it is possible through communication to try to change perceptions of blame and values as well as the extent of offensiveness of an act (Benoit, 2020).

The theory of persuasive attacks is a theory about the messages that criticize the words or deeds—rightly or wrongly—of people, groups, and organizations (Benoit & Dorries, 1996; Benoit, 2017). The goal of a persuasive attack is to increase either offensiveness or responsibility of an act or both. Benoit and Dorries (1996) developed a typology of persuasive attacks based on these two constitutive elements: *increased perceived offensiveness* includes extent of the damage, persistence of negative effects, effects on the audience, inconsistency, victims are helpless/innocent, and obligations to protect victim; *increased perceived responsibility* includes accusations of having committed the act before and planned the act, knowing the likely consequences of the act, and/or benefitting from the act. For a full overview, see Benoit and Dorries (1996) and Frandsen and Johansen (2017, p. 99). Benoit extends the theory to not only include persuasive attacks on actions (what people do), (cf. Benoit & Dorries, 1996) but also include attacks on a person's character (who people are), for example, to increase perceived offensiveness of a character trait (Benoit, 2017).

Insights into the types of attacks and complaints, that is, identifying the attitudes of the critical audiences, are important to know when a defense is needed and how it can be conducted. In fact, this perspective aligns well with the idea of a multivocal approach to crisis communication (see Chapter 16) as well as to the concept of *blame game* that also combines a persuasive attack and image repair.

Applications to Subfields

Image repair theory and the study of crisis response strategies have turned out to be a frequently applied and impactful theory within the study of crisis communication (Avery et al., 2010). Image repair theory has been described as "the definitive work on the strategies used by apologists" (Hearit, 2006, p. 83). The corporate and political crisis subfields have been the primary areas for the application of image repair theory since its beginning. However, the theory has also been applied within national as well as international public sector communication, and within specific subfields such as sport, religion, healthcare, education, tourism, media, and social media. In fact, the high number of scholars applying image repair theory and its inventory of crisis response strategies to various case studies during the past 30 years demonstrates the usefulness of this theory to all areas, where individuals and organizations try to defend themselves against accusations of wrongdoing and/or attacks on their character. It has been useful to the rhetorical and text-oriented study of crisis communication, where focus is on the rhetors, that is, the senders, and the predominantly qualitative analyses of their messages and communication directed toward accusers (and stakeholders) and image repair. However, the theory has also been applied, developed, and extended by scholars within other crisis communication frameworks who attempt to be more strategic, context-oriented, and receiver-oriented, by adding more insights into the role of contextual factors and the reactions among various audiences, stakeholders, and voices for the choice of appropriate crisis response strategies. For instance, *situational crisis communication theory* (Coombs, 2023) looks at the impact and role of crisis type, crisis history, prior reputation, and attributions of responsibility; *contingency theory* identifies 87 contingency factors, including organizational, cultural, political, economic, and publics (Pang et al., 2020; Pang et al., 2023); and *rhetorical arena theory* studies the impact of communication and interferences of multiple voices in the rhetorical arena that opens up during a crisis (Frandsen & Johansen, 2017).

Furthermore, as crisis response strategies can be perceived as *reactive* strategies, that are used once a crisis breaks out, other scholars have added more *proactive* communication strategies to the list of rhetorical strategies. Proactive strategies are useful in some situations before media breaks the news of a crisis to the public or an issue or paracrisis turns into a full-blown crisis. Proactive theories include strategies such as *stealing thunder* (Arpan & Pompper, 2003; Claeys, 2023) and *inoculation* (Wan & Pfau, 2004; Compton, 2025).

As for methods, scholars studying image repair and crisis response strategies primarily use case studies (see list of studies in Benoit, 2020), using the method of rhetorical criticism, conducting rhetorical analysis, text analysis, discourse analysis, or content analysis to identify the type of rhetorical strategies used. However, researchers have also applied image repair theory to quantitative studies conducting surveys or doing experiments (Benoit, 2016; Blaney, 2016). Scholars have studied both the production of image repair, including the frequency of the use of specific strategies, such as denial (e.g., Kim et al., 2009) as well as the reception of image repair messages (e.g., Brown et al., 2016, who studied reactions to transgressions, among athletes within sports). Furthermore, the emergence of social media has added new methods (netnography), models (Social Mediated Crisis Communication), and perspectives (e.g., the role of emotions, online audiences as active communicators, choice of channels) to the study of crisis response strategies (e.g., Austin & Jin, 2018; Glantz & Benoit, 2018).

Practitioner Takeaways

The primary takeaway from the image repair research is that crisis managers need to know about the importance of rhetoric and verbal strategies, including the various crisis response strategies to make an appropriate response that may help an individual or organization in repairing an image that may have been damaged due to wrongdoing or suspected wrongdoing. The bulk of the studies using image repair theory find that it is very important to acknowledge responsibility and to choose the right strategies and words (Coombs, 1995). Practitioners also need to know how to combine and use various sub-strategies, whether they want to deny or apologize for an act perceived as wrongdoing. Finally, they need to have insights on their audiences to choose a proper strategy. However, to be able to account for this, it would be wise to complement knowledge about crisis response strategies with knowledge of strategic and contextual factors as well as about the communicative complexity going on among people during a crisis.

Theoretical Constraints and Concerns

A key theoretical constraint for image repair theory is that it primarily concentrates on a sender perspective: what to say and how to respond when accused of wrongdoing. The theory is less interested in the receiver perspective, as well as into questions such as when to say what and when to choose which strategy to make an appropriate response. This means that except for insights brought by the theory persuasive attacks, image repair theory in itself does not take into account the multiple contextual factors and the communicative complexity, although they have an impact on perceptions, beliefs, and values as well as on the reactions and attributions of responsibility going on among audiences. However, Benoit has slightly adapted his theory following the suggestions by Burns and Bruner

(2000) and other critics, and recently, as seen in Benoit (2024), the theory also attempts to put a stronger focus on audience reactions.

Image repair theory, like a number of other theories, shows little interest in the emotional responses of stakeholders. Finally, IRT does not provide consistent methods for measuring the success or failure of image repair efforts (Ulmer et al., 2019).

Theoretical Engagement Points

1 What type of research methods are most closely associated with image repair theory?
2 Is image repair theory primarily a descriptive, relational, or explanatory theory?
3 Is image repair theory primarily an empirical-analytic, interpretative, or critical theory?
4 How would you evaluate image repair in terms of scope, appropriateness, heuristic value, validity, parsimony, and openness?

Discussion Questions

1 How do the three theoretical traditions (rhetoric, sociology of accounts, and social psychology) that inspire image repair theory contribute to a comprehensive understanding of verbal self-defense? How does the combination of these traditions strengthen the theory?
2 Image repair theory identifies several strategies for responding to accusations, ranging from denial to mortification. Given that some strategies may be more effective in certain situations, what factors should a communicator consider when selecting the most appropriate image repair strategies? For example, when might denial be more effective or less effective than mortification?
3 The chapter discusses the concept of "persuasive attacks," which aim to increase the perceived offensiveness or responsibility of an act. How can an understanding of persuasive attacks enhance the effectiveness of image repair strategies? How can a communicator anticipate these attacks?
4 While image repair theory focuses primarily on the sender's perspective, what are the limitations of this approach, and how might a greater focus on the receiver's perspective improve the practical application of the theory? How has the theory addressed audience reactions?
5 The chapter mentions that the theory has been applied in various fields, such as politics, corporate communication, sports, and religion. How might the specific context of these different fields influence the effectiveness of image repair strategies, and what would be a particularly challenging field to which to apply this theory?

References

Arpan, L. M., & Pompper, D. (2003). Stormy weather: Testing "stealing thunder" as a crisis communication strategy to improve communication flow between organizations and journalists. *Public Relations Review*, *29*(3), 291–308

Austin, L. L., & Jin, Y. (Eds.) (2018). *Social media and crisis communication*. New York: Routledge.

Avery, E. J., Lariscy, R. W., Kim, S., & Hocke, T. (2010). A quantitative review of crisis communication research in public relations from 1991 to 2009. *Public Relations Review*, *36*, 190–192.

Benoit, W. L. (1982). Richard M. Nixon's rhetorical strategies in his public statements on Watergate. *Southern Speech Communication Journal*, *47*, 192–211

Benoit, W. L. (1995). *Accounts, excuses and apologies: A theory of image restoration strategy*. Albany, NY: State University of New York.

Benoit, W. L. (2004). Image restoration discourse and crisis communication. In D. P. Millar and R. L. Heath (Eds.), *Responding to crisis: A rhetorical approach to crisis communication* (pp. 262–280). Mahwah, NJ: Lawrence Erlbaum*.

Benoit, W. L. (2015). *Accounts, excuses and apologies: Image repair theory and research* (2nd ed.). Albany, NY: State University of New York.

Benoit, W. L. (2016). Effects of image repair strategies. In J. R. Blaney (Eds.), *Putting image repair to the test: Quantitative applications to image restoration strategies* (pp. 7–28). Lanham, MD: Lexington Books.

Benoit, W. L. (2017). Criticism of actions and character: Strategies for persuasive attacks extended. *Relevant & Rhetoric*, *8*. http://relevantrhetoric.com/CriticismofActionsandCharacter.pdf

Benoit, W. L. (2020). Image repair theory. In F. Frandsen & W. Johansen (Eds.), *Crisis communication*, Vol. 23. Handbooks of communication science (pp. 105–119). Berlin: De Gruyter Mouton*.

Benoit, W. L. (2024). *Accounts, excuses and apologies: Image repair theory extended* (3rd ed., First ed., 1995, Second ed., 2015). Albany: State University of New York; Suny Press*.

Benoit, W. L., & Dorries, B. (1996). Dateline NBC's persuasive attack on Wal-Mart, *Communication Quarterly*, *44*(4): 463–477*.

Bitzer, L. F. (1968). The rhetorical situation. *Philosophy & Rhetoric*, *1*, 1–14.

Black, E. (1965). *Rhetorical criticism: A study in method*. New York: Macmillan.

Blaney, J. R. (Ed.) (2016). *Putting image repair to the test: Quantitative applications to image restoration strategies*. Lanham, MD: Lexington Books.

Brown, K. A., Billings, A., & Devlin, M. (2016). Image repair across the racial spectrum: Experimentally exploring athlete transgression responses. *Communication Research Reports*, *33*, 47–53.

Burke, K. (1970). *The rhetoric of religion*. Berkeley, CA: University of California Press

Burns, J. P., & Bruner, M. S. (2000). Revisiting the theory of image restoration strategies. *Communication Quarterly*, *48*(1), 27–39

Claeys, A. S. (2023). The benefits and pitfalls of stealing thunder. In W. T. Coombs and S. J. Holladay (Eds.), *The handbook of crisis communication* (2nd ed., pp. 99–111). West Sussex: John Wiley and Sons.

Compton, J. (2025). Inoculation theory. *Review of Communication*, *25*(1), 1–13.
Coombs, W. T. (1995). Choosing the right words: The development of guidelines for the selection of the 'appropriate' crisis-response strategies. *Management Communication Quarterly*, *8*(4), 447–476*.
Coombs, W. T. (2023). *Ongoing crisis communication. Planning, managing, and responding*. Thousand Oaks: Sage
Fishbein, M., & Ajzen, I. (2010). *Predicting and changing behavior: The reasoned action approach*. New York: Psychology Press.
Frandsen, F., & Johansen, W. (2017). *Organizational crisis communication. A multivocal appraoch*. London: Sage.
Glantz, M., & Benoit, W. L. (2018). The world's all Atwitter: Image repair discourse on social media. In L. L. Austin & Y. Jin (Eds.), *Social media and crisis communication* (pp. 168–179). New York: Routledge*.
Hearit, K. M. (2006). *Crisis management by apology: Corporate responses to allegations of wrongdoing*. Mahwah, NJ: Lawrence Erlbaum.
Kim, S., Avery, E. J., & Lariscy, R. W. (2009). Are crisis communicators practicing what we preach? An evaluation of crisis response strategies analyzed in public relations research from 1991 to 2009. *Public Relations Review*, *35*(4), 446–448
Pang, A., Jin, Y., & Cameron, G. T. (2023). The contingency theory of strategic conflict management: Review from three decades of theory development, extension and application. *Journalism and Communication Monographs*, *25*(2), 193–214. https://doi.org/10.1177/15226379231167141
Pang, A., Jin, Y, Kim, S., & Cameron, G. T. (2020). Contingency theory: Evolution from a public relations theory to a theory of strategic conflict management. In F. Frandsen & W. Johansen (Eds.), *Crisis communication*, Vol. 23. Handbooks of communication science (pp. 141–164). Berlin: De Gruyter Mouton.
Scott, M. B., & Lyman, S. M. (1968). Accounts. *American Sociological Review*, *33*(1), 46–62.
Ulmer, R. R., Sellnow, T. L., & Seeger, M. W. (2019). *Effective crisis communication: Moving from crisis to opportunity* (4th ed). Thousand Oaks, CA: Sage.
Wan, H. H., & Pfau, M. (2004). The relative effectiveness of inoculation, bolstering, and combined approaches in crisis communication. *Journal of Public Relations Research*, *16*, 301–328.
Ware, B. L., & Linkugel, W. A. (1973). They spoke in defense of themselves: On the generic criticism of apologßia. *Quarterly Journal of Speech*, *59*, 273–283.

*Requisite Readings

Chapter 10

Situational Crisis Communication Theory

In the 1980s, we witnessed the emergence of sustained writings about crises, crisis management, and crisis communication (Frandsen & Johansen, 2020). The published works included both practitioners writing about their experience with crises and academic research trying to understand crises and crisis communication. These early writings included efforts to develop lists of crisis types and crisis response strategies. The crisis types attempted to capture the range of situations crisis managers were likely to encounter and, therefore, should be prepared to address. The crisis response strategies were the various options for communicating during a crisis. The belief was that communication could improve crisis outcomes if done properly or make the crisis worse if done improperly. Benson (1988) observed the two lists seemed to exist independent of one another and would benefit from integration.

Situational crisis communication theory (SCCT) was developed specifically to integrate crisis types and crisis responses. SCCT sought to provide a theoretical link between crisis types and crisis response strategies. The purpose of this link was to help crisis managers understand which crisis response strategies might make the situation better or worse for the crisis victims and the organizations-in-crisis (Coombs & Holladay, 2002). Since its development, SCCT has been highly influential in the crisis management practice and academic crisis research (e.g., Page et al., 2023).

Theoretical Overview

SCCT sought to link the crisis types with the crisis response strategies because various communication theories hold that the situation influences what constitutes an effective response (e.g., Bitzer, 1968). It follows that the nature of the crisis situation (the crisis type) should influence what makes for an "effective" crisis response (Coombs, 1995). SCCT was influenced by interpersonal communication research about embarrassing situations (Coombs, 2020; Metts & Cupach, 1989). SCCT linked the crisis type

DOI: 10.4324/9781003469964-12

to crisis response strategies through attribution theory. When people perceive events, especially negative events, they seek to create explanations for the cause of the event. People will attribute responsibility for the event to either internal or external factors. For a crisis, an internal attribution would be the organization-in-crisis, while an external attribution might be the weather or a bad actor trying to harm the organization.

SCCT was inspired specifically from Bernard Weiner's (1972) writings on attribution theory. Weiner's view of attribution theory posits that attributions of responsibility are a function of locus of control (external or internal), controllability (can the actor control the event or not), and stability (do such events happen regularly or infrequently). SCCT started by mapping how people make attributions about the common crisis types. The next step was to use attribution to link the crisis types to the crisis responses. The crisis response strategies were evaluated for the perceived amount of responsibility the actor seems to be taking for the crisis with the crisis response strategy. The basic idea is that the level of crisis responsibility in the crisis response should match the perceived level of attribution for the crise evoked by the crisis type (Coombs & Holladay, 2002). As attributions of internal crisis responsibility increase, the threat posed by the crisis the organization increases and requires a crisis response that allows the organization to take responsibility for the crisis (Coombs, 2007).

Moreover, SCCT drew upon Sturges's (1994) conceptualization of crisis responses. Sturges (1994) divided crisis response into instructing information, adjusting information, and reputation repair. Instructing information provided information that helps people to protect themselves physically from a crisis. Adjusting information helps people to cope psychologically with a crisis. Reputation repair seeks to reclaim the reputational assets lost during a crisis (Holladay, 2009). SCCT states that the initial crisis response must address the instructing and adjusting information, which has been termed the ethical base response (Coombs, 2016). It is ethical because it is the right thing to do when following an ethic or care and the base response because the crisis managers can build upon it with reputation repair efforts (Coombs, 2017; Yehya & Coombs, 2017).

Theoretical Conceptualization

The development of SCCT can be divided into three phases: proto, articulation, and boundaries. The proto phase (1995–2001) is when the ideas that became formalized into SCCT were first presented and tested. The articulation phase (2002 to 2018) covers the full presentation and testing of SCCT. This includes the connection between SCCT and paracrises. The boundary phase (2019 to the present) focuses on efforts to identify the boundaries and SCCT and integration of a stronger affective component to SCCT.

The Proto Stage

The origins of SCCT begin with a crisis communication decision tree published by Coombs in 1995. The decision tree used attribution theory as the theoretical link between crisis types and crisis responses. There was a crisis matrix created using two dimensions drawn from attrition they. The dimensions were internal or external locus of control and intentional or unintentional action (controllability). The four crises in the matrix were faux pas, accidents, terrorism, and transgression. Faux pas are external and unintentional and reflect actions an organization takes and believe they are appropriate but some people perceive the actions as inappropriate. An example would be a group being offended by an advertising message. Accidents are internal and unintentional events that happen during the course of organizational operations. An example would be a fire at a manufacturing facility. Terrorism is external and intentional and refers to external agents purposefully trying to harm the organization directly or indirectly. An example would be product tampering. Transgressions are internal and intentional and capture actions managers take that knowingly place people at risk. An example would be a company selling food it knows to be contaminated with a foodborne illness (Coombs, 1995).

A repertoire of crisis response strategies were identified. The emphasis was on strategies identified in prior research used to promote reputation (image) repair. The repertoire identified five types of crisis response strategies differentiated by their potential effect on target audiences. Nonexistence strategies seek to establish that no crisis has occurred. Distance strategies recognize a crisis exists but tries to limit the organization's responsibility for the crisis and/or the seriousness of the crisis. Ingratiation strategies try to enhance the reputation of the organization-in-crisis. Mortification strategies seek win forgiveness for the crisis. Suffering explains that the organization is a victim of the crisis in an effort to evoke sympathy from others (Coombs, 1995).

Three factors drawn from the crisis management literature were identified as potential influences on attributions of crisis responsibility—the degree to which people attribute responsibility for the crisis the organization-in-crisis. Those three factors were veracity of evidence, damage, and performance history. Veracity of evidence was proof that a crisis happened with choices between true and false. False indicates cases, where in reality there was a misperception that a crisis occurred. Damage was the amount of damage created by a crisis with the choices being major or minor. Performance history was how well or poorly an organization treated its stakeholders. Positive performance history should build a perception of trustworthiness by stakeholders in the organization. The decision also tried to differentiate between victims and non-victims in the crisis situation (Coombs, 1995).

In terms of recommendations for the decision tree, mortification was favored when the damage was major in any of the four crisis types. Nonexistence strategies were only used for faux pas crises. The suffering strategy was only used for terrorism, while distance was recommended for accidents with minor damage (Coombs, 1995).

A series of experimental studies were then conducted to test key elements of the decision tree and its underlying theoretical assumptions. During this time, the decision tree was referred to as a symbolic approach because it emphasized the importance of crisis communication (e.g., Coombs & Holladay, 1996, 2001). A fundamental assumption in this emerging theory was the negative relationship between attributions of crisis responsibility and post-crisis reputation. Marketing research had shown a negative effect of attributions of crisis responsibility on customer perceptions of an organization following a product harm crisis (Mowen, 1980). There was a need to prove this relationship held in other crisis situations. Coombs and Holladay (1996) established the connection between attributions of crisis responsibility and reputational damage for accident and transgression crises. Three additional studies also verified this connection (Coombs, 1998, 1999; Coombs & Holladay, 2001). These early studies operationalized reputation as trustworthiness using the organizational reputation scale develop from the credibility research of McCroskey (Coombs & Holladay, 1996).

Coombs and Holladay (1996) did a preliminary test of the recommended crisis response strategies provided by the decision tree. Using accident and transgression crisis types, the recommended crisis responses resulted in more favorable post-crisis reputations than either a no response condition or a non-recommended crisis response. This study also added the stability concept from attribution theory. Stability was operationalized through crisis history. Crisis history was whether or not an organization had had a similar crisis in past. Previous crises would suggest the recent crisis was part of a pattern of behavior suggesting the crisis is not so anomalous. A number of later studies have validated the connection between crisis history and crisis attributions (e.g., crisis history citations).

Coombs (1998) revised both the lists of crisis response strategies and crisis types. Crisis response strategies were organized along a continuum rather than simply being a list. The starting point for the continuum was the mitigation-aggravation continuum of accounts (McLaughlin et al., 1983). Accounts are explanations of behaviors, and crisis response strategies are a form of account (Allen & Caillouet, 1994; Benoit, 1995). The continuum used the term defensive-accommodative because Marcus and Goodman (1991) used those terms in their study of crisis responses. The defensive-accommodative continuum relates to attribution theory because it reflects varying degrees of taking responsibility for a crisis. This study also found little support for either damage severity or external control being relevant to crisis responsibility attributions. A follow-up study came to a similar conclusion about damage severity, and it was dropped (book chapter). External control was also dropped from future studies.

Instructing and adjusting information enter the discussion more fully in 1999 examining the strategies. This study found that the compassion aspect of adjusting information was a valuable response for post-crisis reputations (Coombs, 1999). However, instructing and adjusting information had not yet been fully established as the preferred initial response. In Coombs and Holladay (2001), the effects of performance history on attributions of crisis responsibility were documented. The study operationalized performance as being among the Best Please to Work and contributions to the local community. Later crisis communication studies would refer to this as indicators of corporate social responsibility (CSR) (e.g., Kim & Yang, 2009). Performance history was presented as negative, neutral, or positive. The results found that the negative performance history increased perceptions of crisis responsibility relative to either the neutral or positive performance history conditions (Coombs & Holladay, 2001). This finding was called the Velcro effect because the negative performance history seemed to attract negative perceptions much like Velcro attracts fuzz.

These early studies under the heading of the symbolic approach provided the theoretical and methodological foundations for SCCT. Theoretically, the studies validate key assumptions that would be part of SCCT including the effect of attributions of crisis responsibility on post-crisis reputations and the way both crisis history and performance history (later to be called prior reputation) influenced attributions of crisis responsibility. Methodologically, the measurements used in the early SCCT research were developed. The initial outcome variable of organizational reputation was treated as trustworthiness. The studies also emphasized the importance of assessing account acceptance. As accounts, crisis response strategies should have an effect only if they are accepted. Without monitoring account acceptance, researchers do not know if the failure to find an effect for a crisis response strategy was a result of failure to accept the account or failure of the account to influence the desired outcome (Fediuk et al., 2023). The symbolic approach research focused on reputation as the outcome variable for crisis communication because of the emphasis on the value of crisis response strategies.

The Articulation Phase

The year 2002 marks the first time that the name situational crisis communication was used with the publication in *Management Communication Quarterly* by Coombs and Holladay (2002). The ideas that began with the decision tree and were tested as part of the symbolic approach became formalized into SCCT. Because of its emphasis on attributions, SCCT is a cognitive approach to crisis communication. Moreover, the focus on attribution also gives SCCT a receiver orientation. How people affected by the crisis perceive the crisis, the organization-in-crisis, and crisis responses are central to crisis management.

The seminal work in SCCT focused on crisis responsibility and how it can be used to categorize crisis types. The study began by examining the internal (personal) locus of control and controllability factors from attribution theory. Controllability had already been called blame in the management literature (Griffin et al., 1996). The results indicated that the personal control and controllability were isomorphic. The two factors were combined to create the crisis responsibility variable (Coombs & Holladay, 2002).

The next phase of the study was to assess how crisis responsibility could be used to create clusters of crises. Clustering is useful because people will draw similar perceptions of crisis responsibility from crises with the same cluster—see them similarly. Moreover, the initial attributions of crisis responsibility are an indicator of the level of threat the crisis poses to the organization. To be more precise, the level of crisis responsibility reflects the degree of reputational damage a crisis might inflict upon an organization-in-crisis. Thirteen crisis types were identified in the extant crisis management literature. Table 10.1 presents the original 13 crisis types. Scores for crisis responsibility were used in a hierarchical cluster analysis. The optimal number of crisis clusters was three. The optimal number was a function of the three clusters producing significantly different scores from one another for crisis responsibility and organizational reputation. These differences indicated that the three clusters were distinct from one another.

Table 10.1 Original 13 Crisis Types

Rumor
Natural disaster
Malevolence/product tampering
Workplace violence
Challenge
Technical breakdown accident
Technical error product harm
Megadamage
Human breakdown accident
Human breakdown product harm
Organizational misdeed no injuries
Organizational misdeed management misconduct
Organizational misdeed with injuries

A four-cluster solution did not provide such clear distinctions (Coombs & Holladay, 2002).

The three crisis clusters were named victim, accidental, and preventable. The victim crisis cluster included natural disasters, rumors, workplace violence, and product tampering. In each of these crisis types, the organization and constituents were victims of the crisis. The victim crisis cluster produced minimal attributions of crisis responsibility. The accidental crisis cluster included challenges, megadamage, technical breakdown accidents, and technical breakdown recalls. In these crises, unintentional actions seem to cause the crises. The accidental crisis cluster produced moderate attributions of crisis responsibility. The preventable crisis cluster included human breakdown accidents, human breakdown recalls, and organizational misdeeds. These crises seem intentional because management knowingly places constituents at risk or engaged in inappropriate conduct or involved human errors that could have been avoided. The preventable crisis clusters produced strong attributions of crisis responsibility.

The final stage in the research was to verify the relationship between perceptions of crisis responsibility and post-crisis organizational reputation. Separate analyses were run for each of the three crisis clusters. The analyses involved correlating crisis responsibility and organizational reputation. For each of the three clusters, there was a significant, negative correlation between crisis responsibility and organizational reputation. The results indicated that attributions of crisis responsibility were related to reputational damage from a crisis (Coombs & Holladay, 2002).

Crisis response strategies are the second critical factor in SCCT. From the research in the proto stage, the crisis response strategies were grouped according to potential outcomes. Deny strategies seek to establish that there is no crisis, or the organization has no connection to a crisis. Crisis response strategies in the deal category include attacking the accuser, denial, and scapegoating. Diminish strategies seek to lessen attributions of crisis responsibility. Crisis response strategies in the diminish category include excuses and justifications. Deal strategies seek to influence how people perceive the organization-in-crisis. Crisis response strategies in the deal category include ingratiation, concern, compassion, regret, and apology (Coombs, 2006). The study examined if the crisis response strategies would cluster as anticipated.

A hierarchical cluster analysis was performed using crisis responsibility and protecting victims as the clustering variables. The analysis found a three-cluster solution was optimal. The three clusters matched the anticipated clusters of denial, diminish, and deal exactly (Coombs, 2006). SCCT continued to use these three crisis response clusters with some modifications to the deal category. Compensation was added to the deal category. Ingratiation was removed to create a separate category that was considered secondary. Ingratiation (bolstering) did not seem to work as a primary strategy because it made little sense or had little value if it was the only response used in a crisis (Park, 2017). Concern, compassion, and regret were removed because they were considered part of instructing information rather than a form of reputation repair (Holladay, 2009).

Identifying the crisis type was the first step in assessing the threat posed by a crisis. The crisis type is a frame. The discourse around the crisis has cues which indicate how people are framing the crisis—the crisis type. Crisis managers need to identify the crisis cues being used to define their crisis. Artificial intelligence has been successfully trained to identify the cues for the various crisis clusters (Coombs, 2023). Not all constituents will see a crisis exactly the same, but most people will perceived a crisis type similarly in terms of attributions of crisis responsibility (Coombs, 2007). Identifying the crisis types provides an initial assessment of the crisis threat defining the threat as attributions of crisis responsibility.

The second step in assessing the crisis threat is to consider the contextual modifiers. Originally known as intensifiers, contextual modifiers can alter the people's attributions of crisis responsibility. Intensifier was the original term because the first two variables studied, prior reputation and crisis history, did intensify attributions of crisis responsibility. A negative prior reputation and a history of past crises each intensify attributions of crisis responsibility. The most important finding is that people will perceive an accidental crisis similar to an intentional crisis when either of these contextual modifiers is present. The term contextual modifiers was selected because other factors might reduce attributions of crisis responsibility. Other potential contextual modifiers include cultural differences and the voices of others speaking about the crisis. SCCT is open to adding additional contextual modifiers (Coombs, 2020).

Once crisis managers have assessed the potential threat—the level of crisis responsibility most people are likely to perceive—the focus can shift to selecting crisis response strategies. Remember, the initial response will feature adjusting and instructing information. The assessment of anticipated attributions of crisis responsibility shapes the selection of the reputation management strategies (Coombs, 2020). SCCT argues that the crisis response strategy should match with perceptions of crisis responsibility. The more people are likely to perceive the organization as responsible for a crisis, the more the crisis response should reflect an acceptance of crisis responsibility. It should be noted that studies during the articulation phase expanded the crisis outcomes beyond reputation. Anger (Coombs & Holladay, 2005, 2008; Coombs et al., 2016), negative word-of-mouth intentions (Seo & Jang, 2021), and purchase intentions (Coombs & Holladay, 2006; Hegner et al., 2016) became common crisis outcomes during this phase.

The language shifted from appropriate responses to optimal and suboptimal responses. Optimal responses seek to maximize the benefits to those affected by the crisis and the organization-in-crisis (Claeys & Coombs, 2020). The overarching communication recommendation from SCCT, the primary optimal response, is to provide an ethical base then to utilize accommodative responses when attributions of crisis responsibility are high (Coombs, 2007). Academic research and practitioner research have found support for the value of this optimal response. Various experiments have found that accommodative strategies can improve post-crisis reputations, result in less anger toward the organization-in-crisis, generate less intention to engage in negative word-of-mouth, and produce less of a decrease in purchase intentions compared to more defensive crisis response strategies (e.g., Ma & Zhan, 2016). Raithel and Hock (2021) found that companies that used the accommodative response guidance experienced more favorable stock returns using an event based analysis of stock returns. They also found negative effects when a company used an overly accommodative strategy when one was not called for by the crisis- response match recommendations.

The SCCT studies illuminated the suboptimal responses as well. Denial was shown to be a problematic response if the organization had any connection to the crisis (Coombs et al., 2016). The diminish strategies proved to have little positive effect on crisis outcomes (Zhou et al., 2022). The study results found minimal effects for bolstering on crisis outcomes and the evidence reinforced it was better as a secondary than as a primary crisis response (e.g., Park, 2017).

The meta-analysis of SCCT did find the optimal crisis response did produce some inconsistent results for the preventable crises. Sometimes, the optimal crisis responses provided the desired effects on the crisis outcomes, and sometimes, they had no effect (Ma & Zhan, 2016). These mixed results for the preventable crisis cluster raised the issue of boundaries for SCCT and initiated a new phase of the SCCT research.

Boundary Phase

All theories have boundaries. Boundaries indicate the conditions under which the theory is valid and the point at which they are no longer applicable. Prior SCCT research suggested that a boundary for SCCT might reside within the preventable crisis cluster. Four studies found no effect for some crises situations from the preventable crisis cluster. This lack of effect indicated that SCCT's optimal crisis recommendations may not be applicable to all crises within the preventable crisis cluster. The question became what was this boundary condition and how would crisis managers know they had reacted it? Moral outrage is one answer to that question.

Moral outrage is a negative, moral emotion. It is defined as "negative affect directed toward another in response to a moral violation" (Ginther et al., 2022, p. 2). Moral outrage is evoked "when there are attributions of blame for the event, perceived greed by the corporation and perceived unfairness of the corporate behavior" (Antonetti & Maklan, 2016, p. 75). This explanation of moral outrage reflects cognitive appraisal theory which holds that cues in a situation or event produce predictable emotions (Lazarus, 1991). The cues for moral outrage are the action is intentional, is an injustice, and is motivated by greed. Moral outrage first enters the discussion of SCCT with the exploration of the scansis (Coombs & Tachkova, 2019).

Scansis is a term used to capture the intersection of a scandal and crisis. The roots of a scansis resides in concerns about the need to differentiate the terms scandal and crisis rather than treat them as interchangeable. The base for the distinction was the moral violation aspect of scandal (Clemente & Gabbioneta, 2017). However, there are situations where a "crisis transmogrifies into a scandal" (Coombs et al., 2018, p. 181), because the crisis also involves a perceived moral violation. Perceptions are critical to scandals and scansis, because the same action (crisis) can sometimes be viewed as a moral violation and sometimes not viewed as a moral violation (Entman, 2012).

A scansis emerges "when an organizational crisis is appraised to be an injustice that is driven by greed" (Coombs & Tachkova, 2019, p. 76). The scansis might be a function of the initial crisis event (it is viewed as intentional, an injustice, and linked to greed) or by an inappropriate response to a crisis (Coombs et al., 2018). An inappropriate response can create a double crisis (Grebe, 2013). The response creates the impression of a moral violation that is intentional, an injustice, and driven by greed.

Coombs and Tachkova (2019) treated the scansis as a for preventable crisis and examined the effects of the SCCT the optimal accommodative strategy (including adjusting information) on the common crisis communication research outcomes of reputation, purchase intention, anger, and negative word-of-mouth intention. They found not difference between the optimal response, suboptimal response (justification), and no response. The type of response had no effect on any of the four crisis outcomes.

Coombs and Tachkova (2019) argued that the results suggest the need to add a third appraisal to SCCT. SCCT involves two appraisals, a situation is considered negative and crisis responsibility assigned for the situation. Moral outrage should become the third appraisal. The third appraisal is needed because moral outrage appears to be a boundary condition for SCCT's crisis response recommendations. Furthermore, one possible conclusion from their analysis might be that the crisis response is irrelevant during a scansis. This could mean a suboptimal response was as useful as an optimal response in a scansis. However, a suboptimal response confirms the moral outrage and does nothing to counter it. A second study was performed to uncover potential benefits for an optimal crisis response beyond the initial four crisis outcomes. The second study found that an optimal response (corrective action and accepting the moral violation) did increase the perceived empathy of the response and did reduce moral outrage when compared to corrective action alone. The results indicate that there are benefits to an optimal crisis response in a scansis that moves people away from moral outrage (Coombs & Tachkova, 2019).

The scansis research suggested the use of a triadic appraisal for SCCT and moral outrage as a boundary condition. But these ideas required testing to confirm them. The scansis and the meta-analysis problematized the preventable crisis cluster and problematization is one catalyst for theory building (Colquitt & Zapata-Phelan, 2007). Coombs and Tachkova (2023b) focused on the preventable crisis cluster to demonstrate how moral outrage contributed to a revision of SCCT. The initial preventable crisis cluster includes human-error accidents, human-error product harm, and management misconduct. Human-error accidents are perceived as preventable, that is why they generate perceptions of crisis responsibility similar to management misconduct which are intentional actions (Coombs & Holladay, 2002). That is why the preventable crisis cluster has also been called the intentional crisis cluster (Coombs, 2020).

However, the trust violation literature would suggest the distinction between integrity-based and competency-based trust violations would treat human-error and management misconduct as qualitatively different from one another. Human error is a result of incompetence (competency-based), while management misconduct is a result of a lapse in integrity (integrity-based) (Kim et al., 2006). Because crises are a form of trust violation, the distinction between integrity-based and competency-based violation should apply.

Coombs and Tachkova (2023b) conducted research to reimage the preventable crisis cluster using moral outrage as the third assessment factor. The first step was to determine how the crisis types in the preventable crisis cluster would group using injustice and greed as the factors in a hierarchical cluster analysis. Three crisis scenarios each were included from human-error accidents, human-error product harm, management misconduct, and scansis. Organizational reputation, purchase intention, and negative word-of-mouth intentions were used to help assess the ideal number of clusters. The preventable crisis cluster was revealed to have three distinct sub-clusters. The three sub-clusters were human-error crises, management misconduct crises, and scansis. A closer look at the difference between human-error crises and management misconduct crises reflected the integrity-based/competency-based distinction. The management misconduct crises created much stronger perceptions of injustice, greed, and moral outrage than the human-error crises. This result supported the need to separate human-error crises from the other crises in the preventable crisis cluster. Finally, the scansis scenarios produced the strongest reports of moral outrage and were significantly stronger than the management misconduct or human-error crises.

The study validated the utility of a triadic appraisal for SCCT crises. Moral outrage provided new insights into the preventable crisis cluster and the establishment of a boundary condition. Strong feelings of moral outrage were a boundary condition for SCCT's crisis response recommendations. Moreover, moral outrage could be a boundary condition for other crisis communication theories. The boundary line seems to exist between human-error crises and management misconduct crises. The management misconduct crises and scansis crises seem to produce strong enough feeling of moral outrage to separate themselves from all the other crisis types (Coombs & Tachkova, 2023b).

Moral outrage creates a strong need to punish an offender. It is one of the best predictors of third-party punishment (TPP). TPP occurs when someone affected by an action learns of a violation and feels the need to punish those responsible for the violation even if they do not know the victims of the violation. For crises, those who learn about the crisis and experience moral outrage will want to punish the organization responsible for the crisis. Purchase intention and negative word-of-mouth intention are forms of TTP (Coombs & Tachkova, 2023b). Coombs and Tachkova (2023b) also argued for a reconsideration of the range of crisis outcomes considered by researchers and crisis managers. Value incongruence is an important outcome because it can promote disidentification. When stakeholders disidentify with an organization, the stakeholder relationship is damaged and in the worst case scenario is severed. Moral outrage is a recognition by stakeholders that the organization is not like them—there is value incongruence. Crisis managers need to be cognization of value incongruence and take steps to reverse the increasing sense of value incongruence created by moral outrage (Coombs & Tachkova, 2023b).

Moral outrage suggested a new variant in the gradation of crises. Crisis management has always recognized variations among crises (Coombs, 2007; Jin, 2009; Lu & Huang, 2018). More recently, researchers have begun to draw distinctions between sticky crises and regular crises. Sticky crises are more complex and difficult to manage than regular crises (Reber et al., 2020). Lu and Huang (2018) differentiated crises with high and low intensity emotions. Moral outrage is a high-intensity emotion. Moral outrage, inducing crises, is one form of sticky crisis. Coombs and Tachkova (2023a) argued that moral outrage fundamentally changes the crisis communication dynamic. The beginning of a theoretical extension of SCCT is offered based on moral outrage (affect) being at the center of the extension.

The primary focus of the initial stages of the moral outrage-based theoretical extension was an identification of the new variables shaping the crisis communication process. Those variables include value incongruence, disidentification, felt need for punishment, TPP, and compassion for victims. Moral outrage, inducing crises, should result in higher value incongruence, greater disidentification, along with an increased felt need for punishment and intention to engage in TTP when compared to regular crises. Punishment becomes a key variable. Greater compassion for the crisis victims should increase feelings of moral outrage and create a stronger felt need for punishment and intention to engage in TTP.

The crisis outcomes reflect these new variables. An optimal crisis response, one that includes curative actions and recognition of the moral violation, should increase perceptions of empathy and lessen value incongruence and disidentification. Suboptimal crisis response should intensify perceptions of value incongruence, felt need for punishment, and intention to engage in TPP. It should also increase feelings of compassion for the crisis victims (Coombs & Tachkova, 2023a). The moral outrage research strongly links it to punishment (e.g., Ginther et al., 2022). The felt need for punishment and intention to engage in TPP is the reason that the optimal response has no effect on the short-term crisis outcomes of post-crisis reputation, purchase intention, and negative word-of-mouth intentions. However, suboptimal crisis responses can intensify the negative feelings about the organization and move it further along the road toward infamy. Infamy is an emotion-based social evaluation (the collective perceptions constituents hold for an organization), indicating social disapproval of an organization (Zavyalova et al., 2017). Moral outrage is difficult to manage because of the felt need for punishment, but crisis managers must resist the belief that suboptimal response is fine given the limited effects of optimal responses (Coombs & Tachkova, 2024; Coombs & Tachkova, 2023a; Coombs & Tachkova, 2022).

Unspoken Assumptions

A theory derived from communication, SCCT, has some unspoken assumptions based upon the nature of communication. First, SCCT relies upon stakeholder perceptions because perceptions are central to communication. The definition of crisis used in SCCT is predicated on stakeholder perceptions of expectancy violations (Coombs, 2023). Crisis managers must read the crisis situation and require understanding how stakeholders are defining the crisis. Such information is provided by social and traditional media coverage of a crisis. Moreover, SCCT is concerned with how people perceive and react to crisis messaging. This is evident in the importance of account acceptance in SCCT.

Second, all communication is influenced by the nature of the source and the channel being used. Source credibility is important and relates to prior reputation. Prior reputation is a rough indicator of the organization's source credibility. Remember that SCCT's measure of reputation is based upon the trustworthiness dimension of credibility. Channels can affect how people perceive messages but there is limited evidence of a channel effect in crisis communication. SCCT follows the view that crisis managers should use all available communication channels during a crisis. Repetition and overlap between channels are good things during a crisis. Finally, individual differences in receivers do matter. For instance, we do know that the level of organizational identification does matter during a crisis (e.g., Zavyalova et al., 2016). However, crisis managers can not deliver message just to those with high or low identification (or some other segmentation factor). Rather, public crisis messages must be designed for the least common denominator, those people who will be the least receptive to the crisis message (Coombs, 2023).

Summary

SCCT as formal theory has been in existence for over 20 years and its proto version for over 25 years. A large body of research has verified the core assumptions of SCCT related to understanding attributions of crisis responsibility. Moreover, many of SCCT's crisis recommendations for optimal and suboptimal crisis responses to various crisis types have been supported. Future research needs to expand on the role on moral outrage in SCCT and crisis communication in general. This will help to unpack the way moral outrage is a boundary condition for SCCT and how the theory can be extended to show utility beyond this current boundary.

Application to Subfields

SCCT was developed with a focus on organizational crisis. Therefore, it is logical that SCCT has been applied most often in the corporate subfield (e.g., Claeys & Coombs, 2020; Claeys et al., 2010; Guerber et al., 2020). This includes not only corporations but non-profit organizations (e.g., Sisco et al., 2010). SCCT has been applied in the public subfield as well. A number of researchers have used SCCT to understand public health crises (e.g., Chon & Park, 2021, Lu & Jin, 2022; Sun & Li, 2024), mass shootings (e.g., Barbe & Pennington-Gray, 2018; Domschat et al., 2023), natural disasters (e.g., Edwards, 2011), and crisis management in the public sector (e.g., Chunxia et al., 2022; Sulistyanto et al., 2020). SCCT has not been applied to the political subfield, but a conceptual piece has been written about how the theory could be applied in politics (e.g., Coombs, 2011).

Practitioner Takeaways

SCCT provides a number of insights into the use of crisis response strategies and dynamics of the crisis situation. SCCT has established the value of instructing information, adjusting information, and accommodative responses during a crisis. These responses place the victims at the center of the crisis response and reflect empathy. Crisis researchers have found that empathy is a crucial component to crisis communication (De Waele et al., 2020; Dolamore et al., 2021; Ndone & Park, 2022; Schoofs et al., 2022). SCCT also illustrates the dangers of using denial when the organization has some responsibility for a crisis while justification and excuse have little value as a crisis response.

SCCT has provided a vocabulary for talking about the crisis types—how crises are framed. Understanding the cues for the various types helps crisis managers understand the type of crisis they are experiencing, the potential threat posed by that crisis, and what crisis responses are optimal or suboptimal. Moreover, the introduction of moral outrage helps crisis managers realize when they are in a sticky crisis and the challenges that presents for crisis responses.

Theoretical Constraints and Concerns

An initial concern with SCCT is the theory's roots in Western culture. There are concerns about SCCT application to other cultures and there has been little exploration of culture as a contextual modifier (e.g., Barkley, 2020). SCCT has a strong rational focus as well (Claeys & Coombs, 2020). There is a concern about the limited integration of affect into the theory but resent research (e.g., Coombs & Tachkova, 2023a) has begun to do so. Finally, some have argued that SCCT is poorly suited for complex crises and works best for simpler crises. Ma and Zhan's (2016) meta-analysis of SCCT did indicate SCCT worked better for victim and accident crises than for preventable crises. Preventable crises are the most complex indicating SCCT was more effective for "simpler" crises.

Theoretical Engagement Points

1 What type of research methods are most closely associated with SCCT?
2 Is SCCT primarily a descriptive, relational, or explanatory theory?
3 Is SCCT primarily an empirical-analytic, interpretative, or critical theory?
4 How would you evaluate SCCT in terms of scope, appropriateness, heuristic value, validity, parsimony, and openness?

Discussion Questions

1 How does SCCT's focus on stakeholder perceptions differentiate it from earlier crisis communication models?
2 What are the ethical implications of matching crisis response strategies to the level of attributed responsibility?
3 How can crisis managers effectively identify and analyze the influence of contextual modifiers in a given crisis situation?
4 Discuss the challenges of applying SCCT in the context of "sticky crises" characterized by high moral outrage.
5 How can organizations leverage SCCT to build resilience and enhance their crisis preparedness?

References

Allen, M. W., & Caillouet, R. H. (1994). Legitimation endeavors: Impression management strategies used by an organization in crisis. *Communications Monographs*, *61*(1), 44–62.

Antonetti, P., & Maklan, S. (2016). An extended model of moral outrage at corporate social irresponsibility. *Journal of Business Ethics*, *135*, 429–444.

Barbe, D., & Pennington-Gray, L. (2018). Using situational crisis communication theory to understand Orlando hotels' Twitter response to three crises in the summer of 2016. *Journal of Hospitality and Tourism Insights*, *1*(3), 258–275.

Barkley, K. (2020). Does one size fit all? The applicability of situational crisis communication theory in the Japanese context. *Public Relations Review*, *46*(3), 101911. https://doi.org/10.1016/j.pubrev.2020.101911

Benoit, W. L. (1995). *Accounts, excuses, and apologies: A theory of image restoration*. Albany: State University of New York Press.

Benson, J. A. (1988). Crisis revisited: An analysis of strategies used by Tylenol in the second tampering episode. *Communication Studies*, *39*(1), 49–66.

Bitzer, L. F. (1968). The rhetorical situation. *Philosophy & Rhetoric*, *1*(1), 1–14.

Chon, M. G., & Park, H. (2021). Predicting public support for government actions in a public health crisis: Testing fear, organization-public relationship, and behavioral intention in the framework of the situational theory of problem solving. *Health Communication*, *36*(4), 476–486.

Chunxia, Z., Fei, W., & Wei, F. (2022). Exploring the antecedents to the reputation of chinese public sector organizations during COVID-19: An extension of situational crisis communication theory. *Frontiers in Psychology*, *13*, 818939. https://doi.org/10.3389/fpsyg.2022.818939

Claeys, A. S., Cauberghe, V., & Vyncke, P. (2010). Restoring reputations in times of crisis: An experimental study of the situational crisis communication theory and the moderating effects of locus of control. *Public Relations Review*, *36*(3), 256–262.

Claeys, A. S., & Coombs, W. T. (2020). Organizational crisis communication: Suboptimal crisis response selection decisions and behavioral economics. *Communication Theory*, *30*(3), 290–309*.

Clemente, M., & Gabbioneta, C. (2017). How does the media frame corporate scandals? The case of German newspapers and the Volkswagen diesel scandal. *Journal of Management Inquiry*, *26*(3), 287–302.

Colquitt, J. A., & Zapata-Phelan, C. P. (2007). Trends in theory building and theory testing: A five-decade study of the Academy of Management Journal. *Academy of Management Journal*, *50*(6), 1281–1303.

Coombs, W. T. (1995). Choosing the right words: The development of guidelines for the selection of the "appropriate" crisis response strategies. *Management Communication Quarterly*, *8*, 447–476*.

Coombs, W. T. (1998). The Internet as potential equalizer: New leverage for confronting social irresponsibility. *Public Relations Review*, *24*, 289–304.

Coombs, W. T. (1999). Information and compassion in crisis responses: A test of their effects. *Journal of Public Relations Research*, *11*(2), 125–142.

Coombs, W. T. (2006). The protective powers of crisis response strategies: Managing reputational assets during a crisis. *Journal of Promotion Management*, *12*, 241–259.

Coombs, W. T. (2007). Protecting organization reputations during a crisis: The development and application of a situational crisis communication theory. *Corporate Reputation Review*, *10*(3), 163–176. http://doi.org/10.1057/palgrave.crr.1550049*

Coombs, W.T. (2011). Political public relations and crisis communication: A public relations perspective. In J. Stromback and S. Kiousis (Eds.), *Political public relations: Principles and applications* (pp. 214–234). New York: Routledge.

Coombs, W. T. (2016). Reflections on a meta-analysis: Crystallizing thinking about SCCT. *Journal of Public Relations Research*, *28*(2), 120–122.

Coombs, W. T. (2017). Revisiting situational crisis communication theory: The influences of social media on crisis communication theory and practice. In L. Austin & Y. Jin (Eds.), *Social media and crisis communication*, (pp. 21–38). New York: Routledge.

Coombs, W.T. (2020). Situational crisis communication theory: Influences, provenance, evolution, and prospects. In F. Frandsen and W. Johansen (Eds.), *Crisis communication* (pp. 121–140). De Gruyer Mouton.

Coombs, W. T. (2023). *Ongoing crisis communication: planning, managing, and responding* (6th ed.). SAGE Publications.

Coombs, W. T., & Holladay, S. J. (1996). Communication and attributions in a crisis: An experimental study of crisis communication. *Journal of Public Relations Research*, *8*, 279–295.

Coombs, W. T., & Holladay, S. J. (2001). An extended examination of the crisis situation: A fusion of the relational management and symbolic approaches. *Journal of Public Relations Research*, *13*, 321–340*.

Coombs, W. T., & Holladay, S. J. (2002). Helping crisis managers protect reputational assets: Initial tests of the situational crisis communication theory. *Management Communication Quarterly*, *16*, 165–186*.

Coombs, W. T., & Holladay, S. J. (2005). Exploratory study of stakeholder emotions: Affect and crisis. N. M. Ashkanasy, W. J. Zerbe, & C. E. J. Hartel (Eds.), In *Research on emotion in organizations: Volume 1: The effect of affect in organizational settings* (pp. 271–288). New York: Elsevier.

Coombs, W. T., & Holladay, S. J. (2006). Halo or reputational capital: Reputation and crisis management. *Journal of Communication Management*, *10*, 123–137.
Coombs, W. T., & Holladay, S. J. (2008). Comparing apology to equivalent crisis response strategies: Clarifying apology's role and value in crisis communication. *Public Relations Review*, *34*(3), 252–257.
Coombs, W. T., Holladay, S. J., & Claeys, A. S. (2016). Debunking the myth of denial's effectiveness in crisis communication: Context matters. *Journal of Communication Management*, *20*(4), 381–395.
Coombs, W. T., Holladay, S. J., & Tachkova, E. R. (2018). When a scandal and crisis fuse: Exploring the communicative implications of scansis. In A. Haller, H. Michael, & M. Kraus (Eds.), *Scandalogy* (pp. 172–190). Koln: Herbet Von Halem Verlag.
Coombs, W. T., & Tachkova, E. R. (2019). Scansis as a unique crisis type: Theoretical and practical implications. *Journal of Communication Management*, *23*(1), 72–88.
Coombs, W. T., & Tachkova, E. R. (2022). Elaborating the concept of threat in contingency theory: An integration with moral outrage and situational crisis communication theory. *Public Relations Review*, *48*(4), 102234.
Coombs, W. T., & Tachkova, E. R. (2023a). How emotions can enhance crisis communication: Theorizing around moral outrage. *Journal of Public Relations Research*, *36*(1), 1–17.
Coombs, W. T., & Tachkova, E. R. (2023b). Integrating moral outrage in situational crisis communication theory: A triadic appraisal model for crises. *Management Communication Quarterly*, *37*(4), https://doi.org/10.1177/08933189221151177
Coombs, W. T., & Tachkova, E. R. (2024). How emotions can enhance crisis communication: Theorizing around moral outrage. *Journal of Public Relations Research*, *36*(1), 6–22*.
De Waele, A., Schoofs, L., & Claeys, A. S. (2020). The power of empathy: The dual impacts of an emotional voice in organizational crisis communication. *Journal of Applied Communication Research*, *48*(3), 350–371.
Dolamore, S., Lovell, D., Collins, H., & Kline, A. (2021). The role of empathy in organizational communication during times of crisis. *Administrative Theory & Praxis*, *43*(3), 366–375.
Domschat, L., Stephens, M., & Saeed, H. (2023). Communication to protect brand image during a terrorism crisis: Application of situational crisis communication theory. *Journal of Contingencies and Crisis Management*, *31*(4), 913–927.
Edwards, F. (2011). From Katrina to Sandy: Comparative analysis of crisis communication during a natural disaster. *Language & Communication Quarterly*, *2*(2), 111–126.
Entman, R. M. (2012). *Scandal and silence: Media responses to presidential misconduct*. Maldin, MA: Polity Press.
Fediuk, T.A., Botero, I.C., & Pace, K.M. (2023). Crisis response effectiveness: Methodological considerations for advancement of empirical research about response impact. In W.T. Coombs and S.J. Holladay (Eds.), *The handbook of crisis communication* (2nd ed., pp. 31–52). West Sussex, UK: John Wiley & Sons.

Frandsen, F. & Johansen, W. (2020). Reframing the field: Public crisis management, political crisis management, and corporate crisis management. In F. Frandsen and W. Johansen (Eds.), *Crisis communication* (pp. 59–102). Boston: De Gruyter.

Ginther, M. R., Hartsough, L. E., & Marois, R. (2022). Moral outrage drives the interaction of harm and culpable intent in third-party punishment decisions. *Emotion*, *22*(4), 795–804.

Grebe, S.K. (2013). Things can get worse: How mismanagement of a crisis response strategy can cause a secondary or double crisis: The example of the AWB corporate scandal. *Corporate Communications: An International Journal*, *18*(1), 70–86.

Griffin, M., Babin, B. J., & Attaway, J. S. (1996). Anticipation of injurious consumption outcomes and its impact on consumer attributions of blame. *Journal of the Academy of Marketing Science*, *24*(4), 314–327.

Guerber, A. J., Anand, V., Ellstrand, A. E., Waller, M. A., & Reychav, I. (2020). Extending the situational crisis communication theory: The impact of linguistic style and culture. *Corporate Reputation Review*, *23*, 106–127.

Hegner, S. M., Beldad, A. D., & Kraesgenberg, A. L. (2016). The impact of crisis response strategy, crisis type, and corporate social responsibility on post-crisis consumer trust and purchase intention. *Corporate Reputation Review*, *19*, 357–370.

Holladay, S.J. (2009). Crisis communication strategies in the media coverage of chemical accidents. *Journal of Public Relations Research*, 21, 208–215.

Jin, Y. (2009). The effects of public's cognitive appraisal of emotions in crises on crisis coping and strategy assessment. *Public Relations Review*, *35*(3), 310–313.

Kim, H. K., & Yang, S. U. (2009). Cognitive processing of crisis communication: Effects of CSR and crisis response strategies on stakeholder perceptions of a racial crisis dynamics. *Public Relations Journal*, *3*(1), 1–39.

Kim, P. H., Dirks, K. T., Cooper, C. D., & Ferrin, D. L. (2006). When more blame is better than less: The implications of internal vs. external attributions for the repair of trust after a competence-vs. integrity-based trust violation. *Organizational Behavior and Human Decision Processes*, *99*(1), 49–65.

Lazarus, R. S. (1991). Progress on a cognitive-motivational-relational theory of emotion. *American Psychologist*, *46*(8), 819–834.

Lu, X., & Jin, Y. (2022). Integrating strategy and dosage: a new conceptual formula for overcoming unintended effects in public health crisis communication (PHCC). In W.T. Coombs & S.J. Holladay (Eds.), *The handbook of crisis communication* (2nd ed., pp. 261–282). West Sussex: John Wiley & Sons.

Lu, Y., & Huang, Y. H. C. (2018). Getting emotional: An emotion-cognition dual-factor model of crisis communication. *Public Relations Review*, *44*(1), 98–107.

Ma, L., & Zhan, M. (2016). Effects of attributed responsibility and response strategies on organizational reputation: A meta-analysis of situational crisis communication theory research. *Journal of Public Relations Research*, *28*(2), 102–119*.

Marcus, A. A., & Goodman, R. S. (1991). Victims and shareholders: The dilemmas of presenting corporate policy during a crisis. *Academy of Management Journal*, *34*(2), 281–305.

McLaughlin, M. L., Cody, M. J., & Rosenstein, N. E. (1983). Account sequences in conversations between strangers. *Communications Monographs*, *50*(2), 102–125.

Metts, S., & Cupach, W. R. (1989). Situational influence on the use of remedial strategies in embarrassing predicaments. *Communications Monographs*, *56*(2), 151–162.

Mowen, J. C. (1980). Further information on consumer perceptions of product recalls. *Advances in Consumer Research*, *7*(1). pp. 519–523

Ndone, J., & Park, J. (2022). Crisis communication: The mediating role of cognitive and affective empathy in the relationship between crisis type and crisis response strategy on post-crisis reputation and forgiveness. *Public Relations Review*, *48*(1), 102136. https://doi.org/10.1016/j.pubrev.2021.102136

Page, T. G., Zhou, A., & Capizzo, L. W. (2023). Finding the path beyond reputation repair: A structural topic modeling analysis of the crisis communication paradigm in public relations. *Public Relations Review*, *49*(4), 102349. https://doi.org/10.1016/j.pubrev.2023.102349

Park, H. (2017). Exploring effective crisis response strategies. *Public Relations Review*, *43*(1), 190–192.

Raithel, S., & Hock, S. J. (2021). The crisis-response match: An empirical investigation. *Strategic Management Journal*, *42*(1), 170–184.

Reber, B. H., Yarbough, R. C., Nowak, G., & Jin, Y. (2020). Complex and challenging crises: A call for solutions. In Y. Jin, B. H. Reber & G. J. Nowak (Eds.), Advancing *crisis communication effectiveness: integrating public relations scholarship with practice* (pp. 3–16). New York: Routledge.

Schoofs, L., Fannes, G., & Claeys, A. S. (2022). Empathy as a main ingredient of impactful crisis communication: The perspectives of crisis communication practitioners. *Public Relations Review*, *48*(1), 102150. https://doi.org/10.1016/j.pubrev.2022.102150

Seo, S., & Jang, S. S. (2021). Who spoils the barrel? Negative spillover effect on competitor brands during food crises. *International Journal of Hospitality Management*, *98*, 103047.

Sisco, H. F., Collins, E. L., & Zoch, L. M. (2010). Through the looking glass: A decade of Red Cross crisis response and situational crisis communication theory. *Public Relations Review*, *36*(1), 21–27.

Sturges, D. L. (1994). Communicating through crisis: A strategy for organizational survival. *Management communication quarterly*, *7*(3), 297–316.

Sulistyanto, A., Usmar, U., & Hermiyetti, H. (2020). Model of crisis communication management in the perspective of situational crisis communication theory at the transportation ministry. *Jurnal Komunikasi Ikatan Sarjana Komunikasi Indonesia*, *5*(2), 232–242.

Sun, D., & Li, Y. (2024). Influence of strategic crisis communication on public perceptions during public health crises: Insights from YouTube Chinese media. *Behavioral Sciences*, *14*(2), 91.

Weiner, B. (1972). Attribution theory, achievement motivation, and the educational process. *Review of Educational Research*, *42*(2), 203–215.

Yehya, N. A., & Coombs, W. T. (2017). Catalytic defiance as a crisis communication strategy: The risk of pursuing long-term objectives. *Business Horizons*, *60*(4), 463–472.

Zavyalova, A., Pfarrer, M. D., & Reger, R. K. (2017). Celebrity and infamy? The consequences of media narratives about organizational identity. *Academy of Management Review*, *42*(3), 461–480.

Zavyalova, A., Pfarrer, M. D., Reger, R. K., & Hubbard, T. D. (2016). Reputation as a benefit and a burden? How stakeholders' organizational identification affects the role of reputation following a negative event. *Academy of Management Journal*, *59*(1), 253–276.

Zhou, Z., Zhang, X., & Ki, E. J. (2022). Crisis response strategy manipulation: A systematic review and a test of nuances. *Public Relations Review*, *48*(3), 102208*.

*Requisite Readings

Chapter 11

Stealing Thunder

Research in legal studies found when lawyers first disclosed a weakness in their case, the weakness hurt the case less than when the same weakness was first disclosed by the opposition. This effect was called stealing thunder (Williams et al., 1993). Crisis communication research originated among practitioners. Crisis managers wrote about their efforts to handle crises offering pieces of advice based upon their experiences. Timing emerged as a common theme in these writings. Most crisis managers recommended responding as soon as possible in a crisis situation. If timing mattered in crisis communication, perhaps stealing thunder was relevant to crisis communication. Stealing thunder has proven to have a very robust and positive effect in crisis communication.

Theoretical Overview

Stealing thunder has been associated with the timing aspect of crisis communication. Arpan and Pompper (2003) described stealing thunder as a "highly proactive crisis communication approach" (p. 292). In general, stealing thunder involves "an admission of a weakness (usually a mistake or failure) before that weakness is announced by another party, such as an interest group or the media" (Arpan & Pompper, 2003, p. 294). Claeys (2023) succinctly described stealing thunder as the self-disclosure of a crisis. Research finds that when an organization is the first to disclose a crisis exists, the crisis inflicts less reputational damage upon the organization (Arpan & Pompper, 2003; Claeys, 2017).

The origins of "stealing thunder" reside within legal studies and have been adapted for the crisis context. Legal cases and crisis situations share features, including judgment made about the party linked to a negative event. The organization-in-crisis becomes the defendant in the crisis situation. The findings of stealing thunder are very robust, meaning experiments consistently find support for the value of stealing thunder across a

DOI: 10.4324/9781003469964-13

wide range on contexts including different crisis types, varying cultures, and variability in the initial reputation of the organization-in-crisis (Claeys, 2023). This chapter explores the application of stealing thunder to crisis communication.

Theoretical Conceptualization

Stealing thunder is an established concept with legal studies (e.g., McElhaney, 1987). Stealing thunder centers on a weakness in the defense's case. If lawyers feel the information is known by and will be disclosed by the opposition, the lawyers should divulge the information first. The argument holds that the failure to steal thunder would result in the information having an increased impact upon the jury. The ability to reduce the impact of the weakness in the case was the rationale for stealing thunder. Stealing thunder is a persuasive effort to reduce perceptions of guilt (Dolnik et al., 2003). Williams et al. (1993) were the first to experimentally test the proposed benefits of stealing thunder on mock juries. The experiment provided support for stealing thunder and suggested it worked by enhancing the credibility of the defendant. Williams et al. (1993) also speculated on a number of other reasons for the positive effects of stealing thunder on jury decisions.

Dolnik et al. (2003) explored the range of reasons stealing thunder could be beneficial in court cases including enhanced credibility, framing, commodity theory, and changing meaning. Again, the study found support for using stealing thunder in legal cases. Moreover, the data found the strongest support for the changing meaning interpretation of stealing thunder. As Dolnik et al. (2003) explained, "presenting negative information about oneself may force the evaluative audience to make sense of the information by changing its meaning to be consistent with what they would expect the revealer to be presenting" (p. 269). The idea is that when a defendant says something that is incriminating, those evaluating the defendant change the meaning of the information to be less damaging or even favorable for the defendant (Dolnik et al., 2003).

Arpan and Pompper (2003) were the first to bring stealing thunder to crisis communication with a published, experimental study. This was quickly followed by Arpan and Roskos-Ewoldsen's (2005) study of stealing thunder as proactive disclosure of crisis information. These two early studies provided the foundation for additional crisis communication research exploring the reasons for stealing thunder being beneficial in a crisis (e.g., Claeys & Cauberghe, 2012) and exploring stealing thunder in different contexts (e.g., Beldad et al., 2018; Lee, 2016). An-Sofie Claeys has produced the most extensive and informative line of stealing thunder research.

The core of stealing thunder is an organization knowing that there is a crisis and disclosing that information to stakeholders before anyone else discloses the information. An organization steals thunder when it is the first to disclose a crisis and thunder occurs when a third party discloses a crisis Claeys, 2023. We mistakenly assume that any crisis will become public, but we must accept that some crises can remain hidden by organizations. Stealing thunder is about "the spontaneous revelation of something that might otherwise remain unknown" (Claeys, 2023, p. 104). Claeys, 2023 rightly notes that stealing thunder is more than timing and a simple tactical effort. Rather, stealing thunder is a crisis disclosure strategy. True stealing thunder is spontaneous, meaning that the organization is not forced into the disclosure. Claeys and Opgenhaffen (2021) found that many professionals will engage in pseudo-stealing thunder. The professionals draft statements just in case a third party might disclose the crisis. Those statements are used if the professionals anticipate disclosure by a third party.

Furthermore, stealing thunder having a positive effect is not a given. Similar to the effects in law (Dolnik et al., 2003), crisis stealing thunder has a reduced effect when its use is identified as being strategic (designed to protect the organization-in-crisis) (Lee, 2016). As with other crisis response strategies, pre-crisis reputation does affect stealing thunder. Organizations with unfavorable pre-crisis reputations see less benefits and the risk of generating suspicion when using stealing thunder (Beldad et al., 2018). This diminished effect fits with the problem of stealing thunder being interpreted as a move designed to benefit the organization. Another feature which suggests limits to stealing thunder is the way stealing thunder is operationalized can affect its utility. For instance, expressing emotions in a crisis message, including stealing thunder, alters its effects upon stakeholders. Expression of sadness can enhance the crisis disclosure strategy that is stealing thunder (Claeys et al., 2013).

Three mechanisms have been used to explain stealing thunder in law and crisis communication. Interestingly, the results supporting the various mechanisms vary by the domain being studied. Increased credibility from stealing thunder is the first explanation. People expect an organization to report good news and not report its own failings such as a crisis. Similarly, people expect the defense in a court case to not say anything bad abouts its case. Stealing thunder is an expectancy violation which increases the credibility of the discloser (e.g., Burgoon et al., 1983) and increases trust in the discloser and their messages (Lee, 2016). The evidence of expectancy violations and credibility are mixed in the legal domain (Dolnik et al., 2003) but generally confirmed in the crisis communication research (Arpan & Pompper, 2003). Stealing thunder does improve perceptions of trust and credibility for the organization-in-crisis resulting in less reputational damage (Claeys & Cauberghe, 2012).

Change of meaning is a second explanation. Change of meaning was discussed already in the legal discussion of stealing thunder. To summarize, people perceive the self-disclosed information as less severe than when it is disclosed by a third party. Legal research supports the change of meaning explanation (Dolnik et al., 2003), there is a lack of support for this explanation in the crisis communication research (Claeys, 2023).

Commodity theory is third explanation of stealing thunder. Commodity theory holds that something's value is based upon its availability. A commodity, including information, is more valuable when it is scarce. This is also known as the old-news-is-no-news hypothesis. Stealing thunder makes information about the crisis available to stakeholders, including the news media. Hence, later reports about the crisis have less value and are less interesting to stakeholders, including the news media. Studies have found support for commodity theory as an explanation of stealing thunder (e.g., Zhou & Shin, 2017). As Claeys (2023) observed, "By self-disclosing, the information loses power" (p. 101). Stealing thunder discounts the value of later information reported about the crisis.

Stealing thunder as a crisis disclosure strategy has the potential to be abused. The abuse of stealing thunder involves what is disclosed and when it is disclosed. Organizations can choose what to disclose about the crisis and how they disclose that information. The abuse occurs when the organization seeks to spin the crisis through selective disclosure of information designed to highlight any positive aspects to the situation. Selective disclosure will hurt the organization when additional crisis information becomes known to stakeholders. The timing of stealing thunder relates to waiting until being "forced" to disclose the crisis. This goes back to pseudo-thunder stealing where the organization waits until it knows that a third party will disclose the crisis before it discloses the existence of a crisis (Claeys, 2023).

Any obvious limitation to stealing thunder is an organization must know about the crisis before any of its stakeholders. With many event-based crises, the crises could appear in traditional or social media before an organization can make an announcement about the crisis. Research has shown prior reputation can limit the potential effectiveness of stealing thunder as well (Beldad et al., 2018). Culture influences the degree to which crisis managers are willing to use stealing thunder and the effects it has upon constituents (Zhou & Shin, 2017).

Research with professionals found that organizations are hesitant to use stealing thunder. The rationale is simple: if you do not disclose a crisis exists, stakeholders might never learn about the crisis. If you disclose a crisis, stakeholders will definitely know about the crisis (Claeys & Opgenhaffen, 2021). Again, we have to assume some crises never become public and not that all crises eventually see the light of day. Claeys and Coombs (2020) used behavioral economics to explain the choice not to steal thunder. Stealing thunder will result in loss. When constituents learn about a crisis, that information will affect their social evaluations of the organization, including reputation, and even how they might interact with the organization. Behavioral economics (BE) is a fusion of psychology and economics used to explain patterns in anomalies, violations of the rational theories of economics. BE explores the "irrational" heuristics that influence how people make decisions. A fundamental heuristic is that people fear loss much more than they enjoy gain (Thaler, 2015). Also people value short-term outcomes over longer-term outcomes. Stealing thunder will generate a loss, making it an unattractive choice. The argument for stealing is more long-term. The organization will suffer less in the long-term compared to thunder. However, this assumes the crisis will be revealed (thunder will strike) and some loss is unavoidable in the long run. Not disclosing the crisis might result in the crisis never being known or being known at some future date. The heuristics that favor loss avoidance and a short-term focus pushes crisis managers away from stealing thunder (Claeys & Coombs, 2020).

Applications to Subfields

The corporate crisis subfield is the primary area for the application of stealing thunder. The original stealing thunder (Arpan & Pompper, 2003) and the bulk of later studies (Yao et al., 2024) have examined organizations stealing thunder and the effects upon their stakeholders. A wide range of crisis types have been explored using steaking thunder. A number of moderating variables have been studied in the corporate crisis subfield including the previously discussed pre-crisis reputation (Beldad et al., 2018). Lee and Lee (2021) examined stealing thunder as a moderate on the utility of pre-crisis engagement, efforts to diffuse a negative event before it escalates into a crisis. The stealing thunder research in the corporate crisis subfield includes research that concentrates specifically on the application to employees as part of internal crisis communication (Kim & Lim, 2020). Stealing thunder has been applied to both the political and public crisis subfields as well but to a far lesser extent. Wigley (2011) applied stealing thunder to political scandals and found less media coverage for scandals when stealing thunder was utilized. Fowler (2017) examined the public subfield with an analysis of how a police department used Twitter to steal thunder during a mall shooting crisis. The steaming thunder allowed the police department to become the dominant voice during the public crisis. Lee (2020) explored the use of stealing thunder in the digital environment. Natural disasters, as part of the public crisis subfield, are a poor fit with stealing thunder because they are event-based and those managing the crises are not responsible for the crisis.

Practitioner Takeaways

The primary takeaway from the stealing thunder research is that crisis managers can steal thunder when they have the chance (Claeys, 2017). The bulk of the studies find stealing thunder results in less reputational damage than thunder (crisis disclosure by a third party). However, stealing thunder is not a cure-all. If an organization appears to be forced to disclose or has an unfavorable prior reputation, there may be no positive effect from stealing thunder. Also, crisis managers should be aware that stealing thunder might be a tough sell internally. Other managers may resist the crisis disclosure strategy feeling it is better to wait and even hope that the crisis never does become public knowledge. Crisis managers must be prepared to justify and to advocate for stealing thunder. Crisis managers must be sure to steal thunder properly by disclosing all relevant information no matter how negative that information might be and to capture the proper emotions in the crisis strategy. Limited disclosure during stealing thunder could come back to harm the organization. Stealing thunder is not for every organization nor for every crisis situation.

Theoretical Constraints and Concerns

A key theoretical constraint for stealing thunder is its limited applicability. Not every crisis is amenable to the self-disclosure of a crisis. Some crises happen so quickly that there is no time to steal thunder. Stealing thunder has focused on reputation (social evaluations in general) as the primary outcome variable. Research needs to explore a wider array of outcomes that could be associated with stealing thunder. More research is needed to explore the three reasons given for the positive outcomes of stealing thunder. It could be that different crisis outcomes could be linked to various theoretical explanations for stealing thunder. Additional research also is warranted for understanding the various ways to express stealing thunder and how those expressions can shape the benefits derived from stealing thunder. Researchers have just begun to explore the boundary conditions for stealing thunder. Prior reputation appears to boundary condition for stealing thunder, but we know little beyond that. While a robust crisis response strategy, stealing thunder does have its limitations.

Theoretical Engagement Points

1 What type of research methods are most closely associated with stealing thunder?
2 Is stealing thunder primarily a descriptive, relational, or explanatory theory?

3 Is stealing thunder primarily an empirical-analytic, interpretative, or critical theory?
4 How would you evaluate stealing thunder in terms of scope, appropriateness, heuristic value, validity, parsimony, and openness?

Discussion Questions

1 Under what circumstances is stealing thunder most effective as a crisis communication strategy? Provide examples from real-world crises.
2 How does stealing thunder enhance the credibility of an organization in crisis? What are the potential risks of employing this strategy?
3 Compare and contrast the three main mechanisms used to explain the effectiveness of stealing thunder: credibility enhancement, change of meaning, and commodity theory. Which mechanism do you find most compelling and why?
4 Discuss the ethical implications of stealing thunder. How can organizations ensure that they are not using this strategy to manipulate or deceive stakeholders?
5 How has the rise of social media and the 24/7 news cycle impacted the use and effectiveness of stealing thunder in crisis communication?

References

Arpan, L. M., & Pompper, D. (2003). Stormy weather: Testing "stealing thunder" as a crisis communication strategy to improve communication flow between organizations and journalists. *Public Relations Review*, *29*(3), 291–308*.

Arpan, L. M., & Roskos-Ewoldsen, D. R. (2005). Stealing thunder: Analysis of the effects of proactive disclosure of crisis information. *Public Relations Review*, *31*(3), 425–433.

Beldad, A. D., van Laar, E., & Hegner, S. M. (2018). Should the shady steal thunder? The effects of crisis communication timing, pre-crisis reputation valence, and crisis type on post-crisis organizational trust and purchase intention. *Journal of Contingencies and Crisis Management*, *26*(1), 150–163.

Burgoon, M., Dillard, J. P., & Ooran, N. E. (1983). Friendly or unfriendly persuasion: The effects of violations of expectations by males and females. *Human Communication Research*, *10*(2), 283–294.

Claeys, A. S. (2017). Better safe than sorry: Why organizations in crisis should never hesitate to steal thunder. *Business Horizons*, *60*(3), 305–311*.

Claeys, A. S. (2023). The benefits and pitfalls of stealing thunder. In W. T. Coombs & S. J. Holladay (Eds.), *The handbook of crisis communication* (2nd ed., pp. 99–111). West Sussex: John Wiley and Sons*.

Claeys, A. S., & Cauberghe, V. (2012). Crisis response and crisis timing strategies, two sides of the same coin. *Public Relations Review*, *38*(1), 83–88*.

Claeys, A. S., Cauberghe, V., & Leysen, J. (2013). Implications of stealing thunder for the impact of expressing emotions in organizational crisis communication. *Journal of Applied Communication Research*, *41*(3), 293–308.

Claeys, A. S., & Coombs, W. T. (2020). Organizational crisis communication: Suboptimal crisis response selection decisions and behavioral economics. *Communication Theory*, *30*(3), 290–309.

Claeys, A. S., & Opgenhaffen, M. (2021). Changing perspectives: Managerial and legal considerations regarding crisis communication. *Public Relations Review*, *47*(4), 102080.

Dolnik, L., Case, T. I., & Williams, K. D. (2003). Stealing thunder as a courtroom tactic revisited: Processes and boundaries. *Law and Human Behavior*, *27*, 267–287.

Fowler, B. M. (2017) Stealing thunder and filling the silence: Twitter as a primary channel of police crisis communication. *Public Relations Review*, *43*(4), 718–728.

Kim, Y., & Lim, H. (2020). Activating constructive employee behavioural responses in a crisis: Examining the effects of pre-crisis reputation and crisis communication strategies on employee voice behaviours. *Journal of Contingencies and Crisis Management*, *28*(2), 141–157.

Lee, S. Y. (2016). Weathering the crisis: Effects of stealing thunder in crisis communication. *Public Relations Review*, *42*(2), 336–344.

Lee, S. Y. (2020). Stealing thunder as a crisis communication strategy in the digital age. *Business Horizons*, *63*(6), 801–810.

Lee, S. Y., & Lee, J. Y. (2021). Fixing the barn door before the horse bolts: Effects of pre-crisis engagement and stealing thunder in crisis communication. *Public Relations Rreview*, *47*(1), 101930.

McElhaney, J. W. (1987). *McElhaney's trial notebook* (2nd ed.). Chicago: American Bar Association.

Thaler, R. H. (2015). *The making of behavioral economics: Misbehaving*. New York: W.W. Norton & Company.

Wigley, S. (2011). Telling your own bad news: Eliot Spitzer and a test of the stealing thunder strategy. *Public Relations Review*, *37*(1), 50–56.

Williams, K. D., Bourgeois, M. J., & Croyle, R. T. (1993). The effects of stealing thunder in criminal and civil trials. *Law and Human Behavior*, *17*(6), 597–609.

Yao, H. C., Ling, I. L., Liu, C., & Liao, J. F. (2024). Hospitals with a tarnished reputation: Stealing thunder, concealment intention, and learning from an organizational and industrial history of crisis concealment. *Journal of Public Relations Research*, *36*(1), 45–71.

Zhou, L., & Shin, J.-H. (2017). Does stealing thunder always work? A content analysis of crisis communication practice under different cultural settings. *Public Relations Review*, *43*(5), 1036–1047. https://doi.org/10.1016/j.pubrev.2017.08.004*

*Requisite Readings

Chapter 12

Integrated Crisis Mapping

The early crisis communication theories leaned toward the rational. SCCT and stealing thunder both place a heavy emphasis on a rational approach (Claeys & Coombs, 2020). However, we know that crises are emotion evoking events, yet emotion remained in the background of early crisis communication research (e.g., Coombs & Holladay, 2005). The integrate crisis mapping model shifted emotion from the background to the foreground of crisis communication research and provided the initial energy to what became an emotional turn in the field.

Theoretical Overview

Jin et al. (2007) observed that the early crisis communication theories and research gave scant attention to emotion. Even when emotion was mentioned, it was more of a secondary than a primary concern (e.g., Coombs & Holladay, 2005). The lack of attention to emotion, stakeholder emotions to be more specific, prompted the development of the integrated crisis mapping (ICM) model. ICM filled the need for a "public-based, emotion-driven perspective to crisis communication modeling" (Jin et al., 2007, p. 81).

ICM drew from the works of Lazarus in psychology and Cameron in public relations. Lazarus (1991) identified emotion as a critical stimulus for research in his cognitive appraisal theory research. Cameron et al. (2001) linked emotion to public relations in his contingency theory. Cameron et al. (2001) argued that emotion helps to assess the effectiveness of public relations actions, moderate stakeholder perceptions of organizations, and is a critical factor in organizational decision-making. Jin et al. (2007) drew upon these ideas to craft ICM. ICM mapped the various emotions stakeholders are likely to feel in response to different crisis types. Understanding the emotions evoked by a crisis helps crisis managers to prepare more effective crisis messages by addressing these emotions in the crisis response. Moreover, ICM argued stakeholders will also have preferred ways of coping with different crises and those coping strategies

DOI: 10.4324/9781003469964-14

inform what constitutes an effective response. A series of studies were conducted to test elements of ICM.

Most importantly, ICM helped to inspire crisis communication researchers to explore the importance of emotion. ICM provided energy for the emotion turn in crisis communication research (e.g., Zhang & Adegbola, 2022). Examples of the emotional turn include Lu and Huang's (2018) work on the emotion-cognition dual factor model for crisis communication, Austin et al.'s (2023) work exploring emotions in disaster communication and Coombs and Tachkova's (2022, 2023, 2024) work integrating moral outrage in crisis communication theory and research.

Theoretical Conceptualization

ICM is premised on three assumptions. First, the focus is on the emotions of active, primary publics (constituents). Second, the focus is on the dominant emotions displayed by publics. Third, the crisis response should be predicated upon the emotions of the primary publics. Primary publics are those most affected by the crisis, have an interest in the crisis resolution, and have long-term influence on the organization's reputation or operations. Emotions become central to thinking because they can change what is considered an effective crisis response. Hence, the focus on how people react to a crisis based on the emotions evoked by the crisis Jin et al. (2007).

ICM draws from Lazarus' (1991) concept of appraisal primary appraisals related to one's wellbeing while secondary appraisals relate to one's coping resources and options. Lazarus (1991) identified six emotions: (1) anger, (2) anxiety, (3) fright, (4) sadness, (5) shame, and (6) guilt. ICM's focus is on corporate crises and the emotions were narrowed to the four negative emotions of anger, anxiety, fright, and sadness (Jin & Pang, 2010; Jin et al., 2007. Lazarus (1991) specified two coping strategies. Problem-focused coping is about taking action to create change. Cognitive-focused coping is about how people interpret the situation. ICM labeled them as conative coping (problem-focused) and cognitive coping (cognitive-focused). Core relations theme was another element used in ICM. The core relational theme is "the central harm or benefit in the relational encounters that underlies each specific kind of emotion evoked by either party's expression and behavior" (Jin et al., 2007, p. 87).

The core relational theme of anger is the perception of an offense and a threat to wellbeing. The core relational theme of fright involves confronting uncertainty and threat and need for escape or avoidance. The core relational theme of anxiety is immediate and powerful danger and a need to protect oneself from the organization. The core relational theme of sadness is irrevocable loss and the need to create favorable expectations (Jin et al., 2007). These concepts provided the foundational elements for constructing ICM.

ICM categorizes crisis types using the three criteria of internal-external, personal-public, and unnatural-natural. ICM uses a two-by-two grid to organize crisis types. The Y-axis is an organization's issue involvement ranging from high to low. The level of organizational involvement with a crisis reflects the allocations of resources to the crisis management effort. The X-axis is the public's primary coping strategy ranging from cognitive to conative. This dimension reflects the "dominant choice of the publics in dealing with the crisis situation" (Jin et al., 2007, p. 90). IMC identifies four quadrants of crisis types. Quadrant 1 is high engagement and conative coping. The crises populating Quadrant 1 include industrial matters, reputation, technology breakdown, labor unrest, and regulatory/legislative concerns. Quadrant 2 is high engagement and cognitive coping. The crises populating Quadrant 2 include natural disasters, accidents, economic downturns, and hostile takeovers. Quadrant 3 is low engagement and cognitive coping. The crises populating Quadrant 3 include terrorism/psychopathic acts, rumors, and CEO retirement. Quadrant 4 is low engagement and conative coping. The crises populating Quadrant 4 include security issues, human resources, and transportation failures (Jin et al., 2010).

ICM anticipated the primary and secondary emotions for each quadrant and the primary coping strategy used in each quadrant. Table 12.1 presents the anticipated emotions and coping strategies for each quadrant.

The first test of ICM focused on Quadrant 1. The research method was content analysis of five crisis cases that captured the crisis types found in Quadrant 1. News stories were collected and coded for a number of variables, including public emotions and coping strategies. Anxiety was associated with all five crises, while anger was associated with three of the five cases. Anxiety was the primary emotion in three of the five cases. Anger was the primary emotion in two cases. Conative coping was used in four of the five cases (Jin et al., 2010). This first test of ICM demonstrated that Quadrant 1 did evoke anger and anxiety and did result in conative coping

Table 12.1 Anticipated Emotions and Coping Strategies by Quadrant

Quadrant	*Emotions*	*Coping Strategy*
1	Anger (primary) Anxiety (secondary)	Conative
2	Sadness (primary) Fright (secondary)	Cognitive
3	Fright (primary) Sadness (secondary)	Cognitive
4	Anxiety (primary) Anger (secondary)	Conative

supporting the conceptualization of Quadrant 1 and utility of examining crisis emotions. Researchers could study "the upheaval of emotions in crisis" (Jin et al., 2010, p. 431).

The second test of ICM examined the other three Quadrants and combined the results to assess the overall utility of ICM. The analyses of Quadrants 2, 3, and 4 used three cases for each Quadrant and employed the same content analysis of news stories as used in the analysis of Quadrant 1. Table 12.2 presents the results of the study showing the primary coping strategy in each Quadrant and the emotions found in each Quadrant. Anxiety was found in each quadrant resulting in the observation, "Anxiety could even be argued as the default dominant emotion" (Jin et al., 2012, p. 286). For this reason, anxiety is present across all four quadrants as the "background emotion" (Pang et al., 2023a, 2023b). Anger, fright, and sadness were found with anger being the most common emotional reaction (after anxiety). Conative was the dominant coping strategy. "Evidence suggests strong merit that publics in crisis engage in manifest conative coping" (Jin et al., 2010, p. 287). However, cognitive coping is there but latent. The authors argue that "cognitive coping is the antecedent of conative coping" (Jin et al., 2010, p. 288). People are likely to engage in both forms of coping in reaction to a crisis. Crisis response strategies should address these emotions, especially anxiety, and favor action-oriented advice for stakeholders.

Cheng et al. (2011) applied ICM to Singapore to test the applicability of the Western-based model to the Asian context. Following the method developed in testing ICM, the study examined news reports for four crisis cases, one from each of the four Quadrants. The results found a similar pattern favoring conative coping but some differences in the emotions associated with the four Quadrants. Table 12.3 provides a summary of the emotion results. Quadrants 3 and 4 were especially different from the earlier ICM results for the US (Cheng et al., 2011).

Table 12.2 Emotions and Coping Strategies by Quadrant from Data

Quadrant	*Emotions*	*Coping Strategy*
1	Anger (primary) Sadness (secondary)	Conative
2	Sadness/fright (primary) Anger (secondary)	Conative
3	Fright (primary) Anger (secondary)	No preferred strategy
4	Anger (primary) Sadness (secondary)	Conative and cognitive

Table 12.3 Emotions and Coping Strategies by Quadrant from Singapore

Quadrant	*Emotions*	*Coping Strategy*
1	Anxiety (primary) Anger (secondary)	Conative
2	Fright (primary) Anger (secondary)	Conative
3	Anger (primary) Sadness (secondary)	Conative
4	Fright/anxiety (primary) Anger (secondary)	Conative

ICM identified emotions as a central variable in crisis communication. Building on ICM's emotion focus, Jin et al. (2014) sought to integrate emotions more fully into crisis communication by studying the effects of arousal and valence on the acceptance of crisis response strategies and coping strategies. Emotions vary by both arousal (calm to excited) and valence (positive to negative). These two dimensions have been labeled emotional tone and emotional temperature in crisis communication. Jin's (2014) study was a 2x2 experiment using intensity (high and low) and valence (positive/sympathy and negative/anger). The outcomes were coping strategies and acceptance of crisis response strategies. When sympathy was stronger than anger (valence), coping favored action support, instrumental support, emotional support, and emotional venting. Little effect was found for arousal. When sympathy was greater than anger, respondents reported greater acceptance of full apology while scapegoating acceptance was higher when anger was greater than sympathy. Low intensity crises favored full apology while high intensity favored scapegoating. The study shed light on the potential relationship between emotions and crisis response acceptance (Jin, 2014).

Jin et al. (2014) developed a measure of emotional reactions during crises to help facilitate future crisis communication research utilizing emotions. Three different stakeholder emotions can result from a crisis: emotions toward the crisis, emotions toward the organization-in-crisis, and emotions toward themselves in a crisis. The study began with 13 discrete emotions: anger, anxiety, apprehension, confusion, contempt, disgust, embarrassment, fear, guilt, sadness, shame, surprise, and sympathy. The analysis found the emotions formed three clusters. The first cluster was labeled attribution-independent (AI) emotions composed of anxiety, fear apprehension, and sympathy. The second cluster was labeled internal-attribution-dependent (IAD) emptions composed of guilt, embarrassment and shame. The third cluster was labeled external-attribution-dependent

(EAD) emotions composed of disgust, contempt, anger and sadness. The emotion scale provides an additional research tool for crisis communication researchers. Both of these studies reflect how ICM pushed crisis communication to integrate emotion into the study of crisis communication.

Applications to Subfields

ICM was created for the corporate subfield. This corporate focus is evident in the crisis cases selected to test ICM (Jin et al., 2010). Other corporate subfield research drawing upon ICM included Brummette and Sisco (2015) and Yeo et al. (2020). Kim et al. (2019) and Ndone (2023) also have a corporate focus with research examining internal crisis communication and employees. The public subfield has a number of ICM-inspired studies as well. Guo (2017) examined the Boston marathon bombing, Li et al. (2023) explored public health crises, and Lifang et al. (2020) studied natural disasters. While there are no specific studies utilizing ICM in the political subfield, the focus on emotions is relevant to the subfield. ICM's emphasis on emotions allows it to be applicable to all three crisis communication subfields.

Practitioner Takeaways

ICM helps reinforce the importance of emotions for crisis managers. ICM explains why emotions are important and identifies the key emotions felt when stakeholders encounter crises. Moreover, ICM notes what emotions are most likely in different crisis situations. Another benefit from ICM is understanding how stakeholders cope with crises. Stakeholders focus on conative coping but that is built from cognitive coping. Hence, both forms of coping are relevant to crisis communication. The lessons about emotions and coping can be used when creating crisis response messages. Crisis response strategies can be operationalized in different ways. There is no one, set way to express each crisis response strategy. ICM argues that the construction of the crisis response strategy should reflect both the emotional and coping demands associated with the crisis type (Jin & Pang, 2010).

Theoretical Constraints and Concerns

The initial tests of ICM note the concern of using news reports to study the emotions of people reacting to crises. Moreover, these initial tests on based on a small number of crisis cases. Utilization of more direct assessments of people emotions during a crisis, such as the emotion scale developed by Jin et al. (2014) and an expanded number of crisis cases could increase the confidence in the original ICM tests. ICM tends to be more descriptive than prescriptive. It identifies stakeholder emotions as salient to crisis communication but does not specify the nature of that relationship. Jin's (2014) research sought to add a more prescriptive element to ICM but the move to fully articulate prescriptive claims from ICM has yet to be developed.

Theoretical Engagement Points

1. What type of research methods are most closely associated with ICM?
2. Is ICM primarily a descriptive, relational, or explanatory theory?
3. Is ICM primarily an empirical-analytic, interpretative, or critical theory?
4. How would you evaluate ICM in terms of scope, appropriateness, heuristic value, validity, parsimony, and openness?

Discussion Questions

1. How does the ICM model shift the focus of crisis communication from a rational approach to an emotion-driven perspective?
2. Why is understanding stakeholder emotions important in crisis communication, and how does the ICM model help crisis managers address these emotions?
3. Explain the difference between conative and cognitive coping strategies in the context of crisis communication. How can crisis managers use this understanding to develop more effective responses?
4. The ICM model was initially developed in a Western context. How applicable is this model to crisis situations in different cultural settings, as evidenced by the Singapore study?
5. What are some of the limitations of the ICM model? How can future research build upon and improve this model?

References

Austin, L., Kim, S., & Saffer, A. J. (2023). Emotion as a predictor of crisis communicative behaviors: Examining information seeking and sharing during Hurricane Florence. *Journal of Applied Communication Research*, *51*(5), 1–20.

Brummette, J., & Sisco, H. F. (2015). Using Twitter as a means of coping with emotions and uncontrollable crises. *Public Relations Review*, *41*(1), 89–96.

Cameron, G. T., Cropp, F., & Reber, B. H. (2001). Getting past platitudes: Factors limiting accommodation in public relations. *Journal of Communication Management*, *5*(3), 242–261.

Cheng, L. C., Loh, Y., & Pang, A. (2011). Culture and emotion in crisis communication: Indigenization of the integrated crisis mapping (ICM) model. In *Proceedings of the 10th conference on corporate communication* (pp. 222–239). Corporate Communication.

Claeys, A. S., & Coombs, W. T. (2020). Organizational crisis communication: Suboptimal crisis response selection decisions and behavioral economics. *Communication Theory*, *30*(3), 290–309.
Coombs, W. T., & Holladay, S. J. (2005). Exploratory study of stakeholder emotions: Affect and crisis. In N. M. Ashkanasy, W. J. Zerbe, & C. E. J. Hartel (Eds.), *Research on emotion in organizations: Volume 1: The effect of affect in organizational settings* (pp. 271–288). New York: Elsevier.
Coombs, W. T., & Tachkova, E. R. (2022). Elaborating the concept of threat in contingency theory: An integration with moral outrage and situational crisis communication theory. *Public Relations Review*, *48*(4), 102234.
Coombs, W. T., & Tachkova, E. R. (2023). Integrating moral outrage in situational crisis communication theory: A triadic appraisal model for crises. *Management Communication Quarterly*, *37*(4), 798–820.
Coombs, W. T., & Tachkova, E. R. (2024). How emotions can enhance crisis communication: Theorizing around moral outrage. *Journal of Public Relations Research*, *36*(1), 6–22.
Guo, S. J. (2017). The 2013 Boston marathon bombing: Publics' emotions, coping, and organizational engagement. *Public Relations Review*, *43*(4), 755–767.
Jin, Y. (2014). Examining publics' crisis responses according to different shades of anger and sympathy. *Journal of Public Relations Research*, *26*(1), 79–101.
Jin, Y., Liu, B. F., Anagondahalli, D., & Austin, L. (2014). Scale development for measuring publics' emotions in organizational crises. *Public Relations Review*, *40*(3), 509–518.
Jin, Y., & Pang, A. (2010). Future directions of crisis communication research: Emotions in crisis–The next frontier. In W.T. Coombs and S.J. Holladay (Eds.), *The handbook of crisis communication* (pp. 677–682). Malden, MA: Wiley*.
Jin, Y., Pang, A., & Cameron, G. T. (2007). Integrated crisis mapping: Toward a publics-based, emotion-driven conceptualization in crisis communication. *Sphera Publica*, *7*, 81–95*.
Jin, Y., Pang, A., & Cameron, G. T. (2010). The role of emotions in crisis responses: Inaugural test of the integrated crisis mapping (ICM) model. *Corporate Communications: An International Journal*, *15*(4), 428–452*.
Jin, Y., Pang, A., & Cameron, G. T. (2012). Toward a publics-driven, emotion-based conceptualization in crisis communication: Unearthing dominant emotions in multi-staged testing of the integrated crisis mapping (ICM) model. *Journal of Public Relations Research*, *24*(3), 266–298*.
Kim, Y., Kang, M., Lee, E., & Yang, S. U. (2019). Exploring crisis communication in the internal context of an organization: Examining moderated and mediated effects of employee-organization relationships on crisis outcomes. *Public Relations Review*, *45*(3), 101777.
Lazarus, R. S. (1991). Progress on a cognitive-motivational-relational theory of emotion. *American Psychologist*, *46*(8), 819.
Li, L., Zhou, J., Zhuang, J., & Zhang, Q. (2023). Gender-specific emotional characteristics of crisis communication on social media: Case studies of two public health crises. *Information Processing & Management*, *60*(3), 103299.
Lifang, L. I., Zhiqiang, W. A. N. G., Zhang, Q., & Hong, W. E. N. (2020). Effect of anger, anxiety, and sadness on the propagation scale of social media posts after natural disasters. *Information Processing & Management*, *57*(6), 102313.

Lu, Y., & Huang, Y. H. C. (2018). Getting emotional: An emotion-cognition dual-factor model of crisis communication. *Public Relations Review*, *44*(1), 98–107.

Ndone, J. (2023). Internal crisis communication: The effects of negative employee-organization relationships on internal reputation and employees' unsupportive behavior. *Public Relations Review*, *49*(4), 102357.

Pang, A., Jin, Y., & Cameron, G. T. (2023a). Capturing the complexity and dynamism of decision making in PR: The contingency theory of strategic conflict management. In C. Botan & E. Sommerfeldt (Eds.), *Public relations theory III* (pp. 151–172). Routledge. https://doi.org/10.4324/9781003141396-12

Pang, A., Jin, Y., & Cameron, G. T. (2023b). The contingency theory of strategic conflict management: Review from three decades of theory development, extension and application. *Journalism and Communication Monographs*, *25*(2), 193–214*. https://doi.org/10.1177/15226379231167141

Yeo, S. L., Pang, A., Cheong, M., & Yeo, J. Q. (2020). Emotions in social media: An analysis of tweet responses to MH370 search suspension announcement. *International Journal of Business Communication*, *57*(2), 194–211.

Zhang, W., & Adegbola, O. (2022). Emotional intelligence and public relations: An empirical review. *Public Relations Review*, *48*(3), 102199.

*Requisite Readings

Chapter 13

Threat Appraisal Model

Writings about crisis communication have embraced the idea a crisis is a threat and an opportunity. The opportunity is the chance to manage the crisis so that people consider your efforts to be positive. However, the threat aspect of a crisis is what draws managerial attention to the need for crisis management and crisis communication. Managers are concerned about crises because of the harm they can generate for constituents and the organization-in-crisis. The threat appraisal theory articulates the importance of "threat" within the crisis process and its application to crisis communication.

Theoretical Overview

The threat appraisal theory traces its roots to the development of the contingency theory of conflict management (contingency theory for short) in the 1990s. Contingency theory explores some 87 variables, but threat is one of the most important factors in the theory (Reber & Cameron, 2003). Jin presented a conference paper in 2005 that began the threat appraisal model research. Two studies testing the applicability of the threat assessment model soon followed (Jin & Cameron, 2007; Pang et al., 2006). A number of studies began utilizing elements of the threat appraisal model. Starting in Pang et al., 2020, researchers began to expand upon the threat appraisal model. The temporal distance in crises (Kim & Jin, 2020) and moral outrage (Coombs & Tachkova, 2022, 2023) have been used to revise the model. Crisis communication researchers continue to draw upon ideas from the threat appraisal model to illuminate crisis communication (e.g., Choi et al., 2023).

Contingency theory explores the optimal conflict positioning in conflicts which exist within the organization-stakeholder relationship. When conflict arises, public relations professionals must choose an effective communication stance based on the conflict positioning decisions they have made. Contingency theory places possible communication stances on a continuum

DOI: 10.4324/9781003469964-15

from advocacy to accommodation which further drives strategies that guide organizational responses including communication strategies and tactics. Advocacy seeks to push the organization's position while accommodation seeks to address the concerns of stakeholders (Cancel et al., 1999). Contingency theory posits the most effective stance depends. The contextual factors, reflected in the 87 variables, determine what makes for an effective communicative stance (Pang et al., 2020). Contingency theory divides the variables into predisposing and situational. Predisposing variables capture an organization's favorite stance—how organization's usually communicate in conflict situations. The situational factors can cause an organization to shift from that favorite stance resulting in the final stance utilized by the organization (Yarbrough et al., 1998). As noted earlier, threat is considered an important variable within contingency theory.

Contingency theory defines threat as a "potentially negative situation involving publics" (Cancel et al., 1999, p. 184). The organizational response to a situation becomes faster the greater the threat posed by a public. Contingency theory identified both internal and external threats. Threats are meaningful because they help to shape what is an appropriate response in a given situation. Contingency theory "relies heavily on the concept of threat without fully developing the concept as well as its operationalization" (Jin & Cameron, 2007, p. 255). The threat appraisal model does elaborate on the conceptualization and operationalization of threat.

Theoretical Conceptualization

The threat appraisal model begins with primary and secondary appraisals drawn from contingency theory and cognitive appraisal theory. Cognitive appraisal is "a process through which the person evaluates whether a particular encounter with the environment is relevant to his or her wellbeing, and it so, in what ways" (Folkman et al., 1986, p. 992). Primary appraisals involve relevance to wellbeing, while secondary appraisals concern how a person might prevent harm, including the actions one could take and the feasibility of those actions (Pang et al., 2006). The threat appraisal model translates the primary and secondary appraisals into the crisis context. The primary appraisal involves the situational demands and includes perceived danger, uncertainty (an inability to control and predict), and effort required to address the threat. The secondary appraisal involves the resources needed to address the threat and include knowledge, skills, time, finance, and support from the dominant coalition (Pang et al., 2006).

Threat communication is conceptualized as having three dimensions. The first dimension is the level of threat posed to the organization and can be low, medium, or high (threat level). The second dimension is duration of the threat and can be short term or long term (threat duration).

The third dimension is threat type and can be internal or external (threat type). Examples of internal threats are declines in employee perceptions of the organization and economic loss. Examples of external threats include litigation, regulation, drops in reputation, and attacks from activists. The threat appraisal model argues that "for a threat to occur to a practitioner or for an organization, there has to be some insufficiency of resources to meet situational demands" (Pang et al., 2006, p. 87).

Pang et al. (2006) were the first to publish a test of the threat appraisal model. They used news media account to study the Homeland Security's terror alerts. Coding schemes were developed for the three threat dimensions. The results indicated the threat appraisal model did provide an improved diagnostic framework for assessing threats in crisis situations that captured the "multi-layer nature of threats" (Pang et al., 2006, p. 94).

Jin and Cameron (2007) conducted an experiment to explore the utility of the threat appraisal model for explaining how corporate crisis managers responded to threats and the connection between threats and organizational stances. Jin and Cameron (2007) made a modification to the threat appraisal model. They argued that a crisis creates a high threat level, hence, threat became two-dimensional, threat type and threat duration. The study examined the effects of threat type and threat duration on crisis manager's cognitive and affective reactions to crises and the stances organizations were likely to take in response to the crisis. The cognitive reactions include the perceived demands the crisis would place on the organization and the resources required to management crisis. Affective reactions included the valence of the emotions (positive or negative) and arousal (calm to excited) felt by crisis managers in the various threat scenarios.

Jin and Cameron (2007) noted, "it is clear across all the threat consequences, compared to the short-term threats, long-term threats tend to lead to more cognitive appraisal, stronger affective responses, and more accommodative stances" (p. 274). Long-term compared to short-term threats resulted in increased perceptions of situational demands, resources needed, valence, arousal, and more accommodative stances. External compared to internal threats create increased perceptions of situational demands, resources needed, arousal, and accommodative stances. The analyses indicated that the combination of external and long term were the strongest threats leading to stronger perceptions of situational demands and arousal (Jin & Cameron, 2007). The study linked a clear link between the assessment created by the threat appraisal model and how crisis managers perceived the crisis, emotionally reacted to the crisis, and how they would respond to the crisis. Such insights are valuable insights into the crisis management and crisis communication process.

Temporal distance has been added as a relevant factor to threat appraisal. Temporal distance is the perception of when the negative effects of a crisis will be felt (Kim, 2022). It is similar to the concept of velocity in risk assessment. Velocity is how soon a risk could affect an organization (Wolters Kluwer, 2015). Temporal distance differentiates between the near future and the distant future—if the negative effects will be soon or later. While the threat assessment model focused on crisis managers, temporal distance relates to perceptions of the crisis stakeholders (Kim, 2022). The first published study adding temporal distance utilizes a public health crisis involving people dying from an unknown disease after receiving a flu vaccine in an experiment. Temporal distance had no effect on post-crisis reputation but did affect potential supportive behavior and crisis emotions. Negative emotions were stronger when crises effects are near future, while people were more willing to support the organization-in-crisis and less likely to feel negative emotions when the crisis effects were in the distant future. Emotions were found to have a mediating effect on the relationship between temporal distance and potential supportive behavior (Kim & Jin, 2020).

Kim (2022) used an experiment with a stimulus involving contaminated commercial drinking water to explore temporal distance. While focused on a health concern, the stimuli also had a corporate element given it was commercial drinking water. The study used the original outcomes of the threat assessment model including situational demands and resources along with crisis emotions and potential supportive behavior. Temporal distance was found to lower situational demands (more distant crisis created lower situational demands) but had no effect on perceptions of resources, crisis emotions, or potential supportive behavior. The inconsistency with the earlier study was noted with the problem-focused coping offered as a possible explanation for the differences in findings.

Coombs and Tachkova (2023) argued for the reinstatement and revision of the threat level dimension to the threat assessment model. This reinstatement was predicated upon an increasing realization of that some crises are much more intense than normal crises. For instance, research into sticky crises noted how they are more complicated and challenging than normal crises (Reber et al., 2020). Their position was that crisis level should differentiate between high threat level (normal crises) and extreme threat levels (sticky crises). This builds upon Jin and Cameron (2007) observing all crises are high threat level, hence to need to the original low and medium treat levels. However, sticky crises demand we add the extreme threat level to the mix (Coombs & Tachkova, 2023).

Coombs and Tachkova (2022, 2023) utilized moral outrage to differentiate between high threat levels and extreme threat levels. Moral outrage is a distinct form of anger resulting from cognitive appraisals that a situation involves both injustice and greed. Moral outrage is evoke when people perceive an injustice has occurred and that it was motivated by greed (Antonetti & Maklan, 2016). Prior research had established moral outrage changes the nature of the crisis communication dynamic (Coombs & Tachkova, 2019). The effect of moral outrage was so pronounced that situational crisis communication theory (SCCT) altered its threat assessment to include moral outrage. SCCT now uses a triadic appraisal composed of if a situation is negative, responsibility for the crisis, and moral outrage evoked by the crisis (Coombs & Tachkova, 2022). Extreme threat levels are defined as those that created at least a moderate level of moral outrage.

Coombs and Tachkova (2023) presented a series of propositions of identifying how the revised threat level would affect threat appraisal model. They argued the extreme level crises will produce higher situational demands and perceived need for resources, more negative feelings, and greater emotional intensity than high threat level crise. Coombs and Tachkova (2023) linked moral outrage to threat duration and threat type. Moral outrage is associated with long-term crises and external threats. They posited moral outrage coupled with long-term and external threats will create higher situational demands, a stronger need for resources, and more intense emotional feels than high demand crises that are long-term and external (Coombs & Tachkova, 2023). The moral outrage focus reflected a similar concern with stakeholder threat assessments found in the temporal dimension research.

Applications to Subfields

The threat appraisal model has been applied to all three crisis subfields. The initial publication involved the public subfield because terror alerts relate to public safety (Pang et al., 2006). Temporal distance was explored using public health crises which fall within the public subfield (Kim, 2022). Choi et al. (2023) explored environmental risk and Lee et al. (2022) applied the threat appraisal model to COVID-19. The experimental test of the threat dimensions utilized the corporate subfield (Jin & Cameron, 2007) as did the additional of moral outrage to threat assessment (Coombs & Tachkova, 2023). The threat appraisal model has been applied to the political subfield with analyses of North Korea's nuclear threat (Hwang & Cameron, 2008; Park, 2013). Contingency theory, a key inspiration for the threat appraisal model, is a grand theory of public relations that can be applied to any facet of public relations (Pang et al., 2020). Hence, it is logical that the threat appraisal model has been applied across all three crisis subfields.

Practitioner Takeaways

In crisis management, risks are typically assessed using some mix of impact (how bad), likelihood (odds of occurring), and velocity (how soon it will have an impact) (Coombs & Tachkova, 2023). Threat has become a critical element for crisis managers to consider. A prime example is that the importance of threat the crisis READINESS model developed by the Crisis Communication Think Tank at the University of Georgia to address sticky crises (Jin et al., 2024). The threat appraisal model identifies other aspects of threats that could be useful when crisis managers are assessing threats. In particular, threat duration and threat type are proven to be useful in assessing threats. Temporal distance and the revised threat level hold potential as well. Crisis managers can use the threat appraisal model to create a richer understanding of risks which could evolve into crises.

Theoretical Constraints and Concerns

A concern about threat appraisal model is we still have limited information about its effects on crisis communication. This is to be expected because models are more descriptive than prescriptive. Jin and Cameron (2007) made some connections to crisis communication but the effects of threat type and threat duration on what makes for an appropriate crisis response were tentative. Coombs and Tachkova (2023) proposed some effects of threat level on crisis communication, but that proposition remains largely untested. The threat appraisal model seems to be a useful element for understanding crisis communication. However, it may work better as a supplemental explanation than as the primary explanatory tool for crisis communication.

Theoretical Engagement Points

1 What type of research methods are most closely associated with threat appraisal?
2 Is threat appraisal primarily a descriptive, relational, or explanatory theory?
3 Is threat appraisal primarily an empirical-analytic, interpretative, or critical theory?
4 How would you evaluate threat appraisal in terms of scope, appropriateness, heuristic value, validity, parsimony, and openness?

Discussion Questions

1 How do the three dimensions of threat (threat level, threat duration, and threat type) interact to shape an organization's crisis communication strategy?
2 The threat appraisal model draws on both contingency theory and cognitive appraisal theory. How do these two theories complement each other in understanding threat perception and response?

3 What are the implications of the findings that long-term threats tend to lead to more accommodative stances than short-term threats? How can organizations use this knowledge to improve their crisis communication?
4 How do the concepts of temporal distance and moral outrage enhance the threat appraisal model? What new insights do they offer for understanding stakeholder perceptions and responses to crises?
5 The chapter argues that the threat appraisal model may be more useful as a supplemental explanation than as a primary explanatory tool for crisis communication. Do you agree with this assessment? Why or why not?

References

Antonetti, P., & Maklan, S. (2016). An extended model of moral outrage at corporate social irresponsibility. *Journal of Business Ethics*, *135*, 429–444.

Cancel, A. E., Mitrook, M. A., & Cameron, G. T. (1999). Testing the contingency theory of accommodation in public relations. *Public Relations Review*, *25*(2), 171–197.

Choi, S. I., Zhang, J., & Jin, Y. (2023). The effects of threat type and gain–loss framing on publics' responses to strategic environmental risk communication. *Corporate Communications: An International Journal*, *28*(3), 363–380.

Coombs, W. T., & Tachkova, E. R. (2019). Scansis as a unique crisis type: Theoretical and practical implications. *Journal of Communication Management*, *23*(1), 72–88.

Coombs, W. T., & Tachkova, E. R. (2022). Elaborating the concept of threat in contingency theory: An integration with moral outrage and situational crisis communication theory. *Public Relations Review*, *48*(4), 102234*.

Coombs, W. T., & Tachkova, E. R. (2023). How emotions can enhance crisis communication: Theorizing around moral outrage. *Journal of Public Relations Research*, *36*, 6–22.

Folkman, S., Lazarus, R. S., Dunkel-Schetter, C., DeLongis, A., & Gruen, R. J. (1986). Dynamics of a stressful encounter: cognitive appraisal, coping, and encounter outcomes. *Journal of Personality and Social Psychology*, *50*(5), 992–1003.

Hwang, S., & Cameron, G. T. (2008). The elephant in the room is awake and takes things personally: The North Korean nuclear threat and the general public's estimation of American diplomacy. *Public Relations Review*, *34*(1), 41–48.

Jin, Y., & Cameron, G. T. (2007). The effects of threat type and duration on public relations practitioner's cognitive, affective, and conative responses in crisis situations. *Journal of Public Relations Research*, *19*(3), 255–281*.

Jin, Y., Coombs, W. T., Wang, Y., van der Meer, T. G., & Shivers, B. N. (2024). "READINESS": A keystone concept beyond organizational crisis preparedness and resilience. *Journal of Contingencies and Crisis Management*, *32*(1), e12546.

Kim, S. (2022). It is time that matters in crisis communication: The role of temporal distance and crisis threat appraisal. *Public Relations Review*, *48*(2), 102155.

Kim, S., & Jin, Y. (2020). Organizational threat appraisal by publics: The effects of perceived temporal distance on health crisis outcomes. *International Journal of Communication*, *14*, 21.

Lee, H., Kim, H. J., & Hong, H. (2022). Navigating the COVID-19 pandemic in the contingency framework: Antecedents and consequences of public's stance toward the CDC. *Public Relations Review*, *48*(1), 102149.

Pang, A., Jin, Y., & Cameron, G. T. (2006). Do we stand on common ground? A threat appraisal model for terror alerts issued by the Department of Homeland Security. *Journal of Contingencies and Crisis Management*, *14*(2), 82–96*.

Pang, A., Jin, Y., Kim, S., & Cameron, G. T. (2020). Contingency theory: Evolution from a public relations theory to a theory of strategic conflict management. In F. Frandsen and W. Johansen (Eds.), *Crisis communication* (pp. 141–164). Boston: De Gruyter Mouton.

Park, S. A. (2013). Exploring the perceived impact of threat levels: The case of North Korea's nuclear threat in the US. *Journal of Media and Communication Studies*, *5*(7), 88*.

Reber, B. H., & Cameron, G. T. (2003). Measuring contingencies: Using scales to measure public relations practitioner limits to accommodation. *Journalism & Mass Communication Quarterly*, *80*(2), 431–446.

Reber, B. H., Yarbough, R. C., Nowak, G., & Jin, Y. (2020). Complex and challenging crises: A call for solutions. In Y. Jin, B. H. Reber, & G. J. Nowak (Eds.), *advancing crisis communication effectiveness: Integrating public relations scholarship with practice* (pp. 3–16). New York: Routledge.

Wolters Kluwer. (2015). What is risk velocity and should you track it? Retrieved from https://www.wolterskluwer.com/en/expert-insights/what-is-risk-velocity-and-should-you-track-it#:~:text=In%20the%20realm%20of%20Risk,%2C%20Years%2C%20etc.)

Yarbrough, C. R., Cameron, G. T., Sallot, L. M., & McWilliams, A. (1998). Tough calls to make: Contingency theory and the Centennial Olympic Games. *Journal of Communication Management*, *3*(1), 39–56.

*Requisite Readings

Chapter 14

Social-Mediated Crisis Communication

The advent of the Internet had a significant effect on strategic communication. As the digital environment became populated with new platforms and participants, the digital world had to be integrated into strategic communication efforts. Communicators had to adapt to new channels and the way those new channels changed their environment. Crisis communication needed to integrate the digital world, exemplified by social media platforms, into its efforts. The social-mediated crisis communication (SMCC) model provided the first serious attempt to illuminate the "emerging role of social media in crisis communication" (Jin et al., 2023, p. 151). SMCC explores how social media influences the way people engaged in information seeking and sharing during a crisis and the effects of those actions on crisis communication.

Theoretical Overview

SMCC began life in 2010 as the blog-mediated crisis communication (BMCC) model. Blogs were among the early forms of user-generated digital communication and had the potential to affect crisis communication. The BMCC explored the role of bloggers as opinion leaders and their ability to affect word-of-mouth communication related to a crisis. Bloggers could emerge as an influential source of information during a crisis; hence, they could be important to consider when developing crisis messages (Jin & Liu, 2010). While blogs still exist today, social media platforms have proliferated and become influential sources of information and channels for sharing information. Social media platforms allow more people to become involved in and potentially shape crisis communication efforts. The name changed from blog-mediated to social-mediated to reflect the shift in the digital environment. The reality was that people were increasingly using social media during crises and that usage needed to be understood (Austin et al., 2012: Liu et al., 2011). SMCC became the "first theoretical model to explore the role of social media in crisis communication (Liu et al., 2021,

DOI: 10.4324/9781003469964-16

p. 215). Moreover, SMCC held that emotions were an important factor in crisis communication (Liu et al., 2011).

Theoretical Conceptualization

Since its articulation in 2011, researchers have sought to test and to refine elements of SMCC. SMCC represents a shift in crisis communication focus from a macro- to a micro-level. Prior crisis communication theories focused on the crisis response strategies (e.g., Benoit, 1995; Coombs, 1995). SMCC uses a more micro-level analysis of crisis communication. SMCC moves beyond a focus on the strategies (messages) to include a consideration of the source (sender) and channel as important in the crisis communication process. The source of the message could be the organization-in-crisis or a third party. Social media platforms are one of many channels used in crisis communication along with face-to-face, word-of-mouth, and traditional news media. Along with the message, sources and channels can influence how people perceived the crisis information and their acceptance of the crisis message (Austin & Jin, 2016; Liu et al., 2011). Later researchers added trolling (Ao & Mak, 2021) and information vetting (Lu & Jin, 2020) to SMCC.

Jin et al. (2023) organized the explanation of SMMC around three points: (1) crisis information generation, (2) crisis information consumption, and (3) crisis information transmission. For each of these three points, SMCC considers both publics and the organization-in-crisis. Crisis information generation is driven by the tension a crisis introduces into the organization–public relationship. SMCC posits that publics do create crisis information making them part of the crisis communication process (Zhao et al., 2018). SMMC identifies three types of publics. Influential social media creators produce crisis information. Social media followers consume the crisis information created by the influential social media creators. Social media inactives receive crisis information indirectly through word-of-mouth from social media followers or traditional media (Austin et al., 2012).

There is value in understanding when people seek crisis information—why they seek the information and the factors affecting information seeking. Publics are more likely to seek additional crisis information when traditional media use third party sources for crisis information and when they receive third-party information via social media. SMCC found that people will seek additional information using similar channels to the original information. If the initial information comes from traditional media, they seeking additional information from traditional media but if the initial information is from social media, publics search social media for additional information. Finally, publics are less likely to seek information when the original information is provided by the organization-in-crisis (Austin et al., 2012). The research notes "organizations need to ensure that crisis communication information comes from other trusted sources of information, in addition to coming from the organization" (Austin et al., 2012, p. 203).

Starting with the BMCC model, there was a recognition that misinformation could enter through the digital channels. SMCC has become increasingly concerned about misinformation generation. Misinformation can be defined as "false information about a crisis, initially assumed to be valid but can be later corrected or retracted, that can lead to factual misperception held by people" (Van der Meer & Jin, 2020, p. 561). Social media provides an easy mechanism for misinformation to enter the crisis discussion. Misinformation is dangerous because once misperceptions form, they are difficult to displace (Van der Meer & Jin, 2020). We will return to misinformation in the vetting discussion. SMCC draws upon earlier theories for the analysis of the crisis messages created by organizations. SMCC arrays crisis message strategies from defensive to accommodative, the distinction provided in SCCT. SMCC also includes instructing and adjusting information (Jin et al., 2023). Instructing information tells people how to protect themselves physically from a crisis while adjusting information helps people to cope psychologically with a crisis (Holladay, 2009).

Crisis information consumption explores how crisis information is consumed by publics and organizations. Emotions and vetting are relevant to how publics consume crisis information. Emotions are related to the coping publics enact during crises. Earlier research found publics engage in both cognitive and conative coping. Cognitive coping involves interpretation of the crisis information while conative coping involves the behavioral reactions to crises (Jin et al., 2023). SMCC categorizes emotions into three groups. Attribution-independent emotions are unrelated to attributions of responsibility and include anxiety, apprehension, and fear. Attribution-dependent emotions are linked to attributions of crisis responsibility and include external-attribution-dependent and internal-attribution-dependent emotions. External-attribution-dependent emotions include disgust, anger, and contempt while internal-attribution-dependent emotions include embarrassment, shame, and guilt (Choi & Lin, 2009; Liu et al., 2011). Emotions are related to crisis communication. For instance, crisis information directly from an organization produces lower levels of attribution-independent and external-attribution-dependent emotions than information from a third party (Liu et al., 2011).

Vetting relates to information sharing and has relevance for misinformation. Information vetting studies why and how people vet information before sharing and seeking additional information. Vetting relates to a need to cope with uncertainty and uncontrollability along with expectations of the crisis situation and the information itself. People are more likely to engage in information vetting when the information is inconsistent with memories or common sense, the information is inconclusive, or the person is not sure they are learning from it (unsatisfied with the information) (Lu & Jin, 2020).

There is primary and secondary crisis information vetting. Primary vetting relates to the information accuracy and the characteristics of the information. Primary vetting involves the motivation to vet, emotional coping, and the cognitive processing of information (Lu & Jin, 2020). Secondary vetting focuses on the conclusions people can draw from the information. This includes the nature of the conclusions and how people feel about themselves. How people feel about themselves relates to their satisfaction with the information, their confidence in the information, and any felt need to counterargue the information. Based upon the vetting assessments, people may share the information or seek additional information (Lu & Jin, 2020).

Organizations do consume crisis information as part of monitoring for crises and gauging reactions to their crisis messaging (Coombs & Holladay, 2012; Liu et al., 2012). However, there is limited research that explores the details about how and why organizations consume crisis information (Jin et al., 2023).

Crisis information transmission examines how crisis information is disseminated to others. The crisis information transmission of publics is a function of their coping needs. Public coping is facilitated by learning what happened, who is responsible for the crisis, and what actions they can take on their own in response to a crisis. These coping concerns reflect the ethical base response advocated by SCCT. The ethical base response should be the first response in a crisis and be composed of instructing and adjusting information (e.g., Coombs & Tachkova, 2019). Both cognitive and conative coping shape the crisis information transmission of publics (Jin et al., 2023). Organizations must realize the source of the message and form of the transmission affect how people attend to and share information. Of particular note is how misinformation is more likely to occur when the organization-in-crisis is not the central information source. As noted earlier, information directly from an organization-in-crisis is very powerful and related to stealing thunder. The channels used to transmit the crisis information are important considerations as well (Jin et al., 2023).

Another important theme is SMCC research is the way a social media user establishes influence. Some ways a person becomes an influencer is to display high credibility on the topic, create original and compelling content, and craft content that meets the information and emotional needs of publics (Jin et al., 2023). There are at least three motivators for consuming influencer crisis information: (1) issue relevance, (2) information seeking and sharing, and (3) emotional support and venting (Jin & Liu, 2010).

Mak and Ao (2019) found four categories of influential social media creators. The categories include those people directly involved in the crisis, the news media social media accounts, individuals with strong opinions or attitudes, and self-involved social media influencers.

Of special note are the self-involved who rarely discuss the crisis but instead focus on their position on an issue embedded in the crisis. For instance, Mak and Ao (2019) studied the crisis sparked when Lancôme cancelled a concert by singer Denise Ho. Ho is a Hong Kong activist involved with the issue of the relationship between Hong Kong and Mainland China and the Umbrella Movement. The belief was the cancellation was to prevent negative Mainland views of Ho from spreading to the Lancôme brand. The self-involved social media influencers were focused on the Hong Kong-Mainland China issue. Their posts express strong attitudes and emotions. The self-involved insert themselves into a crisis discussion to advance their own agendas (Mak & Ao, 2019).

Trolling has been used as another concept for segmenting social media publics. Trolling can be defined as "posting provocative and offensive messages" (Ao & Mak, 2021, p. 3). Trolling relates to SMCC and crises because it connects to how people influence one another, how social media spreads negative information by those not directly involved in a crisis, and how publics can work together in a collective effort. Trolls are motivated by a need to reinforce their social identities. "The concept of trolling helps to further segment social media publics by explaining behaviors, emotions, and motivations of them" (Ao & Mak, 2021, p. 8). The trolling analysis of Ao and Mak (2021) of the Lancôme crisis caused by a concert cancellation illustrated how publics can react to one another during a crisis and how publics can work together to create influence.

The regenerative crisis model has also been used with SMCC. The regenerative model takes a non-linear approach to crises. During a crisis, a turning point can occur, causing a redefinition of a crisis and essentially creating a new crisis. The previous crisis response becomes part of the precrisis phase for the new crisis (Coombs, 2017). Influencers were identified as a source for creating crisis turning points (Mak & Ao, 2019). Communicative actions by publics can be the reason a new crisis emerges from the old crisis (Ao & Mak, 2021).

Applications to Subfields

SMCC has been applied to the public and corporate crisis subfields. The original efforts to validate the model included both corporate and public crises (Austin et al., 2012; Liu et al., 2011). Applications to the corporate crisis subfield include Adi's (2020) examination of customers on a commuter train line, Ma et al.'s (2021) analysis of a product recall, Zhang and

Nekmat's (2023) study of industry crises, and Opitz et al.'s (2018) application to internal crisis communication with employees. Applications to the public crisis subfield center on public health crises, including two that applied SMCC to COVID-19 (Bukar et al., 2022; Li et al., 2022), but includes emergency management too (Liu et al., 2021). SMCC has the potential to be applied to the political crisis subfield. We draw this conclusion because the analyses of the Lancôme concert cancellation crisis reflect a strong political dimension to it (Ao & Mak, 2021; Mak & Ao, 2019). This would suggest SMCC could fit comfortably with political crises.

Practitioner Takeaways

SMCC offers a variety of insights into the crisis communication process that hold utility for crisis managers. Overall, SMCC creates awareness of the need to understand the flow of crisis information from, to, and between crisis constituents. Crisis managers are given insights into the various types of social media publics they will encounter during a crisis. SMCC identified a number of segments that exist among the social media publics and how each connects with crisis communication. The social media publics include influential social media creators, social media followers, social media inactives, and trolls. Moreover, SMCC highlights the value of examining the voices of constituents as part of the crisis communication process. The messages from various constituents have the potential to become salient during the crisis communication process. SMCC establishes the importance of identifying influencers before and during a crisis along with some advice on how to identify crisis influencers. SMCC reinforces the value of appreciating emotions that emerge during crises and their important role in the crisis communication process. This includes the strong link between emotions and coping behaviors. Finally, SMCC offers insights into how information, including misinformation, is vetted and shared during a crisis (Jin et al., 2023). SMCC helps to illuminate the complexity that emerges in some crises.

Theoretical Constraints and Concerns

An initial concern about the SMCC model is its complexity. There are a lot of moving parts for SMCC but crises can be very complex. Still, the complexity can make it challenging for crisis managers to utilize the model and to appreciate the benefits of the model. The creators of the SMCC model have identified a number of concerns related to what the model has yet to yield. SMCC has done little to develop the content of the transmission by followers or how social media inactives transmit information. Furthermore, there is a need to integrate message strategies more fully into the SMCC model especially instructing and adjusting information. Finally, the problem of misinformation has yet to be fully integrated into SMMC (Jin et al., 2023).

Theoretical Engagement Points

1 What type of research methods are most closely associated with SMCC?
2 Is SMCC primarily a descriptive, relational, or explanatory theory?
3 Is SMCC primarily an empirical-analytic, interpretative, or critical theory?
4 How would you evaluate SMCC in terms of scope, appropriateness, heuristic value, validity, parsimony, and openness?

Discussion Questions

1 How does the SMCC model differ from traditional crisis communication theories? What are the implications of these differences for crisis managers?
2 The chapter discusses how people seek crisis information. Explain why people might be more likely to seek information from a third party rather than the organization in crisis. What are the implications of this for crisis communication?
3 Explain how social media has changed the way organizations communicate during a crisis. Use examples from the chapter or your own experience to illustrate your points.
4 What are the challenges and opportunities presented by the SMCC model for crisis communication practitioners?
5 The chapter mentions that misinformation can be a significant problem during a crisis. How can the SMCC model be used to address the spread of misinformation?

References

Adi, W. (2020). Simplified social mediated crisis communication model during crisis in Indonesia: A case study on how customers of Indonesia commuter line train company seek information on a train delay due to the double track trial on April 12, 2019. *KnE Social Sciences*, 290–301.

Ao, S. H., & Mak, A. K. (2021). Regenerative crisis, social media publics and Internet trolling: A cultural discourse approach. *Public Relations Review*, *47*(4), 102072*.

Austin, L., Fisher Liu, B., & Jin, Y. (2012). How audiences seek out crisis information: Exploring the social-mediated crisis communication model. *Journal of Applied Communication Research*, *40*(2), 188–207*.

Austin, L., & Jin, Y. (2016). Social media and crisis communication: Explicating the social-mediated crisis communication model. In A. Dudo & L. A. Kahlor (Eds.), *Strategic communication* (pp. 163–186). Routledge*.

Benoit, W. L. (1995). *Accounts, excuses, and apologies: A theory of image restoration*. Albany: State University of New York Press.

Bukar, U. A., Jabar, M. A., Sidi, F., Nor, R. B., Abdullah, S., & Ishak, I. (2022). How social media crisis response and social interaction is helping people recover from Covid-19: An empirical investigation. *Journal of Computational Social Science*, *5*(1), 1–29.

Choi, Y., & Lin, Y. H. (2009). Consumer response to crisis: Exploring the concept of involvement in Mattel product recalls. *Public Relations Review*, *35*(1), 18–22.

Coombs, W. T. (1995). Choosing the right words: The development of guidelines for the selection of the "appropriate" crisis response strategies. *Management Communication Quarterly*, *8*, 447–476.

Coombs, W. T. (2017). Digital Naturals and the rise of paracrises: The shape of modern crisis communication. In S. C. Duhe (Ed.), *New media and public relations* (3rd ed., pp. 281–290). New York: Peter Lang US.

Coombs, W. T., & Holladay, S. J. (2012). Amazon. com's Orwellian nightmare: Exploring apology in an online environment. *Journal of Communication Management*, *16*(3), 280–295.

Coombs, W. T., & Tachkova, E. R. (2019). Scansis as a unique crisis type: Theoretical and practical implications. *Journal of Communication Management*, *23*(1), 72–88.

Holladay, S. J. (2009). Crisis communication strategies in the media coverage of chemical accidents. *Journal of Public Relations Research*, *21*, 208–215.

Jin, Y., Austin, L., & Liu, B. F. (2023). Social-mediated crisis communication research: How information generation, consumption, and transmission influence communication processes and outcomes. In W. T. Coombs & S. J. Holladay (Eds.), *The handbook of crisis communication* (2nd ed., pp. 151–168). West Sussex: John Wiley & Sons.

Jin, Y., & Liu, B. F. (2010). The blog-mediated crisis communication model: Recommendations for responding to influential external blogs. *Journal of Public Relations Research*, *22*(4), 429–455.

Li, Z., Qiu, H., & Zhou, Q. (2022). Social-mediated diffusion of conspiracy theories about COVID-19: A study integrating SMCC and TPB models. *International Journal of Human–Computer Interaction*, *38*(7), 680–689.

Liu, B. F., Austin, L., & Jin, Y. (2011). How publics respond to crisis communication strategies: The interplay of information form and source. *Public Relations Review*, *37*(4), 345–353*.

Liu, B. F., Jin, Y., Austin, A., Kulogoski, E., & Young, C. E. (2021). The social-mediated crisis communication (SMCC) model: Identifying the next frontier. In Y. Jin, B. H. Reber & G. J. Nowak (Eds.), *Advancing crisis communication effectiveness: Integrating public relations scholarship with practice* (pp. 214–230). New York: Routledge.

Liu, B. F., Jin, Y., Briones, R., & Kuch, B. (2012). Managing turbulence in the blogosphere: Evaluating the blog-mediated crisis communication model with the American Red Cross. *Journal of Public Relations Research*, *24*(4), 353–370.

Lu, X., & Jin, Y. (2020). Information vetting as a key component in social-mediated crisis communication: An exploratory study to examine the initial conceptualization. *Public Relations Review*, *46*(2), 101891.

Ma, J., Tse, Y. K., Sato, Y., Zhang, M., & Lu, Z. (2021). Exploring the social broadcasting crisis communication: Insights from the mars recall scandal. *Enterprise Information Systems*, *15*(3), 420–443.

Mak, A. K., & Ao, S. (2019). Revisiting social-mediated crisis communication model: The Lancôme regenerative crisis after the Hong Kong Umbrella Movement. *Public Relations Review*, *45*(4), 101812.

Opitz, M., Chaudhri, V., & Wang, Y. (2018). Employee social-mediated crisis communication as opportunity or threat?. *Corporate Communications: An International Journal*, *23*(1), 66–83.

Van der Meer, T. G., & Jin, Y. (2020). Seeking formula for misinformation treatment in public health crises: The effects of corrective information type and source. *Health Communication*, *35*(5), 560–575.

Zhang, X., & Nekmat, E. (2023). Incorporating competition and comparisons into crisis communication: How competing organizations respond to industry crises. *Public Relations Review*, *49*(3), 102324.

Zhao, X., Zhan, M., & Liu, B. F. (2018). Disentangling social media influence in crises: Testing a four-factor model of social media influence with large data. *Public Relations Review*, *44*(4), 549–561.

*Requisite Readings

Chapter 15

Paracrisis

The emergence of social media has influenced crisis communication and crisis management (Austin et al., 2012). Unfortunately, it also gave rise to the term "social media crisis." Social media crisis was and remains a vague concept referring to anything negative happening in social media often conflating customer service problems with crisis. Reputational crisis is similarly vague. All crises produce some form of reputational damage, hence the outcome becomes inseparable from the crisis. The term paracrisis was introduced in a keynote address to the EUPRERA conference in 2010 to help clarify the difference between actual crises and situations that were just a minor form of the reputational threat. Para means likes, and a paracrisis is like a crisis. Moreover, a paracrisis might event evolve into an actual crisis. A paracrisis in its broadest sense is when an organization (or other entity) must manage a risk in public—where others can see it. Paracrises emerge during the pre-crisis phase. If a crisis is the realization of a risk (Heath, 1997), a paracrisis is the initial emergence of a risk. It would be accurate to consider the paracrisis as a distinct form of issue. Paracrisis is a form of theory as it can be used to diagnosis and to respond to emerging risks.

Theoretical Overview

Paracrises evolved from Lerbinger's (1997) idea of a challenge crisis. A challenge crisis is when some constituents claim an organization is acting irresponsibly or unethically. Challenges are predicated upon perceptions of current organizational practices. Activist groups have used challenges in efforts to change organizational practices. The challenge works by bringing attention to the "problematic behavior" and exerting pressure to change the behavior. Prior to the internet, media advocacy was used to bring attention to the problematic behavior (Ryan, 1991). Pressure was exerted through boycotts and damaging organizational reputations through negative publicity (e.g., Coombs & Holladay, 2012). The Internet,

DOI: 10.4324/9781003469964-17

especially social media platforms, provides new tools with the potential to strengthen activist attention and pressure tactics. Activists could take their messages directly to other constituents and avoid media gatekeepers (Coombs, 2002; Coombs & Holladay, 2018).

Challenges are really a form of risk beginning to emerge rather than a true crisis. Selaković et al.'s (2020) study of the effects of paracrises reinforces how challenges are not true crises. This does not discount the possibility of a paracrisis evolving into an actual crisis if it is mismanaged (Coombs & Holladay, 2012). Because it involves the emergence of a risk, paracrises can be thought of as a special type of issue. Issues management is a proactive form of strategic communication (Jones & Chase, 1979) and is closely affiliated with crisis management (Coombs, 2023). In fact, many organizations combine their issues management and crisis management efforts in one department. However, the primary issue is that management models were developed pre-Internet (Coombs & Holladay, 2018) and are not well suited to the digital environment where most paracrises develop and thrive (Chen, 2022; Lim, 2017). Hence, there was a need to develop a systematic approach for understanding and responding to these unique challenges.

Theoretical Conceptualization

A paracrisis can be considered an effort to publicly manage a risk. Risk management has been part of crisis management since its inception, but prior to the Internet, most risk management was done in private (Coombs, 2023). For instance, activist challenges typically begin with a petition, a formal request for an organization to change its behaviors. An example would be when Greenpeace requested Nestle stop using an irresponsible source of palm oil (Coombs, 2014). The corporations are most likely to reject the petition. Then the activists can launch their pressure tactics and create paracrises, because the corporations have shown they are unresponsive to their demands. The risk for paracrises is the reputational threat created by their argument that the corporation is acting irresponsibly (Coombs & Holladay, 2012; Lange & Washburn, 2012; McDonnell & King, 2013). Paracrises share this element of constituents identifying some problematic behaviors that could damage the organization's reputation (Chen & Holladay, 2023).

Paracrisis are part of the pre-crisis phase of crisis management because they involve risk mitigation efforts (Coombs, 2023). Similar to crises, the basic components of paracrisis are the types of paracrises and possible responses to paracrises. It is important to elaborate on the two key components and then consider various ways of approaching the relationship between the two.

Types of Paracrises

Types of paracrises are the starting point because risk management begins with considering the different types of risk an organization faces because the type of risk can affect risk mitigation efforts (IBM, 2024). The initial articulation of paracrises focused on challenges but the variety of paracrises has expanded to six types: challenges, faux pas, guilt by association, misinformation, social media misuse, and social media account hacking.

The challenge is defined by constituents claiming an organization is acting irresponsibly. The attack on the garment industry in the 1980s for using sweatshops would be a challenge. A faux pas occurs when an organization tries to do something good but instead offends some constituents. A typical example is an advertising or marketing message that some constituents find offensive. Guilt by association happens when an organization becomes linked to some negative actor or event. Spokespersons for organizations can engage in problematic behaviors, and the organization is tainted as well. An example would be when Subway's spokesperson was found to be involved in pedophilia.

Misinformation is when constituents circulate unverified and negative information about an organization, what used to be called rumors. Starbucks, for example, was reportedly not supporting US troops. The online information was inaccurate and did hurt Starbucks' reputation. Social media misuse involves charges by constituents that an organization has violated the ethos or rules for using a social media platform. One example is when organization's use a hashtag for a disaster to promote the sale of products. Social media account hacking is when a bad actor takes control of an organization's social media account and posts malicious content. In 2013, Burger King was hacked with the McDonald's logo appearing and posting negative messages about Burger King's food. Malicious content can include false recall announcements, hate speech, and inflammatory political statements (Chen & Holladay, 2023).

All six types of paracrises are driven by constituent actions. Misinformation and social media account hacking are direct actions by constituents. The other four all involve constituents identifying irresponsible or inappropriate actions taken by an organization (Coombs, 2023).

Responding to Paracrises

The vast majority of Internet postings about corporations are noise and have little effect on corporations. The first step in addressing a paracrisis is deciding whether or not to respond. (Keep in mind not responding is a response.) If the choice is to respond, managers must select a response option. Initially, three response options were identified for paracrises: refute, reform, and refuse. Refute is when management argues that the organization is acting responsibility—they defend the organization. Reform is when management decides to change the target behavior. Refusal is when management ignores the paracrisis, the use of silence (Coombs & Holladay, 2012). The response options for paracrisis have expanded to seven: refusal, refutation, repression, recognition/reception, revision, reference values, and dissociation.

Refusal and refutation are the original refute and reform options. Even if managers decide to ignore the paracrisis, the use of silence is a strategic response (Pang et al., 2022). Repression occurs when managers try to suppress the constituents' actions. Repression is dangerous because it can be viewed as efforts to suppress free speech. Recognition/recognition is when managers publicly recognize a problem but do not take any action on the program. HP used this response when it was first confronted about using rare metals from conflict zones—what are known as conflict minerals (Kim & Davis, 2016).

Revision is similar to reform because managers change the targeted behaviors. There are times organizational practices lag behind socially acceptable practices. Once more the garment industry and the use of sweatshops serve as an example. Reference to organizational values is a type of bolstering because it avoids the problem by talking about positive values. Typically, managers will restate organizational values and their commitment to them. The use of positive information about the organization is a form of counter to the negatives from the paracrisis. Dissociation is when managers deny any connection to a negative actor or action. The response tries to dispel misinformation about the organization.

Research Exploring Paracrises

Paracrisis research has examined response strategies and factors that shape the virality of a paracrisis. The paracrisis response strategy research includes expanding the array of responses and the effects of the responses on potential outcomes. Humor has been examined with mixed results. Honisch and Más Manchón (2020) found humor to be the least effective among four strategies, while Woods (2022) humor to be a useful response. However, Woods (2022) explored a very unique paracrisis for Crock Pot when one of its products was responsible for the death of a beloved television character. Managers should be careful when using humor because it is very easy for humor strategies to end badly.

Reform tends to be a useful response for faux pas. Honisch and Más Manchón (2020) found reform to be the most effective at reducing reputational threats and willingness to boycott (paracrisis intention behaviors). Bogomoletc (2019) found reform, operationalized as apology and corrective, to be effective in faux pas paracrises. Woods (2022) argued for expanding reform to include reassurance, part of the ethical base response from SCCT. This included advice to avoid being aggressive or defensive in a response when the paracrisis was highly emotional. Roh (2017) examined denial as an option when a social media account had been hacked. Denial had a positive effect on reputation, negative emotions, and online word-of-mouth intentions compared to a diminished responsibility response.

Huang and Ki (2023) looked carefully at the operationalization of the paracrisis response. They examined the effects of conversational voice (CHV) versus an organizational tone of voice in messages. Social media research indicates the value of CHV and their study extended it to paracrises. The CHV messages created stronger perceptions of social presence (sense of being together), perceived organizational listening, and reputation. The conclusion was that CHV reduced reputational damage mediated by social presence and perceived organizational listening (Huang & Ki, 2023). Oukropec (2024) explored a number of misinformation paracrises and found a variety of responses were effective, including deliberate silence, legal action, and debunking. The result reinforces the contingent nature of paracrisis responses. While some patterns are emerging indicating certain response fit better with certain types of paracrises, managers must consider the unique element of each paracrisis when selecting a response (Kice & Klyueva, 2022; Woods, 2022).

Lim (2017) found the use of visual mockery when articulating a paracrisis (constituents question the organizational behavior) intensified the outcomes of boycott intention and negative affect. This result suggests factors to consider when considering if a paracrisis might be salient—spread to other constituents. Chen (2022) explored the role of social media influencers in creating a paracrisis. By exploring their network structures, Chen (2022) unpacked the potential role of social media influencers in promoting paracrises and a method for assessing those activities. Smith and Smith (2022) examined what makes people pay attention to paracrises. Their research considered the power of those making the paracrisis claim and the power of the claim itself. They found referencing, social tagging, and calling to action increased attention on paracrises. Reference point involves referring to other companies or individuals that had problems similar to the current paracrisis. Social tagging is tagging others who support the claim of a paracrisis. Calls for action specify what people should do in response to the paracrisis such as boycotting a company or product. Managers are warned they may need to respond when these three factors are increasing social media messages (Smith & Smith, 2022).

Applications to Subfields

Paracrises research has concentrated on applications to the corporate crisis subfield, including non-profits (Persuit, 2017). The studies have situations involving corporations linked to faux pas, misinformation, social media account hacking, challenges, and guilt by association. Logically, the political crisis subfield could have paracrises as well. Politicians could find themselves involved in any of the six paracrisis types. For instance, politicians could engage in social media misuse or a faux pas if their actions intended to do good are considered to be negative by some segment of their constituents. The public crises subfield might have paracrises as well. Misinformation is clear concern for public crises, and actions designed to help constituents could be interpreted in a negative light (faux pas). However, thus far, research has been restricted to the corporate crisis subfield.

Practitioner Takeaways

Paracrises indicate why managers need to be sensitive to the emergence of risk in the digital environment. While paracrisis existed before the digital environment, social media platforms are increasing the need to publicly manage risks (Smith & Smith, 2022). This is especially true for misinformation paracrises (Oukropec, 2024). Paracrises also reveal how complex some paracrises can be (Woods, 2022). Managers need to consider a wide range of concerns when evaluating paracrises and those concerns need to consider the source driving the paracrises and the messages used to frame the paracrisis (Coombs & Holladay, 2012; Smith & Smith, 2022). Early intervention to avoid crises has long been valued in crisis communication (Coombs, 2023). Paracrisis research has identified some of the warning signs of an emerging crisis (e.g., Chen, 2022; Lim, 2017; Smith & Smith, 2022). Paracrisis is one means practitioners can use to avoid potential crises.

Theoretical Constraints and Concerns

Paracrises have been linked to broader theories, including SCCT (Smith & Smith, 2022), SMCC (Honisch & Más Manchón, 2020), and cognitive appraisal theory (Lim, 2017). A complete theory of paracrises has yet to emerge. Moreover, it is not always easy to tell when a paracrisis is becoming a crisis. This is one aspect of crisis management that seems to be more art than science at this point. There is a danger of overreacting to risks, thereby prompting a crisis rather than avoiding a crisis. Not all paracrises require a response (Selaković et al., 2020; Smith & Smith, 2022).

More research is needed to develop a richer theory of paracrises and to help identify when a paracrises needs a communicative response. But trying to determine when a threat warrants an organization's attention is as old as environmental scanning. The problem is some risks are more difficult to assess than others because they are harder to quantify (Cox Jr et al., 2005).

Theoretical Engagement Points

1 What type of research methods are most closely associated with the study of paracrises?
2 Is paracrisis primarily a descriptive, relational, or explanatory theory?
3 Is paracrisis primarily an empirical-analytic, interpretative, or critical theory?
4 How would you evaluate paracrisis in terms of scope, appropriateness, heuristic value, validity, parsimony, and openness?

Discussion Questions

1 Given the blurred lines between a paracrisis and a crisis, how can organizations effectively determine when a situation requires a communicative response? Consider factors such as the severity of the reputational threat, the level of public attention, and the potential for the situation to escalate.
2 Social media platforms play a significant role in the emergence and spread of paracrises. How can organizations leverage these platforms to their advantage in managing paracrises? How might strategies such as proactive engagement, social listening, and building relationships with influencers fit into this?
3 The chapter highlights the importance of considering the source and message framing of a paracrisis when choosing a response strategy. What are some key considerations in this regard? Consider how different types of paracrises might require different approaches and how tailoring the response to the specific audience and context is crucial.
4 Research on paracrisis response strategies has yielded mixed results, suggesting a contingent approach is necessary. What are some of the key contingencies that organizations should consider when selecting a response strategy? Consider factors like the type of paracrisis, organizational values, stakeholder expectations, and the overall communication environment.
5 The chapter primarily focuses on the application of paracrisis management in the corporate context. How can the principles and strategies

discussed be applied to other crisis subfields, such as political or public crises? Consider the unique challenges and opportunities presented by different sectors and how paracrisis management principles might need to be adapted.

References

Austin, L., Fisher Liu, B., & Jin, Y. (2012). How audiences seek out crisis information: Exploring the social-mediated crisis communication model. *Journal of Applied Communication Research*, *40*(2), 188–207.

Bogomoletc, E. (2019). Dialogic communication in faux pas paracrises. What do users want to discuss on brandsâ€™ official Facebook pages? *Journal of Promotional Communications*, *7*(1).

Chen, F. (2022). Unpacking the evolution of a paracrisis: The case of# DeleteUber. *Corporate Reputation Review*, *25*(4), 300–311.

Chen, F., & Holladay, S. J. (2023). Identifying and responding to social media risks: Towards an organizational paracrisis communication framework. *Corporate Communications: An International Journal*, *28*(1), 103–117*.

Coombs, W. T. (2002). Assessing online issue threats: Issue contagions and their effect on issue prioritization. *Journal of Public Affairs*, 2, 215–229.

Coombs, W. T. (2014). *Applied crisis communication and crisis management: Cases and exercise*. Los Angeles, CA: Sage.

Coombs, W. T. (2023). *Ongoing crisis communication: Planning, managing, and responding* (6th ed.). Thousand Oaks, CA: Sage.

Coombs, W. T., & Holladay, J. S. (2012). The paracrisis: The challenges created by publicly managing crisis prevention. *Public Relations Review*, *38*(3), 408–415*.

Coombs, W. T. & Holladay, S. J. (2018). Social issues qua wicked problems: The role of strategic communication in social issues management. *Journal of Communication Management*, *22*(1), 79–95.

Cox Jr, L. A., Babayev, D., & Huber, W. (2005). Some limitations of qualitative risk rating systems. *Risk Analysis: An International Journal*, *25*(3), 651–662.

Heath, R. L. (1997). *Strategic issues management: Organizations and public policy challenges*. Thousand Oaks, CA: SAGE Publications.

Honisch, S. V., & Más Manchón, L. (2020). The effects of paracrisis origin and response strategy on Facebook audience's perceived organisational reputation and behavioural intentions. *Corporate Reputation Review*, *23*(3), 133–144*.

Huang, M., & Ki, E. J. (2023). Protecting organizational reputation during a paracrisis: The effectiveness of conversational human voice on social media and the roles of construal level, social presence, and organizational listening. *Public Relations Review*, *49*(5), 102389.

IBM. (2024). The risk mitigation process. Retrieved from https://www.ibm.com/topics/risk-mitigation#:~:text=The%20first%20step%20in%20risk,of%20risk%20for%20different%20areas

Jones, B. L., & Chase, W. H. (1979). Managing public policy issues. *Public Relations Review*, *5*(2), 3–23.

Kice, B., & Klyueva, A. (2022). Asking for trouble with pure accommodation: Paracrises as rhetorical situations. *Public Relations Review*, *48*(4), 102210.

Kim, Y. H., & Davis, G. F. (2016). Challenges for global supply chain sustainability: Evidence from conflict minerals reports. *Academy of Management Journal*, *59*(6), 1896–1916.

Lange, D., & Washburn, N. T. (2012). Understanding attributions of corporate social irresponsibility. *Academy of Management Review*, *37*(2), 300–326.

Lerbinger, O. (1997). *The crisis manager: Facing risk and responsibility*. Mahwah, NJ: Lawrence Erlbaum.

Lim, J. S. (2017). How a paracrisis situation is instigated by an online firestorm and visual mockery: Testing a paracrisis development model. *Computers in Human Behavior*, *67*, 252–263.

McDonnell, M. H., & King, B. (2013). Keeping up appearances: Reputational threat and impression management after social movement boycotts. *Administrative Science Quarterly*, *58*(3), 387–419.

Oukropec, J. (2024). Strategic defense against misinformation: Empirical findings on paracrisis responses. *International Journal of Strategic Communication*, *19*(1), 54–85.

Pang, A., Jin, Y., Seo, Y., Choi, S. I., Teo, H. X., Le, P. D., & Reber, B. (2022). Breaking the sound of silence: Explication in the use of strategic silence in crisis communication. *International Journal of Business Communication*, *59*(2), 219–241.

Persuit, J. M. (2017). The potential for paracrisis in corporate philanthropy and social media. *International Journal of Organization Theory & Behavior*, *20*(1), 51–71.

Roh, S. (2017). Examining the paracrisis online: The effects of message source, response strategies and social vigilantism on public responses. *Public Relations Review*, *43*(3), 587–596*.

Ryan, C. (1991). *Prime time activism: Media strategies for grassroots organizing*. Boston, MA: South End Press

Selaković, M., Ljepava, N., & Mateev, M. (2020). Implications of the paracrises on the companies' stock prices. *Corporate Communications: An International Journal*, *25*(1), 3–19*.

Smith, S. B., & Smith, B. G. (2022). What amounts to a paracrisis? Interactivity as a lens for evaluating social media-propagated crises. *Journal of Contingencies and Crisis Management*, *30*(2), 204–216*.

Woods, C. L. (2022). Extinguishing a fictional fire: Responding to emotional and misinformed audiences. *Corporate Reputation Review*, *25*(4), 239–252.

*Requisite Readings

Chapter 16

Rhetorical Arena Theory

Crisis communication research often has a focus on the (two-way) communication between an individual, organization, or institution being hit by a crisis, and its communication with victims and stakeholders, trying to understand and respond to the reactions and interactions from the organizational perspective in an appropriate way. This is indeed important. However, multiple voices (e.g., customers, citizens, employees, media, politicians, communication experts), and not just the voices representing the organization, start communicating. This is why a rhetorical arena is defined as a social space that opens up when a crisis hits and where multiple voices communicate *to, with, against, past*, and *about* one another (Frandsen & Johansen, 2010, 2023). All voices are considered crisis communicators of a crisis, and they try to make themselves heard, to interfere, and to influence perceptions, interpretations, and actions in the arena of a crisis. Some of them want dialogue, others do not, and others again, they step in with their own agendas, or just for the sake of interfering.

Rhetorical arena theory (RAT) provides a multivocal approach to crisis communication and studies the communicative complexity represented by the multiple voices (including organizational stakeholders) communicating during a crisis. The theory highlights the importance of getting insights into the various agendas, patterns of interaction, and interdependencies among these multiple voices, and to anticipate the communication of other voices in the arena, to adapt to what is going on, and to protect an organization's reputation. In addition, RAT also has a focus on every single crisis communication process between "senders and receivers" in the arena and how each process is influenced by various contextual factors (e.g., culture, organization type, timing, crisis types) as well as choice of media, genre, and text rhetorics (including words, visuals, artefacts, body language, architecture, and actions). A bad or wrong use of rhetorics may create *a double crisis* "where a communication crisis overlaps the original crisis in so far as the organization in crisis is not able to manage the communication processes that should contribute to the handling of the original crisis"

DOI: 10.4324/9781003469964-18

(Frandsen & Johansen, 2017, p. 38). Thus, the concepts of arena, voice, and rhetoric form the cornerstones of RAT.

Theoretical Overview

Frandsen and Johansen developed RAT at the end of the 1990s to understand the communicative complexity of organizational crises and to identify key parameters (contextual factors) that contribute to the mediation of crisis communication and perceptions of crisis and responsibilities (Johansen & Frandsen, 2000, 2007). Crises are viewed as socially constructed. They started by studying the communication following a series of corporate crises including Daimler-Benz and their Mercedes A class crisis in 1997, Perrier's product recall 1990, Coca Cola and health complaints in Belgium in 1990, Pan Am airline and the Lockerbie bombing 1988, Johnson & Johnson and the tampering of Tylenol 1982 (Johansen & Frandsen, 2000, 2007). During the ensuing years, they developed the theory to not only include corporate crises but also political and public sector subfields. Moreover, RAT was applied to subfield overlapping crises, such as the Cartoon Affair crisis that started as an organizational crisis when the Danish newspaper *Jyllands-Posten* in 2005 published 12 small cartoons depicting Muhammad, the founder of Islam, as part of a debate on self-censorship in Denmark. However, it quickly turned into a global crisis when citizens and governments in some Middle East countries claimed an apology from the Danish government and started boycotting Danish companies and products because they felt offended (Johansen & Frandsen, 2007; Frandsen & Johansen, 2010). In fact, the many studies of the last 25 years have confirmed RAT's application to all types of crises, small or big, national, regional, or global crises, within or across subfields: disasters and emergencies, corporate sector, public sector, health sector, political sector, sports, etc.

In contrast to some of the first crisis communication theories such as image restoration theory (Benoit 1995, 1st ed.), later named image repair theory (Benoit, 2015, 2nd ed.), RAT is based on a multivocal approach to crisis communication and studies the communicative complexity that occurs when multiple voices (consumers, citizens, suppliers, investors, media, politicians, activists, consultants, lawyers, intermediaries, institutions, third parties, etc.) enter the rhetorical arena and communicate from the start to the end of a specific crisis (Johansen & Frandsen, 2007, Frandsen & Johansen, 2020). This approach to crisis communication includes voices communicating in the public sphere (e.g., citizens, consumers, media), the semi-public sphere (e.g., among staff within an organization) and the private sphere (e.g., managers and staff communicating among friends and family).

The most comprehensive presentation of RAT can be found in Frandsen and Johansen's book *Organizational Crisis Communication* (Frandsen & Johansen, 2017, 2nd ed. 2026). This book presents RAT, what it is and what it is not, and demonstrates how different patterns of interaction play out among various voices such as consumers, citizens, activists, media, intermediaries, managers, and employees. The second edition of the book also includes the voices of consultants and politicians and discusses new aspects of third-party interventions.

RAT is inspired by image restoration/repair theory (1995/2015) and situational crisis communication theory (1999/2023) and their lists of crisis response strategies. Furthermore, the theory is inspired by three theoretical traditions that add various perspectives on the complexity of interactions during a crisis: complexity theory, communication theory, and new rhetorical theory.

Within complexity theory, Frandsen and Johansen are primarily inspired by Priscilla Murphy and Dawn Gilpin and their application of game theory and complexity theory (i.e., the study of complex systems) to crisis management (Gilpin & Murphy, 2006, 2008, 2010). The game theory aspect is used in RAT to recognize the strategic interdependencies between actors (e.g., an organization) and voices during a crisis. If an organization starts blaming somebody else for a crisis, the organization is dependent on the reaction and communication of the one who is blamed. Putting the blame on somebody else may in fact increase the criticism and/or make people loose trust in an organization. An organization may also be dependent on the faith-holders, supporters, fans, or loyal consumers that may start communicating to defend a company accused of wrongdoing. It all adds to the communicative complexity in the arena. Another source of inspiration is Seeger, Sellnow, and Ulmer (2003, 2010) and their attempt to transfer chaos theory (another term for complexity theory) from the natural sciences to communication.

Within communication theory, Luhman's theory of social systems (Luhmann, 1995) that defines communication as a triple selection of information, utterance and understanding aligns well with a shift of communication view from transmission and interaction to communicative complexity. Nothing is communicated until it is observed, understood, or interpreted.

Within rhetorics, the theory is inspired by new rhetoric, including Bitzer's ideas around generic criticism and the rhetorical situation (Bitzer, 1968). Text genres have an impact on the choice of rhetorical strategies and wordings used in specific texts. Furthermore, the theory is inspired by image repair theory but applies a semiotic perspective and extends the study of verbal crisis repair strategies of Benoit, to all kind of rhetorical strategies or tactics, based on a semiotic perspective (Eco, 1978). According to semiotics, anything can be a sign, and communicates, for example, words, visuals, artefacts, offices, buildings, architecture, body language, voice pitch and speech rate, and actions. See Frandsen and Johansen (2009) for an example of the use of artefacts as a rhetorical tactic in the shampoo, *Wash & Go*, rumor crisis of Procter & Gamble in 1990.

The theory was named Rhetorical Arena Theory (RAT) for two reasons (1) to highlight the importance of the choice of rhetorical strategies (in attacks or defenses) used, not just by representatives of the organization in a crisis but by all types of voices entering the arena during the crisis and (2) to emphasize that (all kind of) rhetorics matter and can be used in a strategic way to persuade or influence other voices participating in the arena.

According to these perspectives, the theory defines crisis communication in the following way:

> Crisis communication is a complex and dynamic configuration of communicative processes which develop before, during, and after an event or a situation that is interpreted as a crisis by an organization and/or by other voices in the arena. Crisis communication also includes how various actors and voices, contexts and discourses (manifested in specific genres and specific texts) relate to each other.
>
> (Frandsen & Johansen, 2017, p. 148)

Theoretical Conceptualization

In this part, we will present the core concepts of arena and voice of RAT; the two-layered rhetorical arena model with its macro- and micro-levels of analysis; and central patterns of interaction and interdependencies identified among voices in the rhetorical arena.

Key Metaphors: Arena and Voice

The first metaphor, *arena*, highlights how voices in an arena have different perceptions and agree or disagree on how to understand a crisis, its causes or whom to blame. The rhetorical arena is a social and dynamic space, a battlefield, where people meet, compete, debate, negotiate, struggle and conflict around the understandings and responsibilities of a crisis. Some voices are very active in the arena, whereas others are listeners, observing what is going on. Not everyone in the arena strives for dialogue and consensus. Some disagree, taking an agonistic stance, while some deliberately want dissensus, taking a very polarized and antagonistic stance on an issue or crisis. The interactions going on in the arena can lead to changes of the rule of the game, for example, to spillovers to other organizations or politicians. An arena will often be composed of various sub-arenas as well, defined as distinct sub-spaces in the arena where only parts of the voices are heard, see Figure 16.3 on the relationship between the larger rhetorical arena and its sub-arenas.

The second metaphor is *voice*. In the early version of RAT (e.g., Johansen & Frandsen, 2007), the concept of stakeholders was applied to refer to all individuals or organizations who stepped into the rhetorical arena during a specific organizational crisis. However, when studying the arenas of various crises, Frandsen and Johansen realized that some voices do indeed have a stake in the organization in crisis, forming a stakeholder to that organization. Other voices only have a stake in the crisis as such, exploiting the situation to present their own agendas that are not necessarily linked to the organization in crisis. Hence, the concept of *voice* applies not just to the organizational voice but to any person or participant who starts communicating *to, with, against, past* or *about* one another in the rhetorical arena that opens up around a crisis (e.g., customers, citizens, investors, suppliers, partners, employees, media, intermediaries, politicians, NGO's, trolls, lawyers, professional critics). Hence, voices become crisis communicators when they engage in communicating about a crisis or a potential crisis.

A crisis typically attracts the attention of a lot of people. Not only people who are directly affected by the crisis (first and second parties) but also people who have an interest in a crisis situation for various reasons and with specific agendas (e.g., a politician using a crisis of an organization to criticize the government, indirectly saying: "vote for me next time"; or an activist group seeing an opportunity of getting awareness around its cause thanks to a crisis of another organization indirectly saying: "join us to avoid such crises"); as well as people who are just attracted by serious situations and dramas of others or interfere just for the sake of interfering (e.g., trolls). All these voices represent what we call the *communicative complexity* of crises.

The Rhetorical Arena: A Two-Layered Model

The rhetorical arena model has a macro- and a micro-component. The macro-component concentrates on mapping key voices, communicative processes, and interactions that take place in the arena and its sub-arenas during a specific crisis, whereas the micro-component demonstrates how each individual crisis communication process (between a sender and a receiver) in the arena is mediated and formed by four parameters: context, media, genre, and text.

The *macro-component* provides an analytical overview of the patterns of interaction among the voices that enter or are forced to enter the rhetorical arena that opens when a crisis breaks out. The voices in the arena start communicating *with, to, against, past* or *about* one another, and they are often in conflict, disagreeing on how to perceive a crisis and to place responsibility for the crisis. The number of voices entering an arena depends on the length and complexity of a crisis. Patterns of interaction are reflected in communication processes that are combined in specific ways, such as verbal attacks followed by a defense, or a blame game consisting of a series of attacks and defenses among specific voices. Figure 16.1 presents a non-exhaustive excerpt of voices acting in the rhetorical arena.

As it appears from Figure 16.1, an individual or organization hit by a crisis is not necessarily at the center of the arena, and may be the actor that communicates the least, whereas other voices may interact and communicate more according to their specific agendas. Some of them disagree but are still listening to one another (applying an agonistic perspective) whereas others do not even want to listen to others as they have taken a very polarized stance in a crisis (applying an antagonistic perspective), and other voices communicate in sub-arenas where they are not necessarily heard by voices in other parts of the arena or sub-arenas. It is important to identify the voices appearing in the arena. However, it is even more important to try and anticipate the reactions and communication of the other voices, and to have as much insights as possible into the "game," that is, the strategies and politics, played out in the arena, to navigate in an appropriate way. If an organization blames the media for being too aggressive or framing a crisis wrongly, what would then be the reaction of that media? Would it perhaps create even more attacks on the organization? Anticipation may lead to more cautious communication and less confrontation.

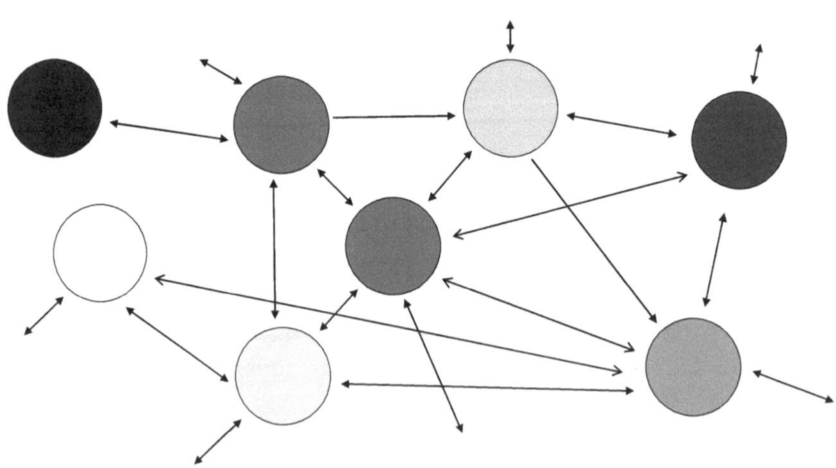

Figure 16.1 The Macro-Component of the Rhetorical Arena (Inspired by Frandsen & Johansen, 2017).

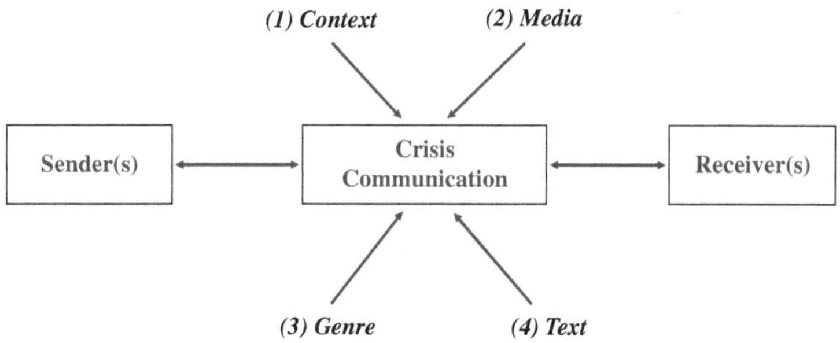

Figure 16.2 The Micro-Component of the Rhetorical Arena (Inspired by Frandsen & Johansen, 2017).

The *micro-component* of the rhetorical arena model (see Figure 16.2) was developed in an attempt, to strengthen and expand the crisis communication theories concentrating on crisis response strategies such as image repair theory (Benoit, 2015) and SCCT (Coombs, 1999). These early models and lists of crisis response strategies mostly had a focus on the communicative function of a strategy (e.g., denial, apology, justification) but did not go into much detail on how these functions were articulated and how they were influenced by various parameters, such as media and text genres. RAT, at the micro-level, has a focus on parameters that influence the articulation of these crisis communication functions or strategies. Figure 16.2 presents four parameters that mediate or form the crisis communication strategies of senders and receivers every time a communication process takes place in the rhetorical arena during a crisis: context, media, genre, and text (rhetoric).

The first parameter is the context. Communication will always be contextualized, and the contextual factors depend on the specific crisis situation, at a specific point in time. Such contextual factors may have an impact on the way an individual or organization attacks, defends or explains itself during a crisis. In the rhetorical arena model, the overarching context can be divided into *national-cultural* contexts such as social structures (political, legal, economic structures and media systems) and social norms and values; *organizational* contexts, such as organizational type (private or public) and organizational (communication) culture; and *situational* contexts such as intensifying factors (crisis type, crisis history, and prior reputation, cf. SCCT of Coombs), timing, changes over time, and the number and type of actors and voices in the arena. The various voices communicating as senders or receivers have their own characteristics as well, including interests, interpretations, agendas, strategic goals, and communicative behavior. According to contingency theory (Pang et al., 2020, 2023), more than 80 different contextual factors can be identified, making it very difficult to manage them all. Hence, identifying central or key contextual elements is important for the navigation during a specific crisis.

The next three parameters of media, genre, and text (rhetorics) also influence the way a crisis communication strategy such as a denial or an apology is articulated. An organization can explain itself in detail on its own corporate website whereas an organization must follow genre conventions when writing a press release for specific newspapers typically (in this case, news criteria and pre-formulation strategies) to make a journalist adapt its words, framing, and information. Similarly, a comment on social media or in a television daily news program often must be very short leaving limited space for explanation. Again, the articulation, wordings, and rhetorical tactics are important. Hence, media, genre and text are important parameters to take into consideration when communicating in a rhetorical arena.

The Larger Rhetorical Arena and Its Sub-Arenas

Two decades ago, Frandsen and Johansen also started discussing the boundaries of the rhetorical arena, including boundaries of social subspaces or sub-arenas within the larger rhetorical arena. Together with Timothy Coombs and Sherry Holladay, they studied the Lance Armstrong doping crisis in 2012 (Coombs et al., 2013a, 2013b; Frandsen & Johansen, 2023). This was one of the first attempts to conceptualize the sub-arena within RAT. According to Coombs & Holladay (2014), "a sub-arena represents a limited space where a message is heard and potentially responded to by a restricted set of actors. Although many actors may speak about the crisis, their voices may be limited, pragmatically, to a sub-arena" (p. 44). A rhetorical arena will typically be composed of a number of sub-arenas that can be populated by "distinctly different people" (Coombs & Holladay, 2014).

Sub-arenas are more or less porous (permeable) and voices from other sub-arenas or the larger rhetorical arena may go in and out or cross over. Some voices may be present in more sub-arenas, others are perhaps only present in one sub-arena. An illustration would be social media which may form the boundaries of a sub-arena during a crisis because it forms a distinct space where a specific number of voices struggle about the understandings of a crisis.

Aligned with the definition of the rhetorical arena, Frandsen and Johansen define sub-arena as

> a dynamic social space that opens during a crisis, where only a distinct part of the voices in the larger rhetorical arena communicate to, with, against, past or about one another, to a large extent, about a crisis in a specific, delimited part of the larger arena.
>
> (Frandsen & Johansen, 2023, p. 176)

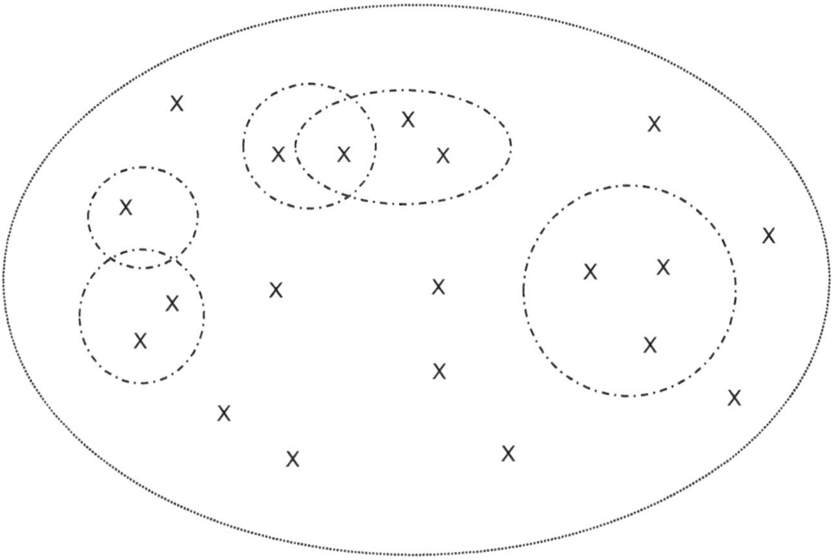

Figure 16.3 Overview of the Rhetorical Arena and Sub-Arenas (Inspired by Frandsen & Johansen, 2023).

Examples of sub-arenas can be the voices talking about the crisis inside a company, in specific social media, or in specific online-news media networks, at specific points in time, forming delimited parts of the larger arena. See Figure 16.3 for the relationship between the larger arena and its sub-arenas.

Crisis managers will have to try to identify the position of the voices (with, against, etc.) in various sub-arenas and to understand the communication transpiring within them. It is beneficial for crisis managers to understand who might be supporting their communicative efforts (communicating with them) or opposing them (communicating against) and why. Moreover, crisis managers need to understand if they are communicating past key crisis-holders. Communicating past one another occurs when actors or voices do not realize who else is talking about the crisis and what they are saying about the crisis. Hence, sub-arenas are a critical tool for the identification of voices that populate the rhetorical arena.

Identifying Patterns of Interactions of Specific Voices and Various Sub-Arenas

Based on RAT, Frandsen and Johansen have conducted a number of studies and identified various patterns of interactions and interdependencies among voices in the arena. A simple pattern is a verbal attack followed by a defense. However, most patterns are more complicated. This is for example the case of third-party interventions, and crisis exploitation (Boin et al., 2009), where politicians, activists, trolls who intervene in a crisis because they can profit from a crisis to create awareness around their own agendas. Some politicians use a crisis of for instance a private or public organization, to attack and criticize the government or officeholders, turning a crisis into a framing contest (Boin et al., 2009).

Specific inter-organizational relations, reputation commons problems (King et al., 2002; Barnett & Pollock, 2012), and interdependencies among organizations within the same industry or sector form another pattern of interactions. When one organization experiences a crisis, it quickly has spillovers or turns into a multi-crisis, involving more organizations within the same industry or supply chain (Frandsen & Johansen, 2017, 2018; Veil & Dillingham, 2020). Other patterns are related to interactions among consumers and citizens toward an organization in crisis, internal crisis communication and to the role and behavior of intermediaries, see below.

Hateholders and Faith-Holders

Studies on social media of consumer and citizen reactions to an organizational crisis have demonstrated the role of "faith-holders and hateholders" (Luoma-Aho, 2010; Coombs & Holladay, 2012; Johansen et al., 2016; Frandsen & Johansen, in press). Organizational wrongdoing typically makes consumers or citizens start blaming and criticizing an organization, and they can turn into negative voices and "hateholders." However, this often leads to another pattern of interaction, that is, faith-holders who support an organization and/or a brand enter the arena to defend an organization or a brand against hateholder attacks. They express support, using denial or bolstering strategies, such as: "we have never experienced this kind of wrongdoing or problem with this organization," and they start attacking and criticizing the hateholders for their behavior or lack of knowledge, for example, "Shame on you, all your filth does not belong to Facebook" (Johansen et al., 2016; Frandsen & Johansen, in press). Faith-holders become co-crisis communicators to an organization hit by a crisis.

Internal Crisis Communication

What is happening inside an organization during a crisis is located in a semi-public sphere which is more difficult to access as a researcher. However, the support of employees during a crisis can be crucial. Frandsen and Johansen started looking at internal crisis communication and interactions among voices such as managers, employees, board rooms, and external consultants, appearing inside an organization, more than fifteen years ago. In fact, they were among the first to enter and conduct research within the new territory of internal crisis communication, in the form of surveys among private and public organizations (Johansen et al., 2012), and they developed an integrative heuristic framework of internal crisis communication (Frandsen & Johansen, 2011). This work marks the beginning of a new stream of research within internal crisis communication among crisis communication scholars, and Frandsen and Johansen are constantly working on expanding this work. Among patterns of interaction, their studies identified employees as active crisis communicators who actively contribute to the solutions of a problem (internal communication) and who can turn into negative or positive ambassadors on behalf of an organization in external communication, e.g., in news media or social media. Heide and Simonsson (2019) also stress the active role of "*co-workers*" as communicators before, during and after a crisis. For the patterns of interaction of communication consultants as internal voices, see Johansen (2017, 2020).

Theory of Intermediaries

A final example of pattern of interactions and interdependencies is the study of intermediaries, defined as

> an actor (individual, organization or a meta-organization) who belongs to a specific area in society (e.g., specific industry, a specific organizational field and/or a specific sector) ... whose primary function is to represent an organization and/or a specific stakeholder group, or intervene between them by furthering or impeding their interests and activities.
>
> (Frandsen & Johansen, 2017, p. 194)

This study led to the development of a *theory on intermediaries* and studies on how intermediaries (e.g., trade associations, trade unions, media, consultants) communicate and interact during crises (Frandsen & Johansen, 2015). This research led to new concepts and to the study of dilemmas of meta-organizations, that is, "organizations of organizations" such as trade associations having organizations from a specific industry or sector as their members. How do they defend a member accused of wrongdoing and protect the reputation of that member, at the same time as they want to protect the reputation of the other members and the whole industry as well as their own reputation as a trade association (Frandsen & Johansen, 2018)? They also identified new communication forms. Intermediaries not only conduct external and internal communication as any kind of organization, but also use *extra-communication*, when an intermediary communicates to its members, for example, about a crisis, issues or dilemmas of one or more of its members (Frandsen & Johansen, 2015, 2017). More research is needed to identify more patterns among the voices communicating in the rhetorical arena of a crisis.

Applications to Subfields

RAT came into existence more than 25 years ago, and it started out with a specific focus on corporate crisis communication but quickly moved to also include public sector and political communication. No matter which type of organization (profit/non-profit, private/public, intermediaries, etc.) that is hit by a crisis, and no matter how big or small the crisis is, multiple voices appear in the arena and its sub-arenas, and communicative complexity becomes an issue to all of them. RAT is an open theoretical framework and applies to all types of crises within all subfields such as emergency or public sector crises, political crises, public health crises, corporate crises, and sports.

An increasing number of researchers have applied RAT and its multivocal approach to understand the complexity of crisis and crisis communication and to expand or add new insights into the theoretical framework. Some have studied the rhetorical arena within the corporate sector such as Johansen et al. (2016), who studied the role of faith-holders in a specific corporate sub-arena; Raupp (2019), who combined the concept of arena with the concept of social network; and Palmieri & Musi (2020), who studied the use of argumentation for trust repair in sub-arenas. Others have applied the theory within the public sector such as Rodin et al. (2019) and Rodin (2023), who studied the relations between three different media and social media sub-arenas and the motivations for online participation during the same public health crisis (Ebola), and Madsen et al. (2023), who did a study on listening in the arena of internal social media in a large Danish hospital during Covid-19. However, within specific areas, such as sports, scholars (e.g., Coombs & Holladay, 2014; Desmarais & Wallace, 2018; Harker, 2023; Kokholm et al., 2025) have found rhetorical arena beneficial because its multivocal approach aligns well with the communicative complexity in sports crisis. As Harker puts it: "RAT is the key to understanding and dissecting sport-related crisis communication" (2023, p. 473). Finally, RAT has also been transferred to other fields, such as to the study of communication in internal social media in organizations during daily business operations, that found that an open organizational communication culture can lead to robustness in crisis (Madsen & Johansen, 2019).

Practitioner Takeaways

One of the key takeaways from RAT for crisis managers is to not just concentrate on the organizational crisis response or defense in a crisis situation but to also anticipate and listen to the reactions and communication of the other voices entering the arena and its sub-arenas. Knowing the "game" of other voices in the arena, knowing their agendas and patterns of interaction may facilitate communication with key voices and stakeholders and can make it possible to navigate strategically among dilemmas and conflicts in the arena. It is important to be aware of the communicative complexity as salient voices may have a huge impact on the understanding of the role and responsibility of an organization in a specific crisis. The more you know about patterns of interaction among conflicting voices, the better prepared you will be for what is coming up, when a crisis situation turns into a battlefield.

Another key take away is related to the use of rhetorics. It is not only a matter of choosing the right overall strategy: denial, excuse, corrective action, apology, etc., it is also a matter of choosing appropriate rhetorics. Words are not just words, they are perceived, interpreted and framed differently among different voices. Also, visuals, artefacts, actions, etc., must be considered crisis communication as they also have an impact on the receivers. Next, be aware of the influence from the context (e.g., what type of crisis is it? and who are the voices present in the arena?). Communicating in specific sub-arenas through specific media and genres also influences how your communication is perceived and understood by other voices. In this regard, another key takeaway is to not worsen a crisis by turning it into a double crisis. Communicating badly or using wrong or non-appropriate rhetorical strategies or tactics may easily make more voices step into the arena and increase criticism. A crisis calls for professional communication.

A final key takeaway is that it is important for a crisis manager to be aware of the communicative complexity and to be able to identify interdependencies, strategies, and agendas of salient voices, to understand how these voices can affect organizational crisis communication actions. To be aware of the "game" in the arena is crucial.

Theoretical Constraints and Concerns

A key theoretical constraint for RAT is that it is impossible to make a full overview of what is going on during a crisis, as a whole crisis typically plays out in all the public, semi-public and private spheres of the arena and its sub-arenas. Multiple voices enter the arena and communicate along the whole process of a crisis. Hence, RAT is subject to various methodological challenges because it will not be feasible to make an exhaustive analysis of all crisis communication processes going on during a crisis.

However, RAT is an open theory that can be refined and expanded, and there is no doubt that we need more studies on the various patterns of interactions among of the multiple voices that enter the arena when a crisis hits.

Theoretical Engagement Points

1. What type of research methods are most closely associated with rhetorical theory?
2. Is RAT primarily a descriptive, relational, or explanatory theory?
3. Is RAT primarily an empirical-analytic, interpretative, or critical theory?
4. How would you evaluate RAT in terms of scope, appropriateness, heuristic value, validity, parsimony, and openness?

Discussion Questions

1. The chapter defines a rhetorical arena as a social space where multiple voices communicate during a crisis. How might the dynamics of a rhetorical arena change depending on the type of crisis (e.g., corporate, political, health) and how might organizations adapt their communication strategies to these changes? Be sure to consider the influence of contextual factors such as culture, organization and crisis type, and timing on the communication process within the arena.
2. RAT emphasizes a multivocal approach to crisis communication, focusing on the various agendas, interactions, and interdependencies among voices. Given that not all voices in the arena strive for dialogue and consensus, how can organizations effectively navigate the complex interplay of voices with different stances (agonistic, antagonistic), and what strategies might be employed to manage these varying perspectives and avoid a "double crisis"?
3. The chapter discusses the concept of sub-arenas as distinct sub-spaces within the larger rhetorical arena. How does the permeability of these sub-arenas affect the flow of information and the overall crisis communication process? What specific communication strategies might organizations adopt to address different voices within various sub-arenas? Be sure to consider the ways voices may be presented in multiple sub-arenas and how messages might be received differently in different spaces.
4. RAT identifies various patterns of interaction including the emergence of "hateholders" and "faith-holders." How can organizations identify and understand the motivations of these groups, and what strategies might they use to leverage the support of faith-holders while addressing the concerns of hateholders? Consider the potential for faith-holders to become co-crisis communicators and how this might impact the overall communication landscape.
5. The chapter outlines the importance of considering context, media, genre, and text when communicating in a rhetorical arena. How might organizations use these parameters to their advantage when choosing

their rhetorical strategies, and what might be the consequences of mismanaging these parameters? Be sure to consider how elements such as visuals, artefacts, and actions can be used as rhetorical tactics.

References

Barnett, M. L., & Pollock, T. G. (Eds.) (2012). *The Oxford handbook of corporate reputation*. Oxford: Oxford University Press.

Benoit, W. L. (1995). *Accounts, excuses, and apologies: A theory of image restoration strategies* (1st ed.). Albany, NY: State University of New York Press.

Benoit, W. L. 2015. *Accounts, excuses, and apologies: Image repair theory and research*, 2nd ed. Albany: State University of New York.

Benoit, W. L. (2024). *Accounts, excuses and apologies: Image Repair Theory Extended* (3rd ed.). Albany, NY: State University of New York.

Bitzer, L. F. (1968). The rhetorical situation. *Philosophy & Rhetoric*, *1*, 1–14.

Boin, A, 't Hart, P., & McConnell, A. (2009). Crisis exploitation: Political and policy impacts of framing contests. *Journal of European Public Policy*, *16*(1), 81–106.

Coombs. W. T. (1999). *Ongoing crisis communication. Planning, managing, and responding* (1st ed.). Thousand Oaks: Sage Publications.

Coombs, W. T. (2023). *Ongoing crisis communication. Planning, managing, and responding* (6th ed.). Thousand Oaks: Sage.

Coombs, W. T., Frandsen, F., Holladay, S. J., & Johansen, W. (2013b). Conceptualizing the Sub-arena: Exploring the boundaries within the rhetorical arena. *Third international conference on crisis communication at the beginning of the 21st century*. Erfurt.

Coombs, W. T., Frandsen, F., Holladay, S. J., & Johansen, W. H. (2013a). LIVESTRONG to livewrong: Analyzing and conceptualizing sub-arenas of crisis communication in the Lance Armstrong doping crisis, Paper presented at *16th International public relations research conference*, Miami, FL, March 9.

Coombs, W. T., & Holladay, S. J. (2012). Faith-holders as crisis managers: The Costa-Concordia rhetorical arena on Facebook. In *Proceedings from Euprera 2012 congress, Istanbul*, September 20–22.

Coombs, W. T., & Holladay, S. J. (2014). How publics react to crisis communication efforts: Comparing crisis response reactions across sub-arenas. *Journal of Communication Management*, *18*(1), 40–57.

Desmarais, F., & Wallace, C. (2018). The force of the national rhetorical arena: Voices in tune against a disrespectful foreign sponsor. *Sport Management Review*, 21(4), 443–558.

Eco, U. (1978). *Theory of semiotics*. Bloomington: Indiana University Press.

Frandsen, F., & Johansen, W. (2009). Wash and communicate: Artifacts and actions in crisis communication. In L. L. Salminen & A. Kankaanranta (Eds.). *The ascent of international business communication* (pp. 67–85). Helsinki: HSE B-90 Series.

Frandsen, F., & Johansen, W. (2010). Crisis communication, complexity and the cartoon affair: A case study. In W. T. Coombs & S. J. Holladay (Eds.), *The handbook of crisis communication*, (1st ed.) (425–448). Malden, MA: Wiley-Blackwell*.

Frandsen, F., & Johansen, W. (2011). The study of internal crisis communication: Towards an integrative framework. *Public Relations Inquiry*, *2*(2), 205–221.
Frandsen, F., & Johansen, W. (2015). Organizations, stakeholders and intermediairies: Towards a general theory. *International Journal of Strategic Communication*, *9*(4), 253–271.
Frandsen, F., & Johansen, W. (2017). *Organizational crisis communication - A multivocal approach* (1st ed.). London: Sage*.
Frandsen, F., & Johansen, W. (in press, 2026). *Organizational crisis communication: A multivocal approach* (2nd ed.). London: Sage.
Frandsen, F., & Johansen, W. (2018). Voices in conflict. The crisis communication of meta-organizations. *Management Communication Quarterly*. *32*(1), 90–120.
Frandsen, F. & Johansen, W. (2020). Arenas and voices in organizational crisis communication. How far have we come? In F. Frandsen & W. Johansen (Eds.), *Crisis communication* (Vol. 23, pp. 195–212). Handbooks of communication science. Berlin: de Gruyter Mouton*.
Frandsen, F., & Johansen, W. (2023). Revisiting and expanding rhetorical arena theory and sub-arenas. In W. T. Coombs, & S. J. Holladay (Eds.), *Handbook of crisis communication* (2nd ed., pp. 169–181). West Sussex: John Wiley and Sons*.
Frandsen, F., & Johansen, W. (in press). The battle between voices in the rhetorical arena of social media crises. In D. Koerber (Ed.), *The culture of the social*, Media crisis: Causes, impact, consequences. University of Toronto Press.
Gilpin, D. R. & Murphy, P. (2006). Reframing crisis management through complexity: In C. H. Botan & V. Hazleton (Eds.), *Public relations theory II* (pp. 375–392). Mahwah, NJ: Lawrence Erlbaum.
Gilpin, D. R. & Murphy, P. (2008). *Crisis management in a complex world*. New York: Oxford University Press.
Gilpin, D. R. & Murphy, P. (2010). Complexity and crisis: A new paradigm. In W. T. Coombs & S. J. Holladay (Eds.), *The handbook of crisis communication* (1st ed., pp. 683–690). Malden, MA: Wiley-Blackwell.
Harker, J. K. (2023). Three decades of sport-related crisis communication: A trends study of the emergence and growth of a crisis communication subfield. In W. T. Coombs, & S. J. Holladay (Eds.), *Handbook of crisis communication* (2nd ed., pp. 471–490). West Sussex: John Wiley and Sons.
Heide, M., & Simonsson, C. (2019). *Internal crisis communication. Crisis awareness, leadership, and coworkership*. Abingdon: Routledge.
Johansen, B. F., Johansen, W., & Weckesser, N. (2016). Emotional stakeholders as 'crisis communicators' in social media: The case of the Telenor customer complaints crisis. *Corporate Communications: An International Journal*, *21*(3), 289–308.
Johansen, W. (2017). Understanding and practicing crisis consulting: A study of public relations and communication firms. *Journal of Communication Management*, *21*(2), 106–123.
Johansen, W. (2020). Crisis management consulting. In F. Frandsen, & W. Johansen (Eds.), *Crisis communication. Handbooks of communication science* (pp. 375–400). Berlin: De Gruyter Mouton.

Johansen, W., Aggerholm, H. K., & Frandsen, F. (2012). Entering new territory: A study of internal crisis management and crisis communication in organizations. *Public Relations Review*, *38*, 270–279.

Johansen, W., & Frandsen, F. (2000). Retorik og krisekommunikation. *Rhetorica Scandinavica 14*, 45–62.

Johansen, W., & Frandsen, F. (2007). *Krisekommunikation. Når virksomhedens image og omdømme er truet [Crisis communication. When image and reputation of organizations are threatened]*. Frederiksberg: Samfundslitteratur.

King, A. A., Lenox, M. J., & Barnett, M. L. (2002). Strategic responses to the reputation commons problem. In A. Hoffmann & M. J. Ventresca (Eds.), *Organizations, policy, and the natural environment: Institutional and strategic perspectives* (pp. 393–406). Palo Alto, CA: Standford University Press.

Kokholm, K., Lott, M., & Johansen, W. (2025). Media framing, sports activism failure and crisis communication – European football and the *One Love* campaign at the World Cup 2022. In W. T. Coombs (Ed.), *Media and crisis communication* (pp. 81–123). New York: Routledge.

Luhmann, N. (1995). *Social systems*. Stanford, CA: Stanford University Press.

Luoma-aho, V. (2010). Emotional stakeholders: A threat to organizational legitimacy? In *Conference paper for the 60th annual conference of the international communication association*, Singapore, June 22–26.

Madsen, V. T., Gode, H. E., & Andersen, M. A. (2023). Vertical and horizontal listening on internal social media during a time of crisis: A case study of a Danish hospital. *Journal of Communication Management*, *27*(4), 563–581.

Madsen, V. T., & Johansen, W. (2019). A spiral of voice? When employees speak up on internal social media, *Journal of Communication Management*, *23*(4), 331–347.

Palmieri, R., & Musi, E. (2020). Trust-repair strategies in crisis rhetorical (sub-) arenas: An argumentative perspective. *International Journal of Strategic Communication*, *14*(4), 272–293.

Pang, A., Jin, Y., & Cameron, G. T. (2023). The contingency theory of strategic conflict management: Review from three decades of theory development, extension and application. *Journalism and Communication Monographs*, *25*(2), 193–214. https://doi.org/10.1177/15226379231167141

Pang, A., Jin, Y, Kim, S., & Cameron, G. T. (2020). Contingency theory: Evolution from a public relations theory to a theory of strategic conflict management. In F. Frandsen & W. Johansen (Eds.), *Crisis communication* (Vol. 23, pp. 141–164). Handbooks of communication science. Berlin: De Gruyter Mouton.

Raupp, J. (2019). Crisis communication in the rhetorical arena. Comparing crisis response reactions across sub-arenas. *Public Relations Review*, *45*(4). https://doi.org/10.1016/j.pubrev.2019.04.002

Rodin, P. (2023). *Voices in the arena: A participation-centred study of multivocal risk and crisis communication on social media*. PhD-thesis, Lund: Lund University, ISBN 78-91-8069-322-6 (PDF).

Rodin, P., Ghersetti, M., & Oden, T. (2019). Disentangling rhetorical subarenas of public health crisis communication: A study of the 2014–2015 Ebola outbreak in the news media and social media in Sweden. *Journal of Contingencies and Crisis Management*, *27*, 237–246.

Seeger, M. W., Sellnow, T. L., & Ulmer, R. R. (2003). *Communication and organizational crisis*. Westport, CT: Praeger.
Seeger, M. W., Sellnow, T. L., & Ulmer, R. R. (2010). Expanding the parameters of crisis communication: From chaos to renewal. In R. L. Heath (Ed.), *Handbook of public relations* (2nd ed., pp. 489–499). Thousand Oaks, CA: Sage.
Veil, S., & Dillingham, L. (2020). Reputational interdependence and spillover: Exploring the contextual challenges of spillover crisis response. In F. Frandsen, & W. Johansen (Eds.), *Crisis communication. Handbooks of communication science* (pp. 363–374). Berlin: De Gruyter Mouton.

*Requisite Readings

Chapter 17

Focusing Event

An interesting question in policy making is "Why some issues gain the attention of policy makers while other languish in obscurity?" Crises are one possibility for raising the visibility and interest in an issue. We are not advocating to precipitate a crisis for fermenting policy change. Rather, the work on focusing events has noted the ability of a crisis to influence policy agendas and actions (Birkland, 1997). The connection between crises and policy decisions is a unique avenue in crisis communication theory.

Theoretical Overview

The focusing event concept closely connects crises with public policy making, the process through which laws and regulations are developed and implemented. Issues compete for space on the policy agenda, the issues (problems) government officials are considering for further action. Space on the policy agenda is limited, so various actors attempt to place their issues on the policy agenda (Cobb & Elder, 1971; Kingdon, 1984). Advocacy coalition is a name given to these policy entrepreneurs who use various communication tactics to influence the policy agenda (Sabatier, 1988). Public and media agendas can influence the policy agenda. The public agenda are issues that the people feel are important, while the media agenda are the issues deemed salient by the media (tradition and social media) (Gilardi et al., 2022). Research has found that the media agenda does influence the public agenda (what has been called agenda setting), and the public agenda can influence the policy agenda (e.g., Barbara et al., 2021; Iyengar & Kinder, 1987). However, the relationship between the three agendas is more one of mutual influence rather than a linear relationship. Moreover, other factors, such as the actions of advocacy coalitions, influence agenda formation too.

Initially, understanding how issues move onto various agendas was called agenda building. Cobb and Elder (1971) formerly defined agenda building as "how issues are created and why some controversies or

DOI: 10.4324/9781003469964-19

incipient issues come to command the attention and concern of decision-makers whole some fail" (p. 905). Media attention helps to create the awareness that is essential to policy agenda formation. Later, the concept of agenda building was supplanted with the term agenda setting. Unnoticed issues will never reach the policy agenda (Graber, 2004). Focus events are one means of generating the attention that is necessary but not sufficient to move an issue on to the policy agenda. Kingdon (2003) was among those interested in how crises could be focusing events moving an issue toward the policy agendas by noting it can be "a crisis or disaster that comes along to call attention to the problem, a powerful symbol that catches on, or personal experience of a policy maker" (pp. 94–95). In this chapter, we explore the development of focusing event as a theory as it relates to crisis communication.

Theoretical Conceptualization

The concept of focusing event is most commonly associated with political scientist Thomas Birkland (1997) and his book *After Disaster: Agenda Setting, Public Policy, and Focusing Events*. However, Birkland was refining the concept of focusing event identified by Kingdon in his (Kingdon, 1984) book *Agendas, Alternatives, and Public Policies*. In his book's introduction, Birkland (1997) quotes Kingdon's definition of focusing event and argues it is too vague. A focusing event was simply a widely used symbol (what today might be called a meme) (Birkland & DeYoung, 2013). Birkland (1997) specified that focusing events were related to agenda setting, "the process by which problems and alternative solutions gain or lose public and elite attention" (p. 8). His refined definition of focus event stated it is "an event that is sudden, relatively rare, can be reasonably defined as harmful or suggests potential harm of interest, and that is known to policy makers and the public virtually simultaneously" (p. 22). Charles Perrow (1984) is another important researcher who mentioned but did not develop the idea of a focusing event.

A focusing event is tied to agenda building and agenda setting, more precisely with efforts to influence the policy agenda. Hence, the roots of focusing events are tied to the early work of Cobb and Elder (1971) and research in agenda setting by McCombs and Shaw (1972). Focusing events provide one means for explaining how issues move onto various agendas with the primary concern being movement of issues on to the policy agenda. Focusing events do not guarantee movement onto the policy agenda, and placement on the policy agenda does not mean policy will be created to combat the issue (Atkinson, 2019). Crises can be focusing events, and focusing events can influence agenda dynamics (Birkland, 1997; Birkland, 1998). Focusing events open a "window of opportunity" for advocacy coalitions (policy entrepreneurs) to push an issue on to the policy agenda. The mobilization of advocacy coalitions and further pressure is required to advance the issue to policy agenda.

Natural disasters and industrial accidents are potential focusing events. Both occur suddenly with very little warning, both are rare making them unpredictable and unplanned, both can affect large numbers of people (harm), and both stimulate virtually simultaneous awareness among the general population and policy makers. Hurricanes, oil spills, and nuclear power plant accidents are used to illustrate the existence of focusing events (Birkland, 1997).

Media coverage is essential to a focusing event. The conceptualization of focusing events pre-dates the Internet, hence, the emphasis on traditional news media coverage for focusing events. Focusing events can attract news media coverage because they possess three desirable news values: an event with a broad scope, visibility of harm, and rarity of an event. The news media are drawn to stories that affect a large number of people (scope), provide strong visual cues (visibility of harm), and standout as unusual (rarity of event) (Golding & Elliott, 1979). Today, social media is another means by which a focusing event can attract attention (Gilardi et al., 2022).

Birkland (1997) identifies three types of focusing events: normal, new, and common events under uncommon circumstances. However, his focus was on normal focusing events. Normal focusing events were Birkland's emphasis because they "occur sufficiently often to allow us to isolate events and model their influence on the agenda" (p. 145). Hurricane Katrina is an example of a normal focusing event. New focusing events are something that "has never happened before, if it has happened, it was so long ago as to have faded from memory" (Birkland, 1997, p. 145). An example of a new focusing event is the 1982 Tylenol product tampering crisis. New focusing events are likely to trigger a search for blame. Common events under uncommon circumstances "gain greater attention due to some unique or unusual feature of the event that makes them newsworthy and, not coincidentally, worthy of greater government attention and potential policy change" (Birkland, 1997; p. 147). Scandals, including political scandals, and some industrial accidents can become common events under uncommon circumstances. The Clintons' involvement in Whitewater scandal is an example of a common event under uncommon circumstances focusing event.

Birkland identified two possible attention foci for focusing events. The first focus is on the victims. Victims are the people who suffer harm from the focusing event. Natural disasters and freak accident are considered acts of God meaning that they could not be prevented. Because the cause was unavoidable, attention is placed upon the victims. The second focus is responsibility and blame. Birkland (1997) noted, "when the disaster is the result of human failings: poor design, operator error, 'corporate greed,' or 'government neglect'—our attention turns to the voluntary acceptance of responsibility for an event or to the coercive process of fixing blame" (p. 2). Consider that the United Nations Office for Disaster Risk Reduction (UNDRR) no longer uses the term natural disaster because disasters are a function of natural hazards and human actions (UNDRR, 2021). When the crisis is considered preventable, people look for some actor to accept responsibly or seek to affix responsibility if no actor willingly accepts responsibility for the crisis.

DeLeo et al. (2021) argued that the COVID-19 pandemic was a focusing event but does fit neatly into Birkland's definition of a focus event because it had a slow onset. This prompted a proposed revision to focusing events using what was called the indicator-event continuum. The indicator-event continuum classifies events along two dimensions: duration and accumulation. Duration of an event is how short or long the event lasts. Rate of indicator accumulation is whether the onset of the event is rapid or gradual. There are four categories for events: long duration and gradual accumulation, short duration and gradual accumulation, long duration and rapid accumulation, and short duration and rapid accumulation. Long duration and gradual accumulation have a gradual buildup with the effects lingering. There is time to observe the indicators, and those indicators should drive policy. Short duration and gradual accumulation do not linger and generally affect a rather limited area. Such events are unlikely to create policy change because they disappear so quickly. Long duration and rapid accumulation create multiple windows of opportunity for policy change because the effects last so long. Short duration and rapid accumulation are sudden events that are short lived. Such events might produce some instrumental policy changes and reflect Birkland's (1997) conceptualization of a focusing event. DeLeo et al. (2021) posit that "timing and duration of a crisis matters" with long duration and gradual accumulation and long duration and rapid accumulation the mostly likely types of events to create significant policy change (p. 23).

Fishman (1999) applied focusing events directly to crises by applying it to the 1996 crash of ValueJet Flight 592 into the Everglades. The crash was caused by a fire in the cargo hold. The fire was ignited by improperly stored chemical oxygen generators used in aircraft. A chemical oxygen generator is at the end of the mask that drops down if a plane loses cabin pressure. When you pull on the mask, a firing pin is triggered causing the oxygen to begin flowing. Investigators believe that the firing pins from the improperly stored chemical oxygen generators created the heat resulting in a fire (Fishman, 1999).

Fishman (1999) concentrated on Birkland's (1997) first two focusing events. Fishman referred to them Type 1 and Type 2. Type 1 was defined as natural disasters, while Type 2 are situations where people struggle to make sense of the events. Fishman (1999) argued that Type 1 had a long history in crisis management discussions. Type 2 was understudied in crisis management. The novelty of Type 2 creates a need to fix blame, a concern in many crises. Fishman's (1999) analysis argued that the crash was a Type 2 event that resulted in policy changes instituted by the Federal Aviation Administration (FAA). Fishman (1999) provided an expanded discussion of Birkland' (1997) "new" focusing event.

Applications to Subfields

Focusing events as a concept originates in and have strong ties to the political crisis subfield with the study of agenda building and agenda setting. The focusing event research centers on policy making and how crise can affect that process. Birkland (1997) was interested in how crises, such as disaster and industrial accidents, could result in policy changes. The political crisis subfield is reflected in focusing events' origins in the works of political scientists such as Cobb, Elder, and Kingdon. Andrejuk (2023) explored the effects of a refugee crisis (political crisis) on policy changes. Birkland (1997) noted that industrial accidents could be focusing events. For instance, the horrific Dow Chemical industrial accident in Bhopal, India, resulted in significant changes to risk communication policies in the US. Farley et al. (2007) examined the policy effects of hurricane Katrina (a disaster) in the US.

Fishman (1999) reinforced the connection between the corporate crisis subfield and focusing events. Fishman articulately revealed how certain corporate crises can be focusing events. The ValueJet Flight 592 airline crash was a focusing event that shaped aviation policy in the US (Fishman, 1999). DeLeo et al. (2021) extended the application of focusing events to the public crisis subfield by studying COVID-19. They explored the way COVID-19 reshaped policies. When applied to the corporate and public crisis subfields, focusing events offer a unique blend of subfields. Regardless of which subfield the crisis originates within, the effects of the focusing event are still political. Hence, both corporate and public crisis subfield-based crises become coupled with effects from the political crisis subfield (policy changes or the lack there of).

Focusing events exemplify the tight coupling of crisis management and issues management (Jaques, 2007). Issues management can be viewed as a form of risk management because it explores changes in public and corporate policies (Jones & Chase, 1979). Issues are the emergence of a risk and proper actions can prevent the risk from fully manifesting into a crisis. (See the chapter on paracrises for more details on this dynamic.) Moreover, issues management can be a consequence of a crisis. New policies can be developed in an effort to prevent future crises. The Bhopal crisis resulting in new requirements for risk communication in the US noted earlier is an example of issues management (Coombs, 2023). An issue can create a crisis, and a crisis can prompt the emergence of an issue. Some researchers have even argued that one goal of a crisis management effort might be to prevent policy changes such as new regulations (Fredriksson, 2014). Successfully managing a crisis becomes a form of issues management as it can reassure stakeholders that policy changes are not needed. The focusing event captures the issue–crisis connection.

Practitioner Takeaways

Focusing events helps crisis communicators to appreciate the connections between issues and crises. Primarily, focusing events emphasize how a crisis can result in policy changes. These policy changes can affect the lives of constituents and organizations. For instance, the Bhopal crisis mandated organizations that use hazardous materials to engage in risk communication with communities near their facilities. The policy changes reshaped the relationship between organizations and their surrounding communities (Coombs, 2023). Crisis communicators need to consider how the crisis might reshape governmental policies, especially if they do a poor job of managing and communicating about the crisis. Focusing events help practitioners to examine the bigger picture surrounding a crisis by considering the broader effects the crisis might have on society.

Theoretical Constraints and Concerns

Focusing events provide an interesting perspective for approaching crises but have a few constraints. A focusing event is not an objective event but socially constructed. The media and powerful politicians can have a significant impact on whether or not an event becomes treated as a focusing event. The influence of media and politicians on framing an event can be one reason a potential focusing event has no effect of policy. There are concerns over the short-term focus of focusing events research that overlooks long-term effect such as learning. Birkland's (1998) own work notes this concern. There are also concerns about the lack of predictive power provided by focusing events and how the concept overlooks many structural and systemic problems that create crises (Atkinson, 2019).

Theoretical Engagement Points

1 What type of research methods are most closely associated with focusing event?
2 Is focusing event primarily a descriptive, relational, or explanatory theory?

3 Is focusing event primarily an empirical-analytic, interpretative, or critical theory?
4 How would you evaluate focusing event in terms of scope, appropriateness, heuristic value, validity, parsimony, and openness?

Discussion Questions

1 What are the necessary components of a focusing event? Which component do you think is the most important and why?
2 Using a recent event that has received media attention, discuss whether that event meets the definition of a focusing event. Be sure to explain your reasoning. If it does not meet the definition, discuss what aspects of the definition are not met.
3 What is the indicator-event continuum and how does it relate to focusing events theory?
4 Compare and contrast focusing events in terms of victims and blame. When does a focusing event tend to focus on victims, and when does it tend to focus on responsibility and blame?
5 How can a crisis communicator apply focusing events theory to their work?

References

Andrejuk, K. (2023). Rapid evolution of refugee policy in Poland: Russian invasion of Ukraine as a focusing event. *Journal of Immigrant & Refugee Studies*, *21*, 1–14.

Atkinson, C. L. (2019). Focus event and public policy. *Global Encyclopedia of Public Administration, Public Policy, and Governance*, 1–5.

Barbara, J., Haley, N., McMahon, H., & Turnbull, T. (2021). Building inherently impactful research programs: The role of organizational context. *Policy Design and Practice*, *4*(3), 357–371.

Birkland, T. A. (1997). *After disaster: Agenda setting, public policy, and focusing events*. Washington, DC: Georgetown University Press*.

Birkland, T. A. (1998). Focusing events, mobilization, and agenda setting. *Journal of Public Policy*, *18*(1), 53–74*.

Birkland, T. A., & DeYoung, S. E. (2013). Focusing events and policy windows. In E. Araral Jr., S. Fritzen, M. Howlett, M. Ramesh and X. Wu (Eds.), *Routledge handbook of public policy* (pp. 175–188). New York: Routledge.

Cobb, R. W., & Elder, C. D. (1971). The politics of agenda-building: An alternative perspective for modern democratic theory. *The Journal of Politics*, *33*(4), 892–915.

Coombs, W. T. (2023). *Ongoing crisis communication: Planning, managing, and responding* (6th ed.). Los Angeles: SAGE.

DeLeo, R. A., Taylor, K., Crow, D. A., & Birkland, T. A. (2021). During disaster: Refining the concept of focusing events to better explain long-duration crises. *International Review of Public Policy*, *3*(1)*.

Farley, J., Baker, D., Batker, D., Koliba, C., Matteson, R., Mills, R., & Pittman, J. (2007). Opening the policy window for ecological economics: Katrina as a focusing event. *Ecological Economics*, *63*(2–3), 344–354.
Fishman, D. A. (1999). ValuJet Flight 592: Crisis communication theory blended and extended. *Communication Quarterly*, *47*(4), 345–375*.
Fredriksson, M. (2014). Crisis communication as institutional maintenance. *Public Relations Inquiry*, *3*(3), 319–340.
Gilardi, F., Gessler, T., Kubli, M., & Müller, S. (2022). Social media and political agenda setting. *Political Communication*, *39*(1), 39–60.
Golding, Peter, & Elliott, Philip. (1979). *Making the news*. London: Longman.
Graber, D. (2004). Mediated politics and citizenship in the twenty-first century. *Annual Review Psychoogy*, *55*(1), 545–571.
Iyengar, S., & Kinder, D (1987). *News that matters: Television and American opinion*. Chicago: University of Chicago Press.
Jaques, T. (2007). Issue management and crisis management: An integrated, non-linear, relational construct. *Public Relations Review*, *33*(2), 147–157.
Jones, B. L. Chase, W. H. (1979). Managing public policy issues. *Public Relations Review*, *5*(2), 3–23.
Kingdon, J. W. (1984). *Agendas, alternatives, and public policies*. Boston: Little, Brown and Co.
Kingdon, John W. (2003). *Agendas, alternatives, and public policies*. 2nd ed. Longman classics in political science. New York: Longman.
McCombs, M. E., & Shaw, D. L. (1972). The agenda-setting function of mass media. *Public Opinion Quarterly*, *36*(2), 176–187.
Perrow, C. (1984). *Normal accidents: Living with high-risk technologies*. New York: Basic Books.
Sabatier, P. A. (1988). An advocacy coalition framework of policy change and the role of policy-oriented learning therein. *Policy Sciences*, *21*(2), 129–168.
United Nations Office for Disaster Risk Reduction (UNDRR). (2021). Journalists told "No such thing as a natural disaster." Retrieved From https://www.undrr.org/news/journalists-told-no-such-thing-natural-disaster

*Requisite Readings

Chapter 18

Crisis Exploitation Theory

Crises in politics can have implications for public policy and political careers. Crises can be the impetus of political change when new policies are created to address the problems revealed by the crisis. Moreover, crises can erode confidence in office-holders. Consider how hurricane Katrina affected policies in the US and views of sitting President Bush (Boin et al., 2009). Crisis exploitation theory has been recognized as "the most detailed articulation of political crisis communication" (Coombs, 2011, p. 220). Crisis exploitation theory highlights the importance of frames and communication in the political crisis subfield (Boin et al., 2008).

Theoretical Overview

Large-scale crises (aka emergencies, scandals, or fiascos) can disrupt the dominant social or political discourses meaning structural change is possible because the current power and authority relationships are delegitimized ('t Hart, 1993). Two types of political spaces begin to open when a crisis occurs (Boin and 't Hart, 2003). One, the crisis can be used as a political weapon. The media focuses attention on an issue and the damage related to it. Questions arise about how the situation was allowed to occur and how the issue should be addressed. Second, "crises help 'de-institutionalise' hitherto taken-for-granted policy beliefs and practices" ('t Hart and Tindall, 2009, p. 22). The crisis indicates flaws in current policies and practices. The more severe the effects of the crisis, the more serious the flaws will appear to be. These severe crises can benefit those who stand in opposition to the status quo (Boin et al., 2008). Yet significant crises often fail to create any new policies. Crisis exploitation theory has been advanced to help explain why policies may or may not change following a significant crisis.

Crisis exploitation theory pulls together research from public policy, political science, and crisis management. The theory explores the ways

DOI: 10.4324/9781003469964-20

political actors leverage crises to promote their agendas, secure power, and justify decisions. Crisis exploitation holds a crisis that creates a window of opportunity for political actors to shape public opinion, introduce new policies, and promote changes likely to have faced resistance (Boin et al., 2009). The window emerges because the crisis causes people to question the status quo, thereby providing a chance for change.

Theoretical Conceptualization

Crisis exploitation has been defined "the purposeful utilization of crisis-type rhetoric to significantly alter levels of political support for public office-holders and public policies" (Boin et al., 2009, p. 83). Crisis exploitation takes a social construction perspective on crises. It is not the event itself that matters but how it is perceived by constituents. A crisis is defined as "events or developments widely perceived by members of relevant communities to constitute urgent threats to core community values and structures" (Boin et al., 2009, pp. 83–84). These social crises can include disasters, economic crises, violence, protests, and emergencies. The constructed nature of crises can result in three outcomes: Type 1, Type 2, and Type 3. Type 1 is when there is no crisis. The political stance is no blame for the crisis, and the policy stance is no need for change. Type 2 is when the crisis is a threat to the status quo. The political stance is diffusion of blame, and the policy stance is to defend the status quo. Type 3 is when the crisis is an opportunity to expose deficiencies. The political stance is to focus blame on office-holders, and the policy stance is to attack the status quo (Boin et al., 2009).

Similar to focusing events, crisis exploitation views crises as an opportunity for policy change and has roots extending to agenda setting. However, crisis exploitation theory seeks to illuminate why some opportunities materialize and some fail. Crises create a heightened public attention and perceived urgency for the exercise of power, framing, and agenda setting. Political actors try to shape policies by exploiting the unpredictability and urgency to push for actions that might not be possible under ordinary circumstances (Boin et al., 2009; 't Hart and Tindall, 2009). The key resource with crisis exploitation theory is persuasion. Crisis exploitation is presented as a framing contest between the various factions seeking to exploit the "crisis-induced opportunity space" (Boin et al., 2009, p. 82). The outcome of the framing contest is one means of understanding why a crisis does or does not produce change (Boin et al., 2009).

Crisis exploitation involves two types of framing contests: significance of the event and causality. The significance of the event is important because it effects if the event demands attention or can be safely ignored. The significance can be minimal, can require recognition, or can have maximized significance. Causality becomes an issue when the event cannot be denied. People want to assign responsibility for the event and consider the degree to which an event is foreseeable and controllable. An exogenize view sees outside forces as being responsible (not our doing) and is found in Type 2. An endogenize view blames the system (the government has failed) itself and is found in Type 3 (Boin et al., 2009).

There are two spheres of crisis exploitation as well: the political game and the policy game. The political game is a battle between the government (office-holders) and the opposition. The policy game is a battle between those defending the status quo and those wanting change. There are four groups of political actors. The political game has oppositional forces and office-holders, while the policy game has status quo and change-oriented. Oppositional forces want to undermine the authority of office-holders or remove them from office, while office-holders seek to deflect responsibility or accept some responsibility for the event. The change-oriented want wholesale or incremental change to policies while the status quo defends existing policies. The political implications for office-holders can be elite damage, careers, reputations, and aspirations go down; elite escape the blame is diffused or displaced; or elite rejuvenation, praise, and support. The policy implications run a range of the "degree of crisis-induced policy change" (Boin et al., 2009, p. 94). Sabatier's (1998) taxonomy is used to characterize the policy changes in a deep core, core, and secondary aspects (Boin et al., 2009).

The political game can result in blame minimization (elite escape), blame acceptance (elite damage), blame avoidance (elite escape), or blame showdown (elite escape, elite rejuvenation, or elite damage is possible). The policy game can result in a policy stalemate, policy stalemate or incremental adjustment, major and swift symbolic change or incremental substantive change, or negotiated incremental adjustment (Boin et al., 2009). The nature of the crisis itself places a critical role in shaping the outcomes of the political and policy games. How obvious the fault is for the crisis and if the crisis hits at the "heart of the existing policy domains" (Boin et al., 2009, p. 98) are two crisis characteristics shaping how the crisis might or might not lead to change. Temporal factors matter as well, including the point in an office-holder's political career and timing relative to an election (Boin et al., 2009).

The initial presentation of the crisis exploitation theory included 15 case studies to illustrate the theory. A general conclusion is that crisis exploitation strategies/efforts do matter. The crisis exploitation efforts help to determine is oppositional forces can dismantle policies and weaken/remover office-holders. Or if office-holders can contain the crisis and the status quo can survive the destabilization. In the political game, officer-holders are in the best position to win when they have strong pre-crisis political capital (especially with the media); they actively and cogently communicate their frames and have been in office for a short time; the cause of the crisis is considered external (exogenous), and an expert commission is used for the official inquiry. Oppositional forces are more likely to win if the crisis is viewed as internal (endogenous), the office-holder has served a long time, the office-holder has had recent bad media coverage, and the inquiry is political (non-expert). In the policy game, incremental change seems to be the most likely outcome for the policy game when a crisis opens a political window (Boin et al., 2009). Crisis exploitation theory offers valuable insights into how crises might shape policy decisions and power dynamics resulting in progressive change or a defense of the status quo.

Application to Subfields

Given its origins in political science, it is not surprising that the primary application of crisis exploitation theory has been in the political crisis subfield. Crisis exploitation theory has been applied to political crises in various countries including China (Liu, 2022) and various levels of government, including the mayoral level (Pille & Prins, 2018). These political applications include economic crises ('t Hart and Tindall, 2009), climate change (Kreuder-Sonnen, 2020), radical mobilization on social media (Jost & Dogruel, 2023), and terrorism (Olsson & Nord, 2015). Crisis exploitation theory has been applied to the public crisis subfield as well. The theory has been applied to disasters (Boin et al., 2009) and public health crises (Hu & Zhong, 2023; Hunt, 2022). Crisis exploitation theory's utility in explaining change following a crisis has potential application to the corporate crisis subfield too. The theory could be used to help explain why significant changes do or do not occur in corporations following a crisis.

Practitioner Takeaways

Practitioners coping with political and public crises learn the value of efforts to exploit a crisis. While some critics dislike the term exploitation, crises can be used to leverage necessary changes such as improving preparedness for disasters or public health crises. Just because a crisis reveals flaws in the system does not mean meaningful change will ensue. Those in power will act to protect their positions and defend the status quo. Crisis-related change must be given a push if it is to have a chance to occur. Crisis exploitation theory identifies some of the resources that can be used in the framing battles that do emerge from crises. A valuable resource is framing the crisis as caused by flaws within the system, not some external factors.

Defining the problem associated with a crisis is an essential step in moving people to accepted the changes necessary to redress the problem.

Theoretical Constraints and Concerns

While an important development in understanding political crises, crisis exploitation does bring with it a number of concerns and constraints. Crisis exploitation theory lacks predictive power. The analyses utilizing the theory are retrospective. It is difficult to anticipate if a crisis will be successfully exploited for change or maintenance of the status quo. There is an overemphasis on opportunism with the focus on political actors motivated by self-interests and little concern for well-intentioned political actors (Boin et al., 2009). Jessop (2002) argues crisis exploitation theory emphasizes agency over structure, thereby underestimating the role of systemic conditions. Moreover, crisis exploitation theory underestimates the role of public backlash and resistance to perceived exploitation (McConnell, 2010). Still, crisis exploitation theory is a critical tool for explaining how political actors navigate the political landscapes reshaped by crises.

Theoretical Engagement Points

1 What type of research methods are most closely associated with crisis exploitation theory?
2 Is crisis exploitation theory primarily a descriptive, relational, or explanatory theory?
3 Is crisis exploitation theory primarily an empirical-analytic, interpretative, or critical theory?
4 How would you evaluate crisis exploitation theory in terms of scope, appropriateness, heuristic value, validity, parsimony, and openness?

Discussion Questions

1 How do crises create opportunities for political change? What factors make a crisis more or less exploitable?
2 What are the different ways political actors can frame a crisis? What are the potential consequences of different framing strategies?
3 How does crisis exploitation theory account for the role of the media in shaping public perceptions of a crisis?
4 What are some of the ethical concerns surrounding crisis exploitation? Can crises be exploited for positive change?
5 Can you think of any recent crises that have been successfully exploited for political or policy change?

References

't Hart, P. & Tindall, K. (2009). Leadership, rhetoric and framing contests in response to the economic meltdown. In P. 't Hart & K. Tindall (Eds.), *Framing the global economic downturn: Crisis rhetoric and the politics of recessions* (pp. 21–42). Canberra, Australia: ANU E Press.

't Hart, P. (1993) Symbols, rituals and power: the lost dimensions of crisis management. *Journal of Contingencies and Crisis Management, 1*(1), 36–50*.

Boin, A., & 't Hart, P. 2003, 'Public leadership in times of crisis: Mission impossible?', *Public Administration Review, 63*(5), 544–553.

Boin, A., 't Hart, P. & McConnell, A. (2009). Crisis exploitation: political and policy impacts of framing contests. *Journal of European Public Policy, 16*(1), 81–106*.

Boin, A., McDonnell, A., & 't Hart, P. (2008). Governing after a crisis. In A. Boin, A. McConnell, & P. 't Hart (Eds.), *Governing after crisis: The politics of investigation, accountability and learning* (pp. 3–32). Cambridge: Cambridge University Press*.

Coombs, W. T. (2011). Political public relations and crisis communication: A public relations perspective. In J. Strömbäck and S. Kiousis (Eds.), *Political public relations: Concepts, principles, and applications* (pp. 214–234). New York: Routledge.

Hu, Q., & Zhong, W. (2023). State-level politicization of crisis communication on Twitter during COVID-19: Conceptualization, measurement, and impacts. *Public Administration Review, 83*(5), 1266–1280.

Hunt, K. (2022). Exploiting a crisis: Abortion activism and the COVID-19 pandemic. *Perspectives on Politics, 20*(2), 396–411.

Jessop, B. (2002). *The future of the capitalist state.* Malden, MA: Polity Press.

Jost, P., & Dogruel, L. (2023). Radical mobilization in times of crisis: Use and effects of appeals and populist communication features in Telegram channels. *Social Media+ Society, 9*(3), 1–12.

Kreuder-Sonnen, C. (2020). Political secrecy in Europe: Crisis management and crisis exploitation. In *Secrecy in European politics* (pp. 134–156). Routledge.

Liu, Y. (2022). Toward understanding crisis exploitation in China. In *Crisis rhetoric and policy change in China* (pp. 29–53). Singapore: Springer Nature Singapore.

McConnell, A. (2010). Policy success, policy failure and grey areas in-between. *Journal of Public Policy, 30*(3), 345–362.

Olsson, E. K., & Nord, L. W. (2015). Paving the way for crisis exploitation: The role of journalistic styles and standards. *Journalism, 16*(3), 341–358.

Pille, C., & Prins, R. (2018). The framing contest unravelled: Mayors, framing strategies and political outcomes in the wake of three riot-related crises in the Netherlands. *Journal of Contingencies and Crisis Management, 26*(4), 469–479.

Sabatier, P. A. (1998). The advocacy coalition framework: revisions and relevance for Europe. *Journal of European Public Policy, 5*(1), 98–130.

*Requisite Readings

Part III

General Theories Relevant to Crisis Communication

Chapter 19

Stress Inoculation Theory

We know that crises create stress, and stress can have negative consequences for those experiencing it. Stress affects those experiencing the crisis and managing the crisis. Moreover, those observing the crisis, such as the news media and those consuming the crisis-related stories, can experience stress vicariously. The negative effects of stress during a crisis range from an inability to understand crisis messaging to powerful emotions and distress caused by stress (e.g., Covello, 2022). Stress is an important factor to consider when managing a crisis. Stress inoculation theory (SIT) provides a proactive approach to stress management by building up stress resistance prior to encountering a crisis.

Theoretical Overview

SIT was developed by Donald Meichenbaum in the 1970s as a mechanism to manage and to cope with stress. SIT is derived from cognitive-behavioral principles. SIT facilitates resilience through a structured preparation process that trains people how to handle stress. SIT "enhances individuals' ability to anticipate, identify, and cope with stressful situations and stress-induced emotional responses" (Morrissey & Reser, 2003, p. 47). By exposing people to moderate stress in training situations along with a chance to practice coping skills, SIT prepares people to be able to adapt to future stressors. It is the exposure to moderate stress that is the inoculation part of the theory. Exposure to small amounts of stress enhances coping abilities (Meichenbaum & Meichenbaum, 1977).

SIT utilizes a transaction view of stress and coping reflecting the works of Lazarus and Folkman (1984). Stress is created when people perceive the resources needed to cope with the situation are greater than the perceived resources they have to meet those demands. People perceive they do not have enough resources to meet the demands of the situation. The transaction is perceptual and involves a transaction between the environment (situation) and themselves (Meichenbaum, 2017; Meichenbaum & Deffenbacher, 1988).

DOI: 10.4324/9781003469964-22

Theoretical Conceptualization

SIT follows a three-step model. Step one is conceptualization and education. People come to understand and to be aware of stress and various coping resources. Step two is skill acquisition and rehearsal. People are trained in coping skills for stress. This will include a chance to try the various coping skills. Step three is application and follow-through. People are provided an opportunity to apply their newly learned coping skills in stress situations they are likely to encounter in their lives. A variety of methods can be used to deliver the training and to practice the skills (Meichenbaum, 2017). The general goal of the three steps is to bolster people's coping repertoires.

SIT has been linked to the specific goals of reducing anxiety and enhancing performance. A meta-analysis review of SIT-based training found a reduction in anxiety and an increase in performance following the training in stress inducing situations. The reduction of anxiety showed a strong magnitude (r = .37), while performance enhancement demonstrated a moderate magnitude (r = .30). The authors of the review concluded, "Results of this analysis indicate that the stress inoculation training approach is an effective method to reduce anxiety and enhance performance in stressful environments" (Saunders et al., 1996).

Application to Subfields

Crisis research has generally not included SIT. Morrissey and Reser (2003) applied SIT to the study of cyclone preparedness in Australia, the public subfield. The research was concerned with the way anxiety can block preparation. The authors argued for the need to consider psychological preparedness as part of the crisis. The SIT training resulted in respondents having lower anxiety, lower fear, great physical preparedness, and greater psychological preparedness after the training (Morrissey & Reser, 2003). SIT has been applied in healthcare indicating an applicability to the public health crisis aspect of the public crisis subfield (Janis, 1983). SIT has proven value in the public crisis subfield.

SIT has potential for the corporate crisis subfield. Saunders et al.'s (1996) meta-analysis was driven by a desire to improve training for reducing stress in organizations. Examples of stress in organizations included accidents at nuclear facilities and airline emergencies. Hence, the meta-analysis fits with crisis situations creating stress and how SIT can moderate the stress. The crisis team and other employees affected by a corporate crisis should benefit from SIT. These employees should experience less stress and improved performance during the stressful crisis situations. More research is needed to test the effects of SIT in the corporate crisis subfield but the potential benefit exists.

Practitioner Takeaways

SIT offers practitioners an additional tool for crisis preparation. Including SIT training in crisis preparedness should facilitate the ability of the crisis team to handle the stress generated during a crisis event. Moreover, even potential victims of a crisis can benefit from SIT training. The most obvious application would be for disasters and public health crises. Populations likely to experience public crises could receive SIT training. SIT training illustrates how crisis preparation is linked to resilience. Individual resilience should be enhanced when the ability to cope with stress is strengthened.

Theoretical Constraints and Concerns

While proven to be helpful in many situations, SIT does have constraints and concerns. SIT's cognitive focus does little to address the emotional reactions to stress. SIT may not apply well to people who have more affective reactions to stress. Moreover, SIT may oversimply the stress process and is not well suited for those experiencing trauma. We must be aware of the limits of SIT and that some people and situations may require more refined and detailed interventions. An example would be transportation accidents that result in mass casualties. Such crises warrant more advanced forms of counseling necessary to combat the trauma associated with a mass casualty event.

Theoretical Engagement Points

1 What type of research methods are most closely associated with SIT?
2 Is SIT primarily a descriptive, relational, or explanatory theory?
3 Is SIT primarily an empirical-analytic, interpretative, or critical theory?
4 How would you evaluate SIT in terms of scope, appropriateness, heuristic value, validity, parsimony, and openness?

Discussion Questions

1 How does the concept of "inoculation" apply to stress management in SIT? Consider the analogy to medical inoculation and discuss how exposure to moderate stress can enhance coping abilities.
2 Explain the transactional view of stress adopted by SIT. How does this perspective influence the way SIT approaches stress management?
3 What are some practical examples of how the three steps of SIT can be implemented in a crisis preparedness program? Provide specific examples for each step, such as educational materials, skill-building exercises, and real-world application scenarios.

4 Discuss the potential benefits and limitations of using SIT in corporate crisis management. Consider the unique stressors and challenges faced by organizations in crisis situations and how SIT might address them.
5 How does SIT contribute to individual resilience in the face of crises? Discuss the link between stress management skills and the ability to adapt and recover from challenging events.

References

Covello, V. T. (2022). *Communicating in risk, crisis, and high stress situations: Evidence-based strategies and practice*. Hoboken: Wiley.

Janis, I. (1983). Stress inoculation in health care. In *Stress reduction and prevention* (pp. 67–99). New York: *Plenum Press*.

Lazarus, R., & Folkman, S. (1984). *Stress, appraisal and coping*. New York: Springer.

Meichenbaum, D. (2017). Stress inoculation trainingv: A preventative and treatment approach. In *The evolution of cognitive behavior therapy* (pp. 101–124). New York: Routledge*.

Meichenbaum, D., & Meichenbaum, D. (1977). *Stress-inoculation training* (pp. 143–182). Springer US.

Meichenbaum, D. H., & Deffenbacher, J. L. (1988). Stress inoculation training. *The Counseling Psychologist*, *16*(1), 69–90*.

Morrissey, S. A., & Reser, J. P. (2003). Evaluating the effectiveness of psychological preparedness advice in community cyclone preparedness materials. *The Australian Journal of Emergency Management*, *18*(2), 46–61.

Saunders, T., Driskell, J. E., Johnston, J. H., & Salas, E. (1996). The effect of stress inoculation training on anxiety and performance. *Journal of Occupational Health Psychology*, *1*(2), 170*.

*Requisite Readings

Chapter 20

Communication Theory of Resilience

Crises are stressful events that disrupt people's lives and routines. Crisis communication should consider the variety of ways crises affect people. Resilience helps to explain how people cope with the effects of crises. The study of crises naturally has included the study of how people recover from a crisis. Most emergency management models, for instance, include recovery as the final phase of a crisis (Drabek, 1985) including the model used by the Federal Emergency Management Agency (FEMA) in the US. The interest in crisis recovery results in a close connection between crises and resilience.

Theoretical Overview

It is nature to consider how individuals, organizations, communities, and societies "bounce back" from crises. Resilience is about the ability to adapt to and to recover from shocks. One specific definition of resilience is the "dynamic process that is influenced by both neural and psychological self organisations, as well as the transaction between the ecological context and the developing organism" (Curtis & Cicchetti, 2007, p. 811). Resilience is a reaction to some adverse event or situation. Resiliency reflects an ability to adapt, recover, and maintain some level of functionality.

Insights into why resilience occurs or fails to occur can help other entities to adapt, recover, and thrive when facing crises. Resilience can improve crisis preparedness (Berkes & Ross, 2013), inform public policy (Cutter et al., 2008), support mental health and well-being (Norris et al., 2008), improve risk communication (Stoffle & Minnis, 2008), and facilitate adaptation (Pfefferbaum et al., 2017). Because of this strong connection, resilience is an essential element in crisis management and communication.

Theoretical Conceptualization

Interest in resilience began in the 1970s with a focus on ecology. Researchers were interested in the way ecological systems could maintain function after

DOI: 10.4324/9781003469964-23

experiencing a disturbance. Norris et al. (2008) began the expansion of resilience to the study of social systems in the 1980s. The research considered how communities can adapt and even grow when facing adversity (Norris et al., 2008). In the 1990s, resilience migrated to psychology by examining a person's ability to adapt positively to adversity (e.g., Masten, 2002). By the 2000s, resilience research was exploring the connections ecological, social, and individual resilience. We see this integration in the social-ecological resilience framework developed by Berkes and Ross (2013). In the 2010s, resilience research began to emphasize the dynamic and adaptive nature of resilience. This included an interest in learning as part of resilience (Pfefferbaum et al., 2017). The 2020s saw an interest in global resilience (Cutter, 2019). Throughout its history, resilience has been viewed as an outcome and a process. Research treats resilience as a process when evaluating if an entity was resilient or not. Research treats resilience as a process when it studies how resilience develops and how it is enacted in the face of adversity. Moreover, resilience is dynamic and changes over time (Rutter, 2012). The general focus of the resilience research has been on identifying factors contributing to or inhibiting an entity's ability to adapt, to recover, and to retain some functionality when confronting an adverse event.

Resilience research is very broad. We have selected Patrice Buzzanell's (2010) communication theory of resilience (CTR) because it takes a communicative approach to resilience and covers the three often intersecting levels of individuals (micro), organizations (meso), and societies (macro). All three levels can be relevant to crisis communication. CTR approaches resilience from the perspective of organizational communication defining it as "the processes by which individuals and organizations reintegrate and foster productive change during and after career setbacks, material and personnel losses, disasters, or other obstacles" (Buzzanell, 2018, p. 14). For Buzzanell (2010, 2018), resilience is an adaptive-transformative process that is communicatively constituted by people. The resilience process is a trigger event or turning point that results in loss or disruption.

Central to CTR's conceptualization of resilience as process are five subprocesses: creating a new normalcy, affirming important identities, utilizing relevant social communication networks, employing alternative logics to see beyond conventional thinking, and backgrounding negative feelings while foregrounding productive behaviors (Buzzanell, 2010).

Crafting new normalcy is about how people put their lives back together. This would include the functioning of organizations and other collectives. Buzzanell (2010) posits that people "talked normalcy into being" (p. 4). People use communication to establish normalcy by defining their lives as normal through their discourse. People and other entities seek to affirm identities following disruption. The focus is on the identity anchor, "a relatively enduring cluster of identity discourse upon which individual and their familiar, collegial, and/or community members rely when explaining who they are for themselves and others" (p. 4). For instance, organization identity is an accepted concept among those studying organizations with a focus on "who we are an organization" (e.g., Gioia et al., 2013, p. 123). Crises can be viewed as attacks on identity, hence the need to reassert an identity after a crisis.

Maintaining and using communication networks reflect the work of Granovetter (1973) and the value of social capital. Social capital refers to the "resources embedded in organization-to-organization relationships" (Buzzanell, 2010, p. 6). Those who utilize communication networks fare better after a crisis than those who are isolated. That is why creating and maintaining communication networks are essential for resilience (Buzzanell, 2010). New logics is about people reframing the situation. Old logics fail to make sense of the world, so people must develop alternative logics allowing them to reframe the situation. Here we see the evidence of the social construction view the permeates Buzzanell's (2010) resilience approach.

People need to both legitimize negative feelings while foregrounding productive actions. Crises will create negative emotions. Those negative emotions should be legitimized—people have a right to feel that way. However, people also must recognize the negative feelings can be counterproductive. Therefore, people must background the unproductive behaviors and negative feelings while they foreground (emphasize) the productive actions they can take after the crisis (Buzzanell, 2010, 2018). For instance, a crisis can make people angry but that anger must be backgrounded in favor of taking actions that will allow those involved to move past the crisis.

Resilience is not accomplished in isolation but with the help and support of others. Resilience is not a trait or a characteristic but "is cultivated interactively for the present and the future" (Buzzanell, 2018, p. 15). Anticipatory resilience captures the future dimension of resilience. When people make sense of a disruptive event (crisis), they build a new narrative to be used to make sense of future events. Anticipatory resilience is "a system of reasoning about the world, through which they understand the possibility of future normal" (Betts et al., 2022, p. 212). Wilson et al. (2021) developed the Communication Resilience Process Scale. The scale uses the five subprocesses in CTR for the basis of the measure.

Applications to Subfields

CTR has been applied to the public and corporate subfields with a focus on the individual level of analysis. CRT's primary application has been to public crises. Agarwal and Buzzanell (2015) examined disaster relief workers using CTR. Olsson (2014) argued for CTR's relevance to public organizations during crises while Jiang et al. (2022) and Lillie et al. (2021) applied CTR to the COVID-19 public health crisis. Kim (2018) utilized CTR to examine employee resilience with a focus on the sense making aspect of CRT and applied resilience directly to internal crisis communication (Kim, 2020). Kim's (2020) work builds a direct link between employee and organizational resilience. Buzzanell (2010, 2018) has argued for CTR's applicability to organizational crises as well within her articulations of the theory.

Practitioner Takeaways

CTR highlights the importance of reliance and how it is related to crisis communication. For instance, Kim (2020) linked internal communication to positive outcomes related to resilience. Others have proven the value of resilience to public crisis victims and workers (e.g., Agarwal & Buzzanell, 2015; Lillie et al., 2021). The Communication Resilience Process Scale provides a means for crisis managers to assess resilience. Crisis managers should consider how a communication-based approach to resilience fits in with their approach to crisis management.

Theoretical Constraints and Concerns

Two general concerns about resilience are how it places more of the crisis burden on communities and less on the state and ignores underlying causes of vulnerability. Essentially resilience shifts attention to those dealing with the crisis and away from those tasked to manage crises (including prevention) (Rushton et al., 2022). For CTR, there is a lack of concern about the structural elements that can impede or facilitate resilience. How do organizational factors or the structure of public organizations inhibit or facilitate resilience? This would include a richer understanding of how crisis communication can contribute to resilience. Moreover, while CTR is multi-level, the research has concentrated primarily on the micro-level (individuals and families) (e.g., Buzzanell, 2017). More research is needed that explores CTR at the meso- and macro-levels (Kim, 2020). While anticipatory resilience is a start, more research is needed that explores how resilience can be cultivated prior to crises.

Theoretical Engagement Points

1 What type of research methods are most closely associated with CTR?
2 Is CTR primarily a descriptive, relational, or explanatory theory?

3 Is CTR primarily an empirical-analytic, interpretative, or critical theory?
4 How would you evaluate CTR in terms of scope, appropriateness, heuristic value, validity, parsimony, and openness?

Discussion Questions

1 How does the concept of "new normalcy" in CTR differ from simply returning to the pre-crisis state? How is communication used to establish this new normalcy?
2 Why is affirming identity crucial for resilience after a crisis? How can communication help individuals and organizations reaffirm their identities?
3 Discuss the role of communication networks and social capital in fostering resilience. How can individuals and organizations leverage these networks during and after a crisis?
4 Explain the process of employing "alternative logics" in CTR. How does this process contribute to reframing the crisis situation and promoting adaptive thinking?
5 Discuss the tension between legitimizing negative feelings and foregrounding productive actions in CTR. How can crisis communicators navigate this tension effectively?

References

Agarwal, V., & Buzzanell, P. M. (2015). Communicative reconstruction of resilience labor: Identity/identification in disaster-relief workers. *Journal of Applied Communication Research*, *43*(4), 408–428*.

Berkes, F., & Ross, H. (2013). Community resilience: Toward an integrated approach. *Society & Natural Resources*, *26*(1), 5–20.

Betts, T., Hintz, E. A., & Buzzanell, P. M. (2022). Emplotting anticipatory resilience: An antenarrative extension of the communication theory of resilience. *Communication Monographs*, *89*(2), 211–234.

Buzzanell, P. M. (2010). Resilience: Talking, resisting, and imagining new normalcies into being. *Journal of Communication*, *60*(1), 1–14*.

Buzzanell, P. M. (2017). Communication theory of resilience: Enacting adaptive-transformative processes when families experience loss and disruption. In D.O. Braithwaite, E.A. Suter & K. Floyd (Eds.), *Engaging theories in family communication* (pp. 98–109). New York: Routledge*.

Buzzanell, P. M. (2018). Organizing resilience as adaptive-transformational tensions. *Journal of Applied Communication Research*, *46*(1), 14–18*.

Curtis, W. J., & Cicchetti, D. (2007). Emotion and resilience: A multilevel investigation of hemispheric electroencephalogram asymmetry and emotion regulation in maltreated and nonmaltreated children. *Development and Psychopathology*, *19*(3), 811–840.

Cutter, S. (2019). *US emergency management in the 21st century: From disaster to catastrophe*. Routledge.

Cutter, S. L., Barnes, L., Berry, M., Burton, C. G., Evans, E., Tate, E. C. & Webb, J. 2008. Community and regional resilience: Perspectives from hazards, disasters, and emergency management. *CARRI Research Report 1*. Oak Ridge: Community and Regional Resilience Institute, http://www.resilientus.org/library/FINAL_CUTTER_9-25-08_1223482309.pdf

Drabek, T. E. (1985). Managing the emergency response. *Public Administration Review*, *45*, 85–92.

Gioia, D. A., Patvardhan, S. D., Hamilton, A. L., & Corley, K. G. (2013). Organizational identity formation and change. *Academy of Management Annals*, *7*(1), 123–193.

Granovetter, M. S. (1973). The strength of weak ties. *American Journal of Sociology*, *78*(6), 1360–1380.

Jiang, Q., Zhang, Y., & Pian, W. (2022). Chatbot as an emergency exist: Mediated empathy for resilience via human-AI interaction during the COVID-19 pandemic. *Information Processing & Management*, *59*(6), 103074.

Kim, Y. (2018). Enhancing employee communication behaviors for sensemaking and sensegiving in crisis situations: Strategic management approach for effective internal crisis communication. *Journal of Communication Management*, *22*(4), 451–475.

Kim, Y. (2020). Organizational resilience and employee work-role performance after a crisis situation: Exploring the effects of organizational resilience on internal crisis communication. *Journal of Public Relations Research*, *32*(1–2), 47–75.

Lillie, H. M., Chernichky-Karcher, S., & Venetis, M. K. (2021). Dyadic coping and discrete emotions during COVID-19: Connecting the communication theory of resilience with relational uncertainty. *Journal of Social and Personal Relationships*, *38*(6), 1844–1868.

Masten, A. S. (2002). Resilience comes of age: Reflections on the past and outlook for the next generation of research. In M.D. Glantz and J.L. Johnson (Eds.), *Resilience and development: Positive life adaptations* (pp. 281–296). London: Springer Nature.

Norris, F. H., Stevens, S. P., Pfefferbaum, B., Wyche, K. F., & Pfefferbaum, R. L. (2008). Community resilience as a metaphor, theory, set of capacities, and strategy for disaster readiness. *American Journal of Community Psychology*, *41*, 127–150.

Olsson, E. K. (2014). Crisis communication in public organisations: Dimensions of crisis communication revisited. *Journal of Contingencies and Crisis Management*, *22*(2), 113–125.

Pfefferbaum, B., Van Horn, R. L., & Pfefferbaum, R. L. (2017). A conceptual framework to enhance community resilience using social capital. *Clinical Social Work Journal*, *45*(2), 102–110.

Rushton, S., Balen, J., Crane, O., Devkota, B., & Ghimire, S. (2022). Re-examining critiques of resilience policy: Evidence from Barpak after the 2015 earthquake in Nepal. *Disasters*, *46*(3), 768–790.

Rutter, M. (2012). Resilience as a dynamic concept. *Development and Psychopathology*, *24*(2), 335–344.
Stoffle, R., & Minnis, J. (2008). Resilience at risk: Epistemological and social construction barriers to risk communication. *Journal of Risk Research*, *11*(1–2), 55–68.
Wilson, S. R., Kuang, K., Hintz, E. A., & Buzzanell, P. M. (2021). Developing and validating the communication resilience processes scale. *Journal of Communication*, *71*(3), 478–513*.

*Requisite Readings

Chapter 21

Concluding Remarks and Observations

It is important to think of theory as a "living thing." Scientific theory is not statistic but rather it evolves and changes over time based on new evidence provided by research and new variables introduced such as social and technological changes. Think of a theory much like a living organism that adapts to its environment. Theory is refined and updated as new data emerges. Those changes might be significant modifications to a theory or even the rejection of the original theory. Consider how the discovery of the archaeological site of Göbekli Tepe in Turkey altered archeological theory. The date of the site changed how the Neolithic period is viewed and challenged the conventional view of the rise of civilization being predicated on agriculture. The site is at least 11,000 years old, making it the earliest known monumental structures created by humans and was constructed by nomadic hunter-gatherers (Curry, 2021).

Risk and crisis communication theory have had to adapt to digital world and is adapting to artificial intelligence (AI). An example of such adaptation can be found in Chapter 3 on the Social Amplification of Risk and Chapter 14 on Social-Mediated Crisis Communication (SMCC) in this book. The theories presented in this book might change as new evidence emerges but will remain essential to practice and theorizing. The theories we have presented are essential to enhancing risks and crisis communication efforts by providing frameworks to guide development those communicative efforts. The theories are also essential elements for future theories as they are refinements of existing theories, a fusing of existing theories or the groundwork from which new theories will be construed.

It is important for crisis and risk communication theory to retain its practical nature. Both are applied forms of communication designed to solve problems. Theories are critical to the development of evidence-based approaches to interventions for crisis and risk. An evidence-based approach to an intervention emerges from a fusion of evidence and practitioner experience. Theory guides the research that provides the evidence dimension of the evidence-based approach. Practitioners then interpret the

DOI: 10.4324/9781003469964-24

evidence through the lens of their experiences to determine if and how the evidence can be applicable to their needs. Both crisis and risk communication have a strong track record of being utilized by practitioners. Examples are the way the Extended Parallel Process model (EPPM) and Situational Crisis Communication Theory (SCCT) have been embraced by those tasked with managing risks and crises. We consider the practical nature of the theories included within this book to be a complement. As noted in Chapter 1, "there is nothing so practical as a good theory."

We have included both risk and crisis communication theories because crisis communication frequently is intertwined with risk communication. It is more productive for practice and research to think of it as crisis/risk rather than to consider crisis and risk communication as two separate disciplines. A builder would not use just one tool to construct a house so why should a practitioner use just one theory to construct crisis/risk interventions? While explained in isolation, practitioners and researchers should be able to combine various theories presented in this book. Which theories are used depends upon the problems faced by the practitioner and the questions the researchers are trying to answer. There is a strength in combining crisis and risk communication theories, especially when the crisis intervention must contain an element of risk.

Concluding Thoughts on Theorizing for Researchers

In Chapter 1, we provided a discussion of theory including how to build theory. It is instructive to return to the discussion of theory for researchers. Theory is an important component of research and an important aspect of evaluations for journal publications. For instances, the first line of the scope for the *Journal of Public Relations Research* states "The *Journal of Public Relations Research* publishes research that creates, tests, or expands public relations theory" (About this Journal, n.d.). But how does research contribute to crisis communication theory?

In their analysis of the management literature, Corley and Gioia (2011) evaluated the theoretical contributions of research using two dimensions. The first dimension was originality. Research must provide original insights into the field. Originality can be incremental or revelatory: incremental advances of our understanding of theory in small steps (increments). The research extends current thinking about theory often by adding a new variable. An example would be research that explores how to operationalize the various crisis response strategies employed by the various crisis communication theories. However, the incremental change should not be trivial or marginal, a subjective element in evaluating the theoretical contributions of a manuscript. Revelatory research reveals something new we have not seen before. The manuscript provides a novel view and/or new insights into crisis communication. Revelatory research offers a new way of seeing crisis communication that can be considered unexpected and interesting, another subjective criterion (Corley and Gioia, 2011). RAT's introduction of the multi-vocal approach to crisis communication is an example of revelatory research.

While researchers aspire to produce revelatory research, most crisis communication research is incremental. There is nothing wrong with incremental research because it does advance the field. Let us return to the example of operationalizing crisis response strategies. The research examining voice and the value of a human voice in creating crisis response strategies is incremental because it is refining existing elements of theory. And the research is important because it provides a greater understanding of how to improve the benefits of crisis interventions. A problem in many manuscripts seeking publication is an overselling of the incremental. Sometimes this involves presenting incremental research as revelatory by overstating the contributions of the research.

A common overstatement is claiming one contrary finding of a minor part of an existing theory indicates the existing theory is wrong. If the core relationships of a theory still hold true, the theory is not proven "wrong." The more likely conclusion is that the new research indicates a boundary condition for the existing theory. We have done a poor job in crisis communication research in establishing the boundaries for our theories. As interventions, it is necessary to understand what works, for whom, and in what circumstances. These are questions about boundaries for theories that are answered by realistic reviews. Realistic (aka realist synthesis) reviews are a form of systematic review that illuminates how why, and under what circumstances an intervention or theory works (e.g., Barbier et al., 2021). As an intervention, crisis communication has similarities to implementation science.

Implementation science emphasizes evidence-based practices (EBP), similar to crisis communication, to understand health-related interventions. Nilsen (2020) defined implementation science as "the scientific study of methods to promote the systematic uptake of research findings and other EBPs into routine practice to improve the quality and effectiveness of health services and care" (Nilsen, 2020, p. 2). As interventions, it is important for crisis communication theory to understand the conditions for when specific crisis interventions (crisis response strategies) produce or fail to produce the desired results. In short, there is a need to map the boundaries of crisis communication theories. The research into moral outrage inducing crises is an example of efforts to demarcate the boundaries of a crisis communication theory (Coombs & Tachkova, 2019, 2023).

Crisis communication research can learn from implementation sciences about exploring theoretical boundaries through realistic reviews and other forms of research. We need better evidence about the conditions under which our crisis interventions have the desired effect or fail to produce the desired effect. The need to understand boundaries has a direct relationship to the practice. The identification of boundaries helps crisis managers know when to use or to avoid the use of specific crisis response strategies. For instance, we know crisis managers should avoid the use of the denial crisis response strategy if there is any chance the organization bears some responsibility for the crisis (Coombs et al., 2016). The strategic use of realistic reviews and scoping studies can illuminate boundaries by indicating how why, and under what circumstances a specific crisis intervention or theory create or fail to create the desired effect (aka work).

The discussion of boundaries relates to Corley and Gioia (2011) second dimension of utility. A theoretical utility can be practical and/or scientific. Practice utility means the theory informs the practice while scientific utility is about academic insights. While scientific utility has a place when academics debate larger theoretical concerns among themselves, it should be a small percentage of the crisis communication research. This claim is based on the value crisis communication research offers for addressing problems in crisis management such as Sutton's work to improve warning messages (Cain et al., 2024; Sutton et al., 2024). Practical utility emphasizes how theory can be used to solve problems in crisis communication. Researchers can get lost in larger philosophical debates or the pursuit of the effects of some minor variable within crisis communication. A strength as the field of crisis communication developed was its connection to EBP and helping to enhance the practice of crisis communication. Those seeking to develop crisis communication theory should not lose sight of this important contribution.

One final though is about how crisis communication theory captures The famous sociologist Robert Merton's notion of theories of the middle range or middle-range theories (MRT). According to Merton (1949), "Middle-range theories deal with delimited aspects of social phenomenon" (p. 39). MRT stands in contrast to grand theories which are very abstract because they seek to explain all aspects of social behavior. Crisis communication theory is delimited in two ways. First, crisis communication theory seeks to explain crisis-related behaviors. While crisis communication theories can include risk communication, the theories still have a specific and limited focus.

Second, we need to return to the idea of boundaries. Crisis communication theories are delimited by its boundaries. Part of the boundaries can be the specific subfield for which a theory was developed. The theories might focus on behaviors within specific subfields of crisis communication. A crisis communication theory might be designed for corporate crises while another might work best for public crises. That is why it is often problematic for researchers to mix studies from different crisis subfields in literature reviews. The results of the studies from different crisis subfields are more likely to have important differences than to share meaningful similarities. Researchers must be mindful of those potential differences when constructing literature reviews, an essential step in building rationales for research studies. Mixing research from different crisis subfields can raise questions about the validity of the study's fundamental rationales.

Discussion Questions

1 How does the idea of a scientific theory as a "living thing" that evolves over time apply to the field of crisis and risk communication? In what ways might these theories adapt to new technologies like AI?
2 The chapter discusses how theories are essential for enhancing risk and crisis communication by providing frameworks to guide communicative efforts. How do you see the relationship between theory, research, and practice in developing evidence-based approaches to crisis and risk interventions?
3 Consider the role of practitioner experience in interpreting evidence and applying theories. Given that crisis and risk communication are intertwined, the text suggests a more productive approach is to think of them as "crisis/risk" rather than two separate disciplines. How can practitioners and researchers combine various theories to address problems and answer research questions in crisis/risk situations?
4 The chapter highlights two dimensions of research contributions: originality (incremental or revelatory) and utility (practical and/or scientific). How should researchers balance the pursuit of incremental versus revelatory research in crisis communication, and how does this balance impact the practical application of their findings? How does the pursuit of utility impact the research questions and methods used by researchers?
5 The chapter introduces the concept of "middle-range theories" (MRT). How do the boundaries of crisis communication theories, including the specific subfields for which they were developed, impact the validity of research and literature reviews? What are some ways researchers can identify the boundaries of crisis communication theories?

References

About this Journal (n.d.). Retrieved from https://www.tandfonline.com/journals/hprr20/about-this-journal

Barbier, M., Schulte, C., Kornadt, A., Federspiel, C., Steinmetz, J. P., & Vögele, C. (2021). Using social marketing for the promotion of cognitive health: A scoping review protocol. *BMJ Open*, *11*(10), e049947.

Cain, L. B., Sutton, J., & Olson, M. K. (2024). Wireless emergency alerts and organisational response: Instructing and adjusting information in alerts. *Journal of Contingencies and Crisis Management*, *32*(1), e12516.

Coombs, W. T., Holladay, S. J., & Claeys, A. S. (2016). Debunking the myth of denial's effectiveness in crisis communication: Context matters. *Journal of Communication Management*, *20*(4), 381–395.

Coombs, W. T., & Tachkova, E. R. (2019). Scansis as a unique crisis type: Theoretical and practical implications. *Journal of Communication Management*, *23*(1), 72–88.

Coombs, W. T., & Tachkova, E. R. (2023). Integrating moral outrage in situational crisis communication theory: A triadic appraisal model for crises. *Management Communication Quarterly*, *37*(4), 798–820.

Corley, K. G., & Gioia, D. A. (2011). Building theory about theory building: What constitutes a theoretical contribution? *Academy of Management Review*, *36*(1), 12–32.

Curry, A. (2021). The last stand of the hunter-gathers? Retrieved from https://archaeology.org/issues/may-june-2021/features/turkey-gobekli-tepe-hunter-gatherers/

Merton, R.K. (1949). *Social theory and social structure*. New York: Simon& Schuster, The FreePress.

Nilsen, P. (2020). Making sense of implementation theories, models, and frameworks. *Implementation Science*, *3*, 53–79.

Sutton, J., Olson, M. K., & Waugh, N. A. (2024). The warning Lexicon: A multi-phased study to identify, design, and develop content for warning messages. *Natural Hazards Review*, *25*(1), 04023055.

Index

Pages in **bold** refer to tables.

FSC
www.fsc.org
MIX
Papier | Fördert gute Waldnutzung
FSC® C083411

Kolibri 360 GmbH
Ferdinand-Jühlke-Straße 7
99095 Erfurt, Deutschland
produktsicherheit@kolibri360.de